CAPTAIN AMERICA

Castaway in Dimension Z Part Two

WRITER: RICK REMENDER
PENCILER: JOHN ROMITA JR
INKERS: KLAUS JANSON,
SCOTT HANNA AND
THOMAS PALMER
COLOURS: DEAN WHITE AND RACHELLE ROSENBERG
LETTERS: VC's JOE CARAMAGNA

ASSISTANT EDITOR: JACOB THOMAS
EDITORS: TOM BREVOORT
AND LAUREN SANKOVITCH
EDITOR IN CHIEF: AXEL ALONSO
CHIEF CREATIVE OFFICER: JOE QUESADA
PUBLISHER: DAN BUCKLEY
EXECUTIVE PRODUCER: ALAN FINE

COVER ART: JOHN ROMITA JR

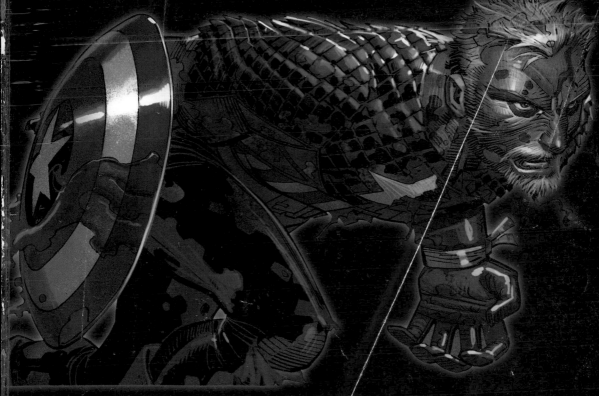

Do you have any comments or queries about this graphic novel? Email us at graphicnovels@panini.co.uk

TM & © 2013 Marvel & Subs. Licensed by Marvel Characters B.V. through Panini S.p.A., Italy. All Rights Reserved. First printing 2013. Published by Panini Publishing, a division of Panini UK L...
Mike Riddell, Manag... ...upoi, Publishing
Director Europe. Bra... ...: Brockbourne House,
77 Mount Ephraim, T... ...alers, and is sold subject
to the condition tha... ...a mutilated condition.
Printed in Italy by Te...

CAPTAIN AMERICA™

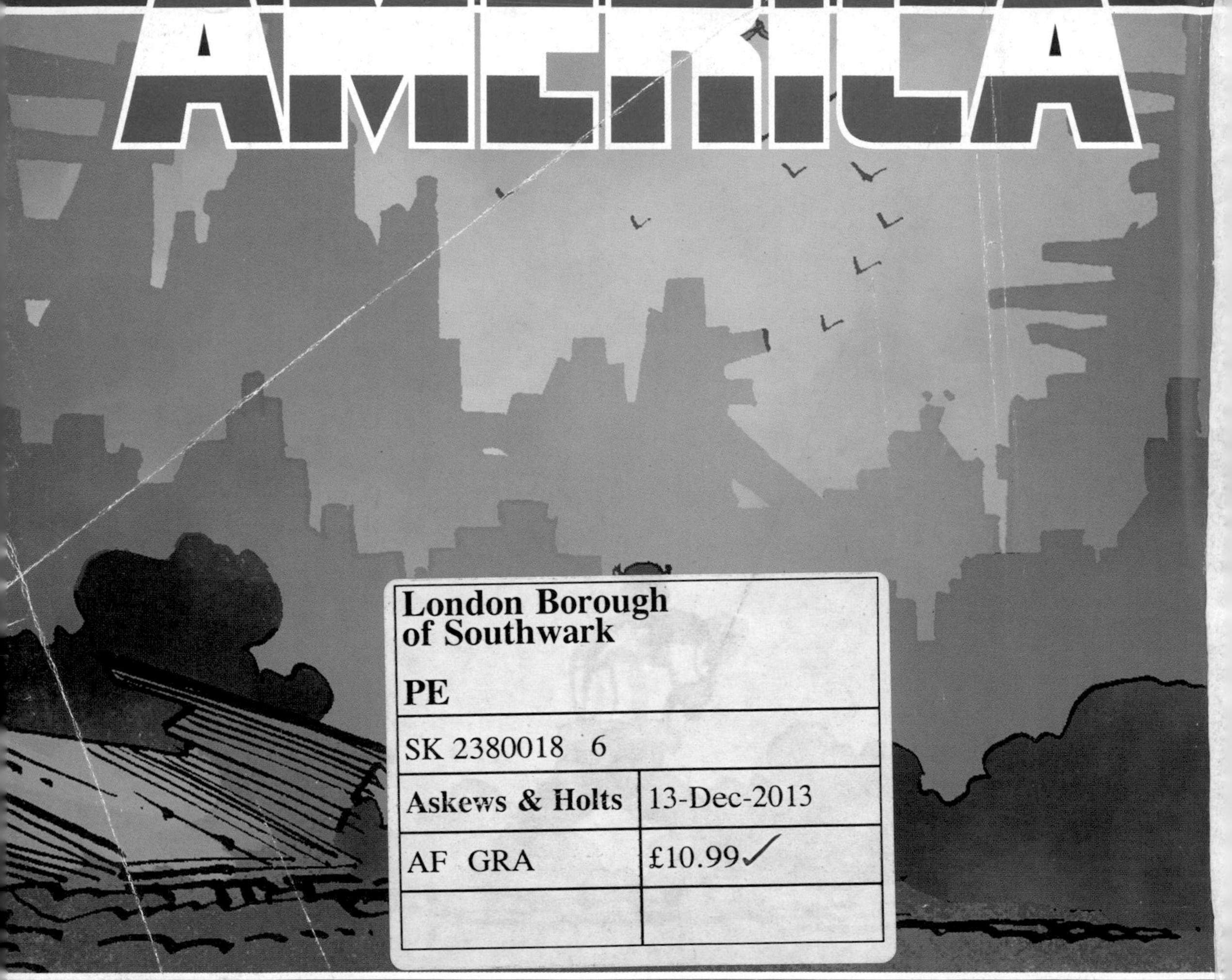

PREVIOUSLY...

Twelve years ago, evil scientist Arnim Zola trapped Captain America in Dimension Z to run genetic experiments on him. Steve escaped Zola's fortress, absconding with an infant he named Ian. He raised Ian among the Phrox, Dimension Z natives who oppose Zola's reign. After a bloody battle between the Phrox and Zola's Mutates, led by his deadly daughter Jet Black, Zola took Ian and blasted Steve off a cliff.

Steve survived, and swore an oath of retribution.

Now, he's coming for his son...

MARVEL GRAPHIC NOVEL

CAPTAIN AMERICA #6

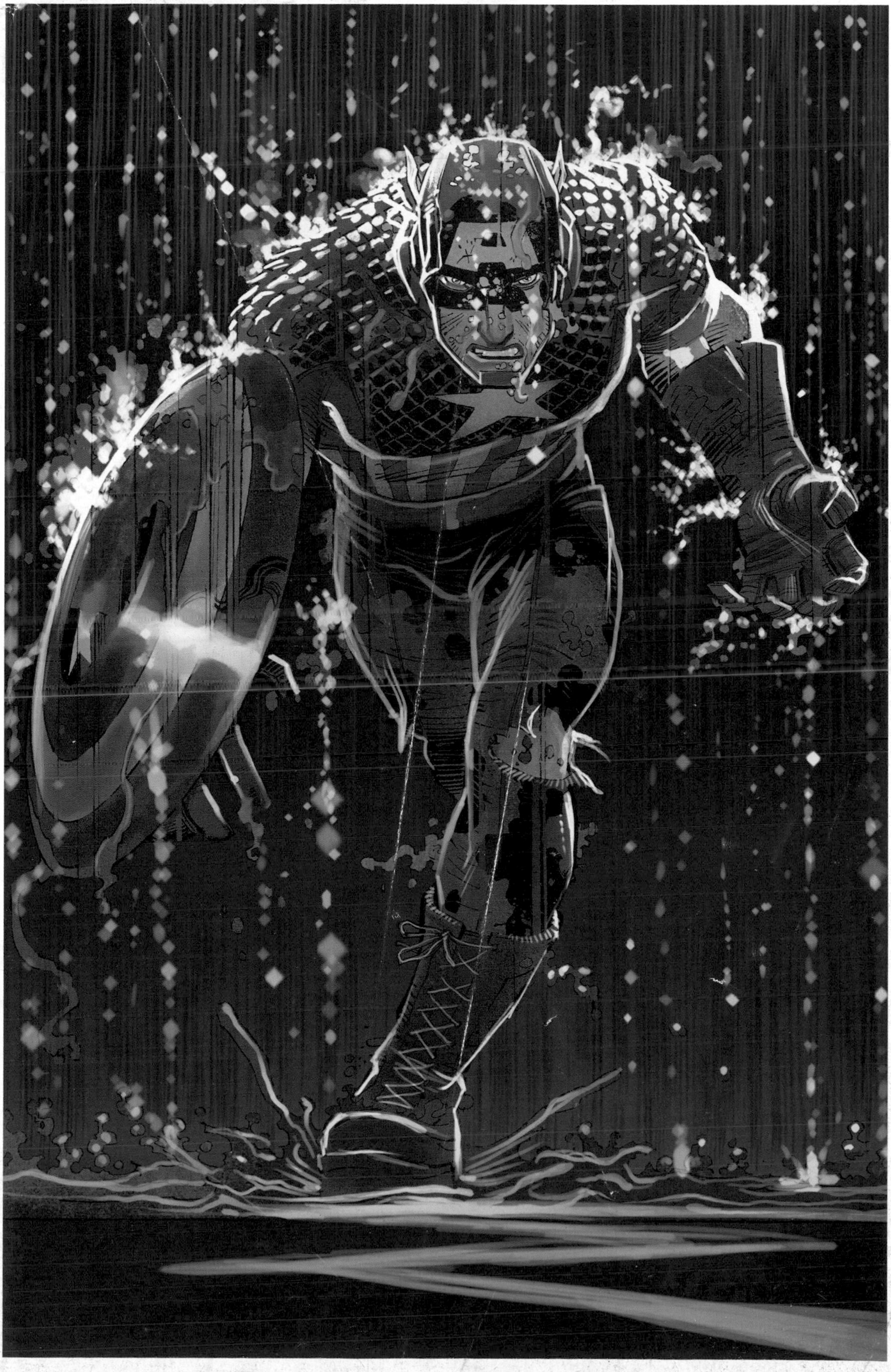

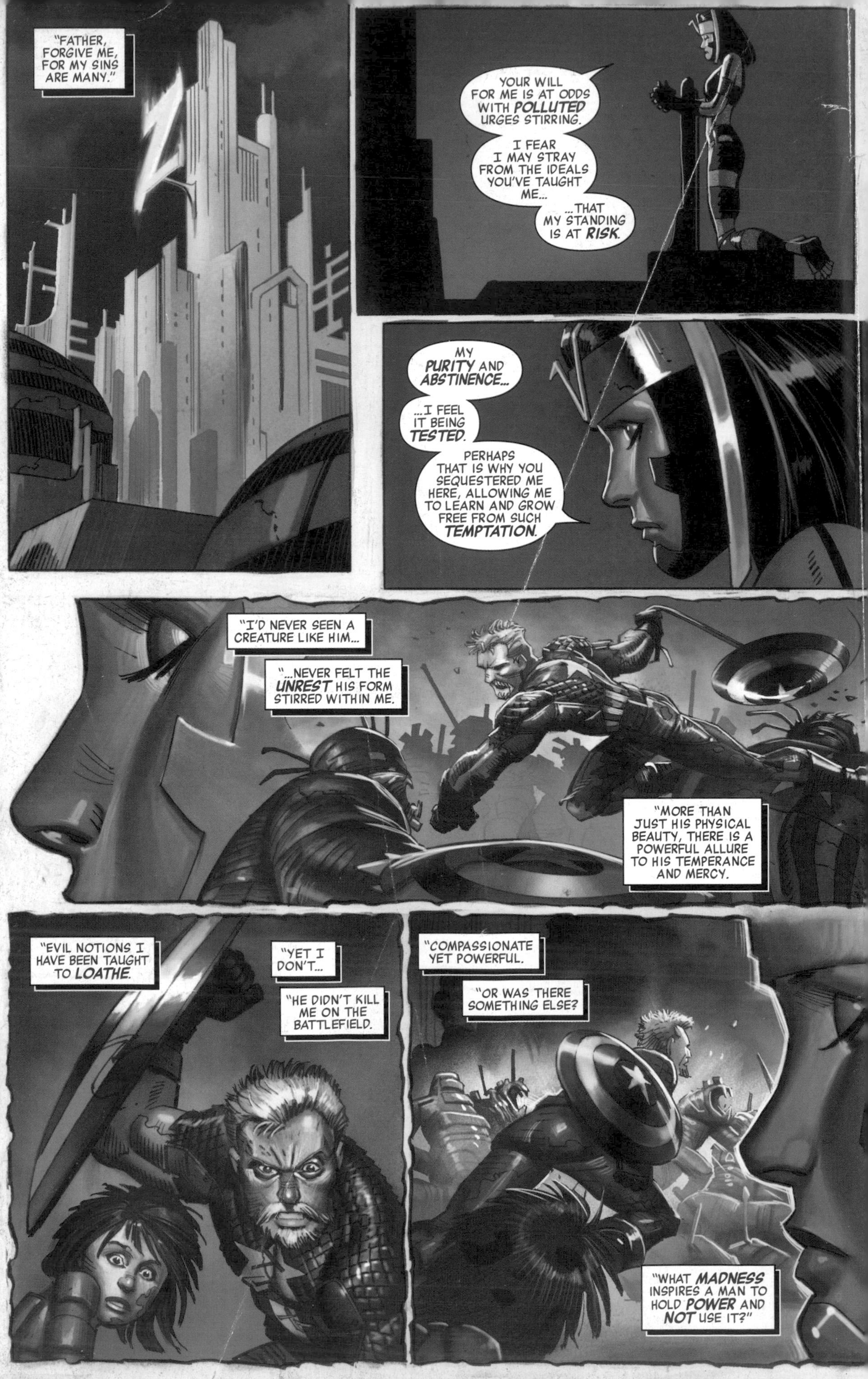
"FATHER, FORGIVE ME, FOR MY SINS ARE MANY."
YOUR WILL FOR ME IS AT ODDS WITH POLLUTED URGES STIRRING.
I FEAR I MAY STRAY FROM THE IDEALS YOU'VE TAUGHT ME...
...THAT MY STANDING IS AT RISK.
MY PURITY AND ABSTINENCE...
...I FEEL IT BEING TESTED.
PERHAPS THAT IS WHY YOU SEQUESTERED ME HERE, ALLOWING ME TO LEARN AND GROW FREE FROM SUCH TEMPTATION.
"I'D NEVER SEEN A CREATURE LIKE HIM...
"...NEVER FELT THE UNREST HIS FORM STIRRED WITHIN ME.
"MORE THAN JUST HIS PHYSICAL BEAUTY, THERE IS A POWERFUL ALLURE TO HIS TEMPERANCE AND MERCY.
"EVIL NOTIONS I HAVE BEEN TAUGHT TO LOATHE.
"YET I DON'T...
"HE DIDN'T KILL ME ON THE BATTLEFIELD.
"COMPASSIONATE YET POWERFUL.
"OR WAS THERE SOMETHING ELSE?
"WHAT MADNESS INSPIRES A MAN TO HOLD POWER AND NOT USE IT?"

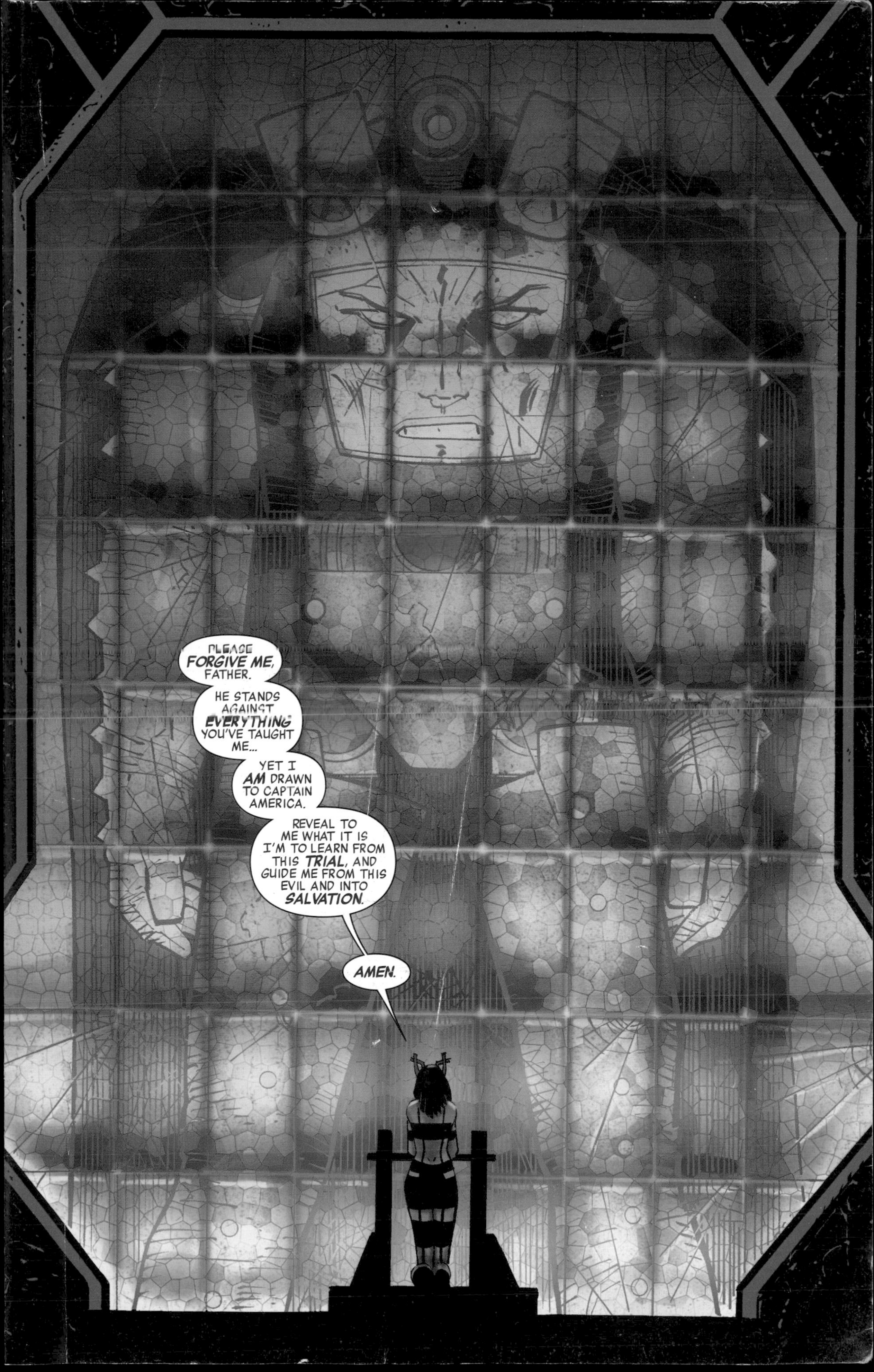

PLEASE FORGIVE ME, FATHER.
HE STANDS AGAINST EVERYTHING YOU'VE TAUGHT ME...
YET I AM DRAWN TO CAPTAIN AMERICA.
REVEAL TO ME WHAT IT IS I'M TO LEARN FROM THIS TRIAL, AND GUIDE ME FROM THIS EVIL AND INTO SALVATION.
AMEN.

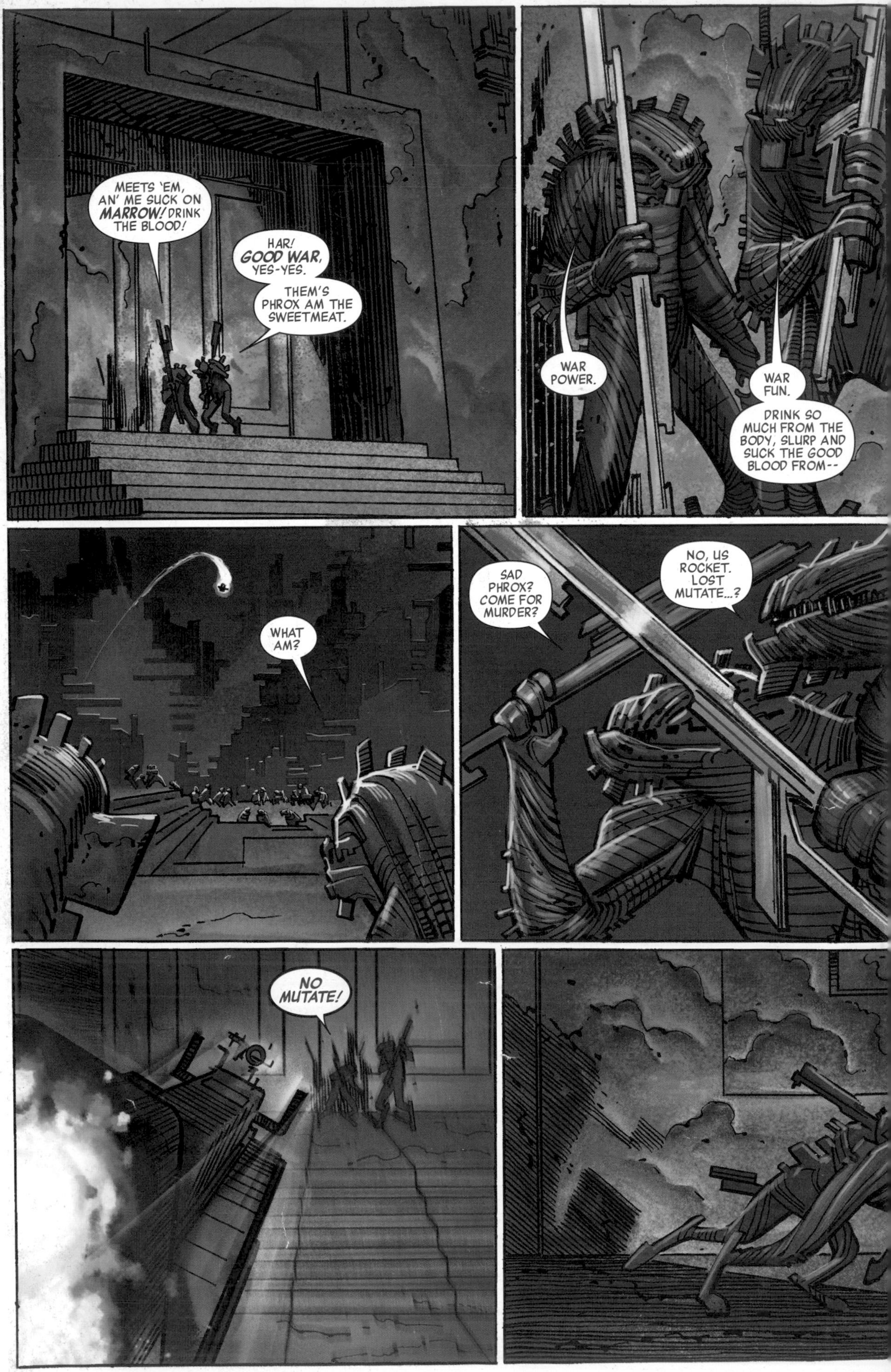

MEETS 'EM, AN' ME SUCK ON MARROW! DRINK THE BLOOD!
HAR! GOOD WAR, YES-YES.
THEM'S PHROX AM THE SWEETMEAT.
WAR POWER.
WAR FUN.
DRINK SO MUCH FROM THE BODY, SLURP AND SUCK THE GOOD BLOOD FROM--
WHAT AM?
SAD PHROX? COME FOR MURDER?
NO, US ROCKET. LOST MUTATE...?
NO MUTATE!

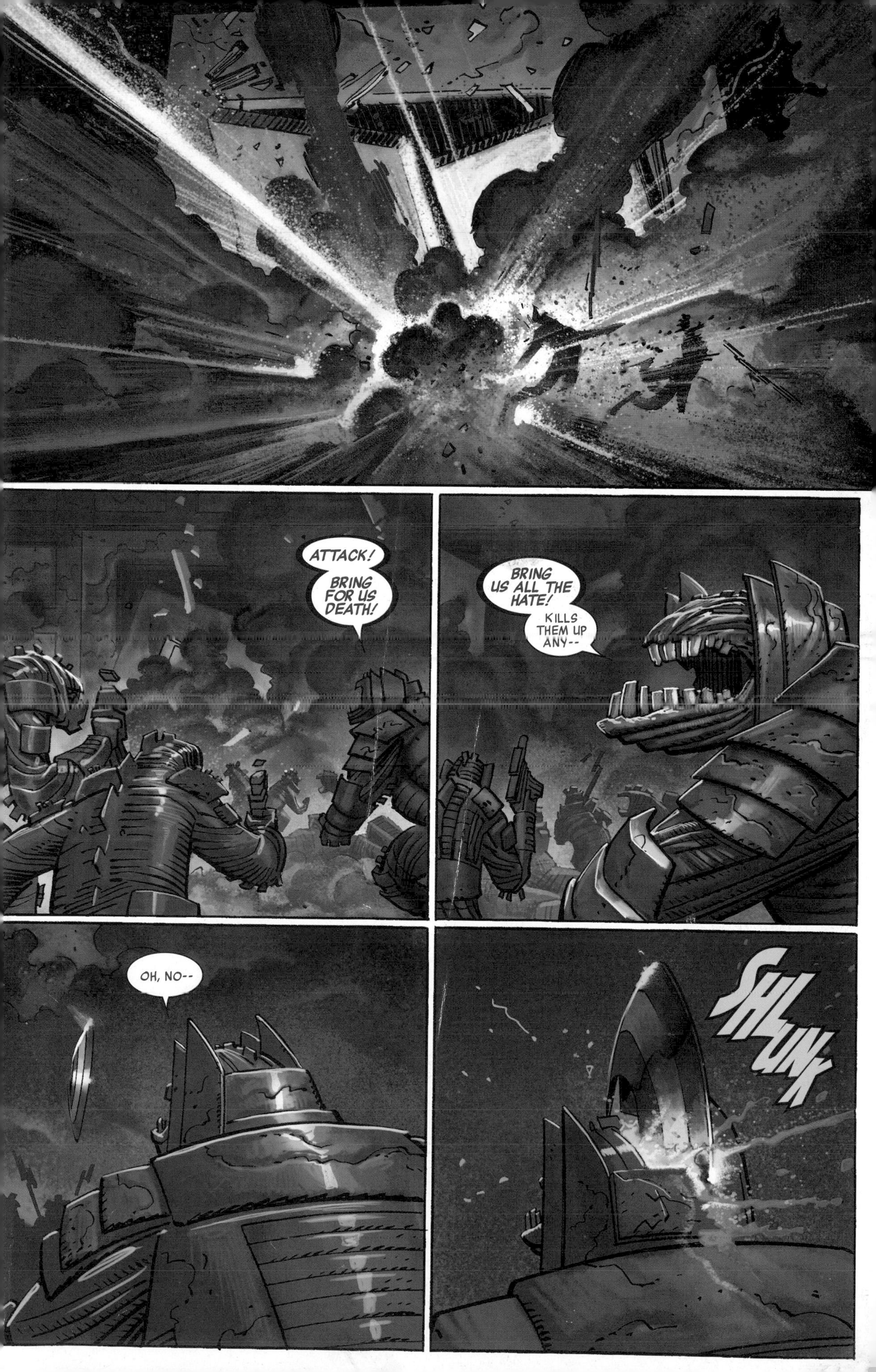
ATTACK!
BRING FOR US DEATH!
BRING US ALL THE HATE!
KILLS THEM UP ANY--
OH, NO--
SHLUNK

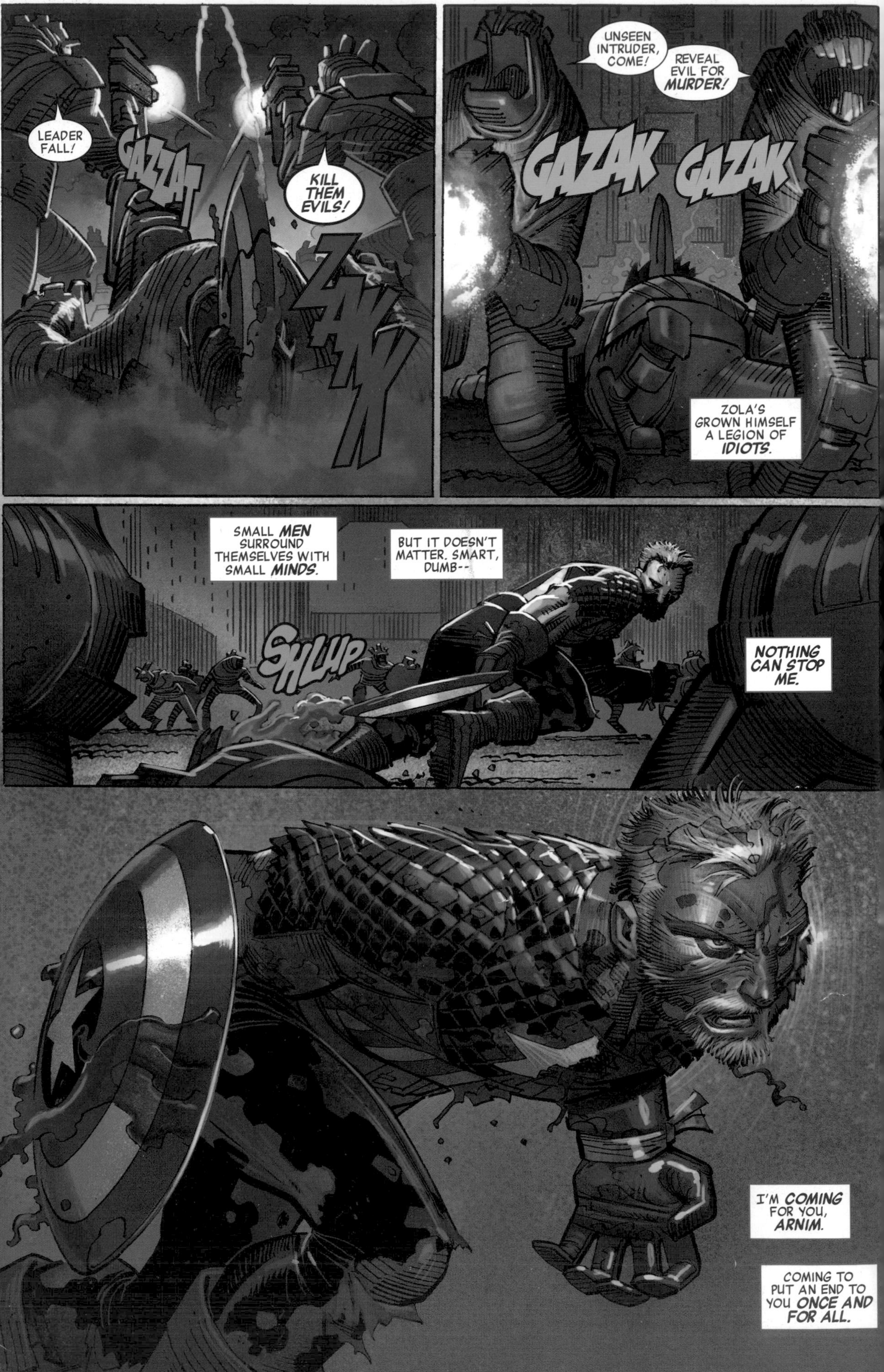
LEADER FALL!
GAZZAT
KILL THEM EVILS!
ZAK
UNSEEN INTRUDER, COME!
REVEAL EVIL FOR MURDER!
GAZAK GAZAK
ZOLA'S GROWN HIMSELF A LEGION OF IDIOTS.
SMALL MEN SURROUND THEMSELVES WITH SMALL MINDS.
BUT IT DOESN'T MATTER. SMART, DUMB--
SHLUP
NOTHING CAN STOP ME.
I'M COMING FOR YOU, ARNIM.
COMING TO PUT AN END TO YOU ONCE AND FOR ALL.

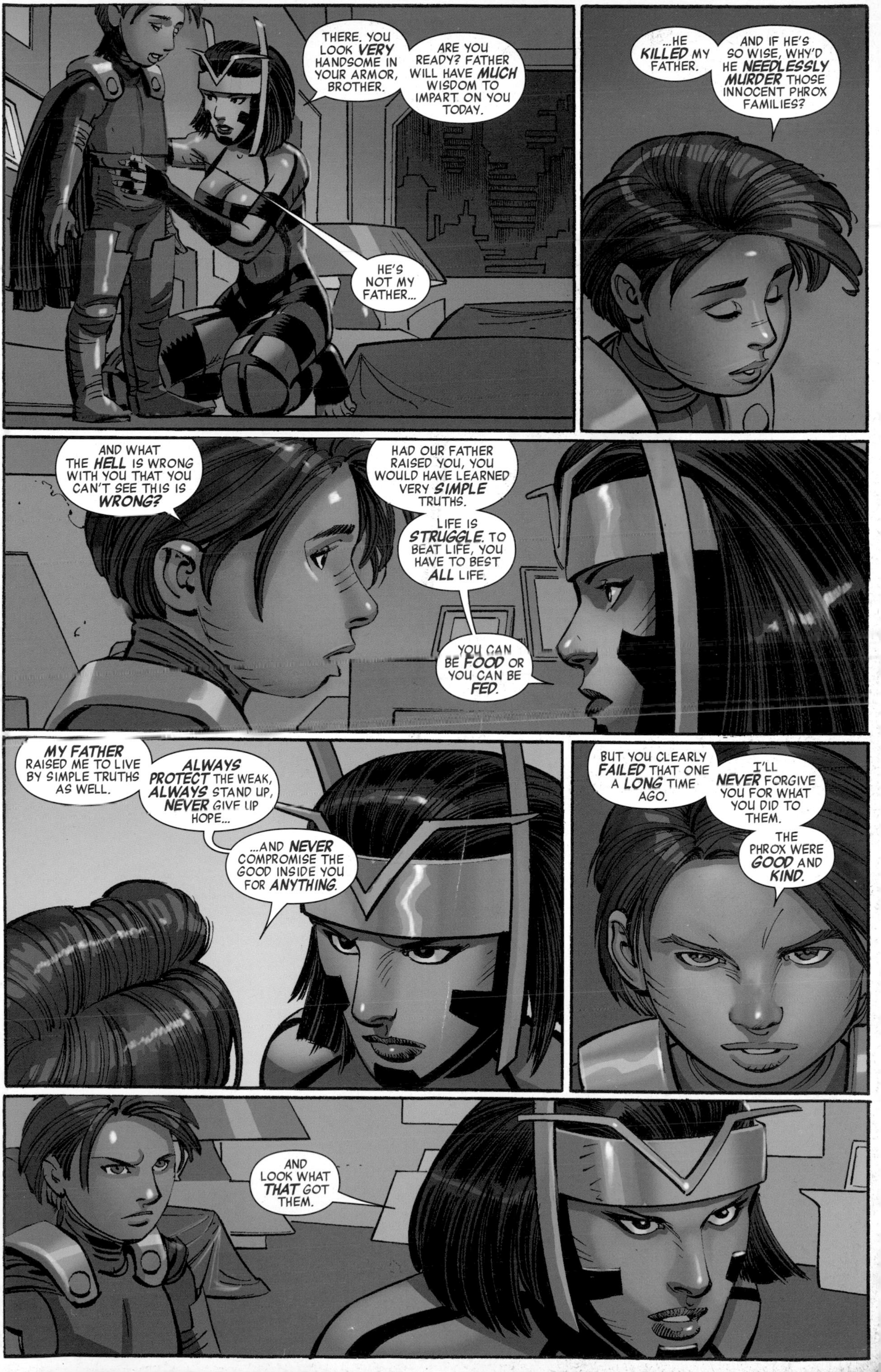
THERE. YOU LOOK VERY HANDSOME IN YOUR ARMOR, BROTHER.
ARE YOU READY? FATHER WILL HAVE MUCH WISDOM TO IMPART ON YOU TODAY.
HE'S NOT MY FATHER...
...HE KILLED MY FATHER.
AND IF HE'S SO WISE, WHY'D HE NEEDLESSLY MURDER THOSE INNOCENT PHROX FAMILIES?
AND WHAT THE HELL IS WRONG WITH YOU THAT YOU CAN'T SEE THIS IS WRONG?
HAD OUR FATHER RAISED YOU, YOU WOULD HAVE LEARNED VERY SIMPLE TRUTHS.
LIFE IS STRUGGLE. TO BEAT LIFE, YOU HAVE TO BEST ALL LIFE.
YOU CAN BE FOOD OR YOU CAN BE FED.
MY FATHER RAISED ME TO LIVE BY SIMPLE TRUTHS AS WELL.
ALWAYS PROTECT THE WEAK, ALWAYS STAND UP, NEVER GIVE UP HOPE...
...AND NEVER COMPROMISE THE GOOD INSIDE YOU FOR ANYTHING.
BUT YOU CLEARLY FAILED THAT ONE A LONG TIME AGO.
I'LL NEVER FORGIVE YOU FOR WHAT YOU DID TO THEM.
THE PHROX WERE GOOD AND KIND.
AND LOOK WHAT THAT GOT THEM.

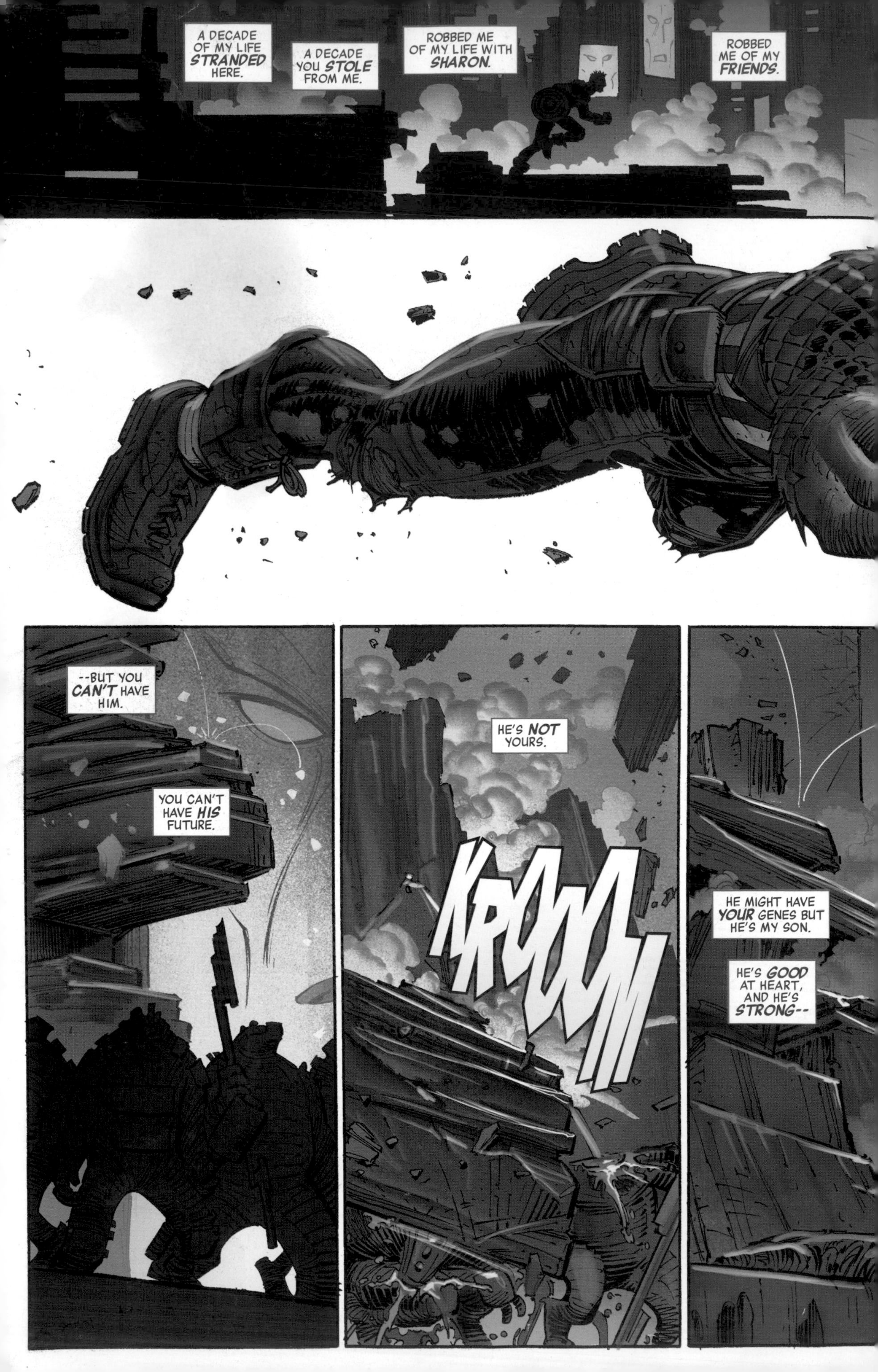
A DECADE OF MY LIFE STRANDED HERE.
A DECADE YOU STOLE FROM ME.
ROBBED ME OF MY LIFE WITH SHARON.
ROBBED ME OF MY FRIENDS.
--BUT YOU CAN'T HAVE HIM.
YOU CAN'T HAVE HIS FUTURE.
HE'S NOT YOURS.
KROOOM
HE MIGHT HAVE YOUR GENES BUT HE'S MY SON.
HE'S GOOD AT HEART, AND HE'S STRONG--

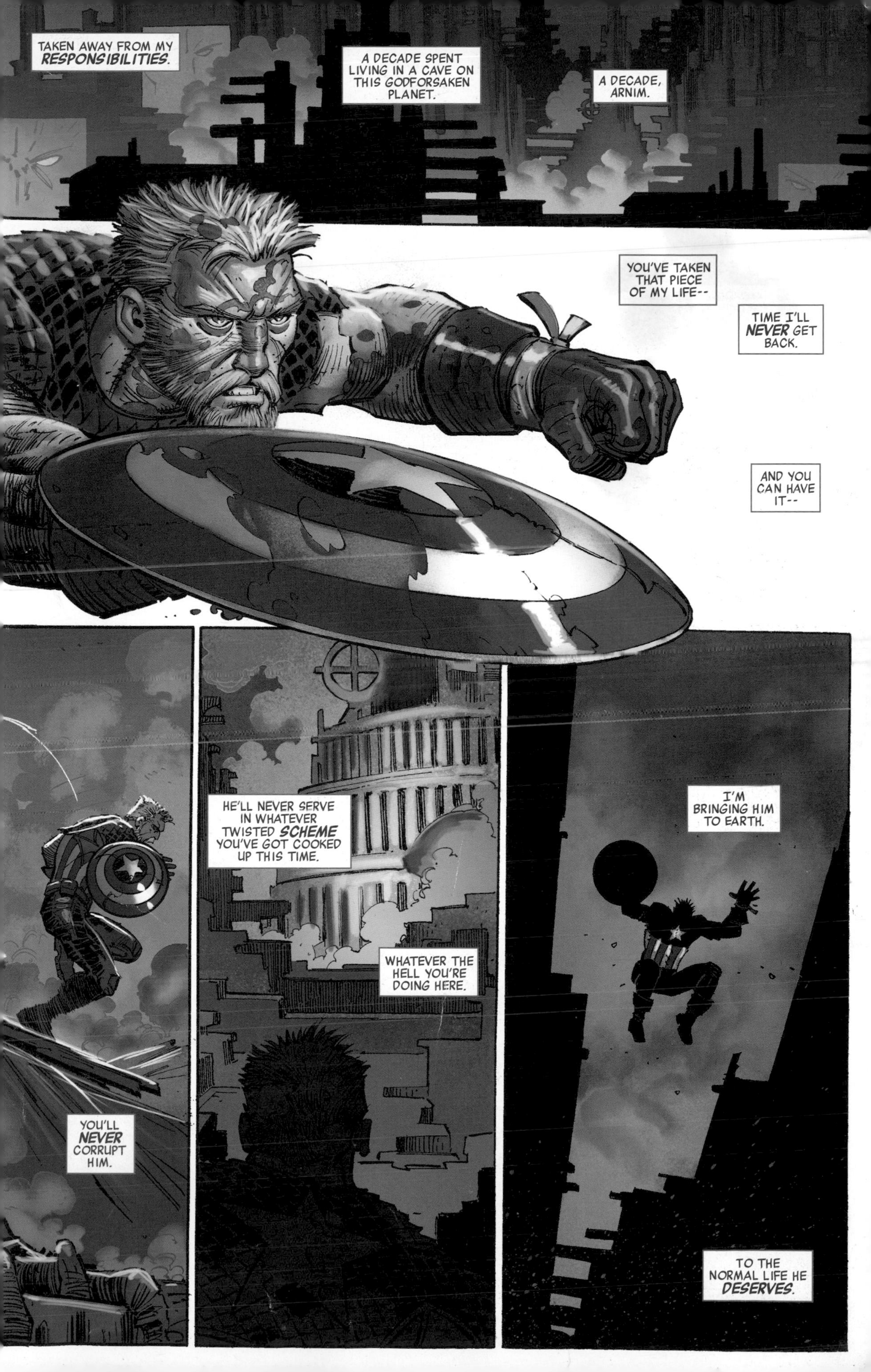
TAKEN AWAY FROM MY RESPONSIBILITIES.
A DECADE SPENT LIVING IN A CAVE ON THIS GODFORSAKEN PLANET.
A DECADE, ARNIM.
YOU'VE TAKEN THAT PIECE OF MY LIFE--
TIME I'LL NEVER GET BACK.
AND YOU CAN HAVE IT--
YOU'LL NEVER CORRUPT HIM.
HE'LL NEVER SERVE IN WHATEVER TWISTED SCHEME YOU'VE GOT COOKED UP THIS TIME.
WHATEVER THE HELL YOU'RE DOING HERE.
I'M BRINGING HIM TO EARTH.
TO THE NORMAL LIFE HE DESERVES.

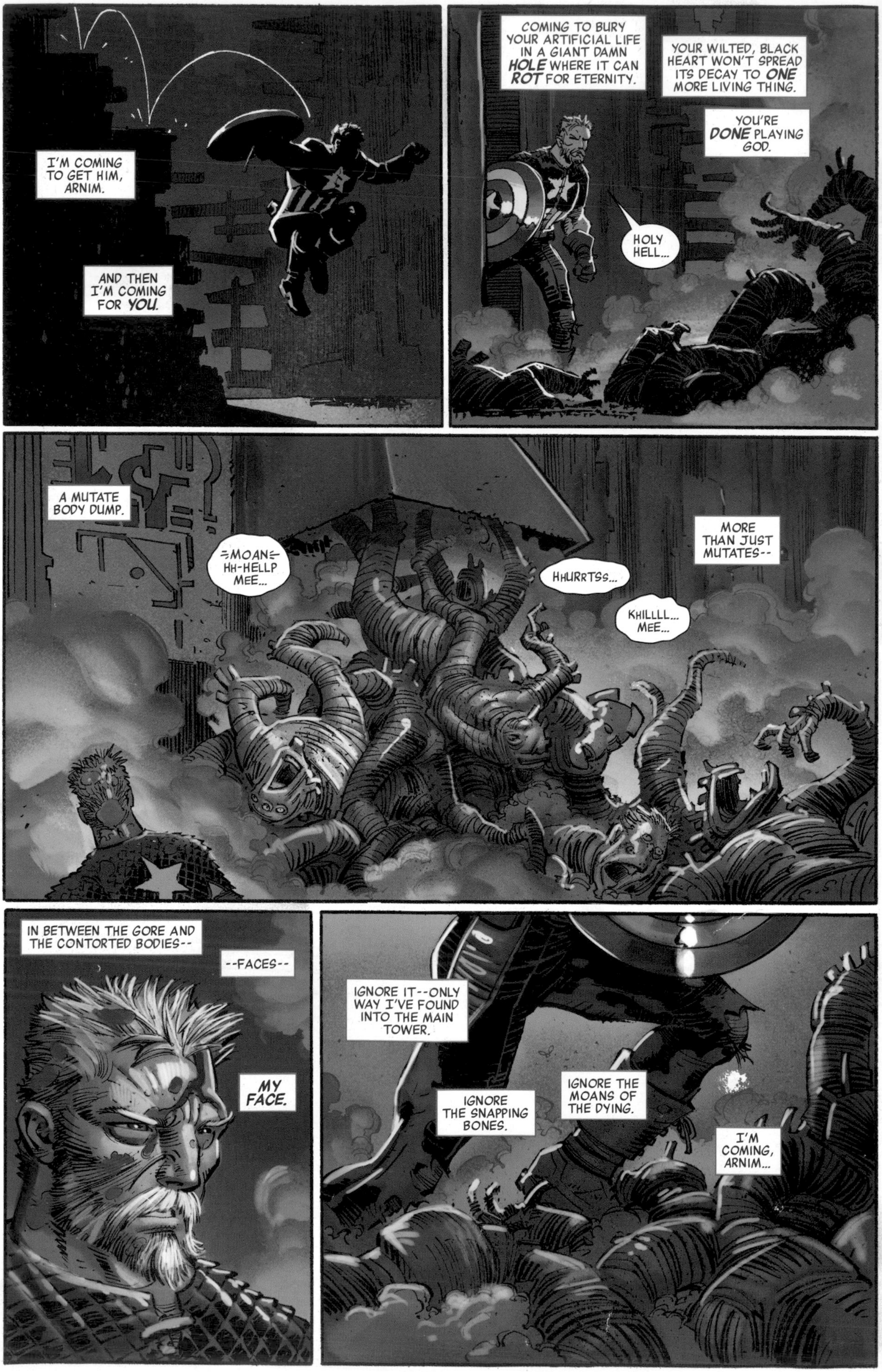
I'M COMING TO GET HIM, ARNIM.
AND THEN I'M COMING FOR YOU.
COMING TO BURY YOUR ARTIFICIAL LIFE IN A GIANT DAMN HOLE WHERE IT CAN ROT FOR ETERNITY.
YOUR WILTED, BLACK HEART WON'T SPREAD ITS DECAY TO ONE MORE LIVING THING.
YOU'RE DONE PLAYING GOD.
HOLY HELL...
A MUTATE BODY DUMP.
MOAN HH-HELLP MEE...
HHURRTSS...
KHILLLL... MEE...
MORE THAN JUST MUTATES--
IN BETWEEN THE GORE AND THE CONTORTED BODIES--
--FACES--
MY FACE.
IGNORE IT--ONLY WAY I'VE FOUND INTO THE MAIN TOWER.
IGNORE THE SNAPPING BONES.
IGNORE THE MOANS OF THE DYING.
I'M COMING, ARNIM...

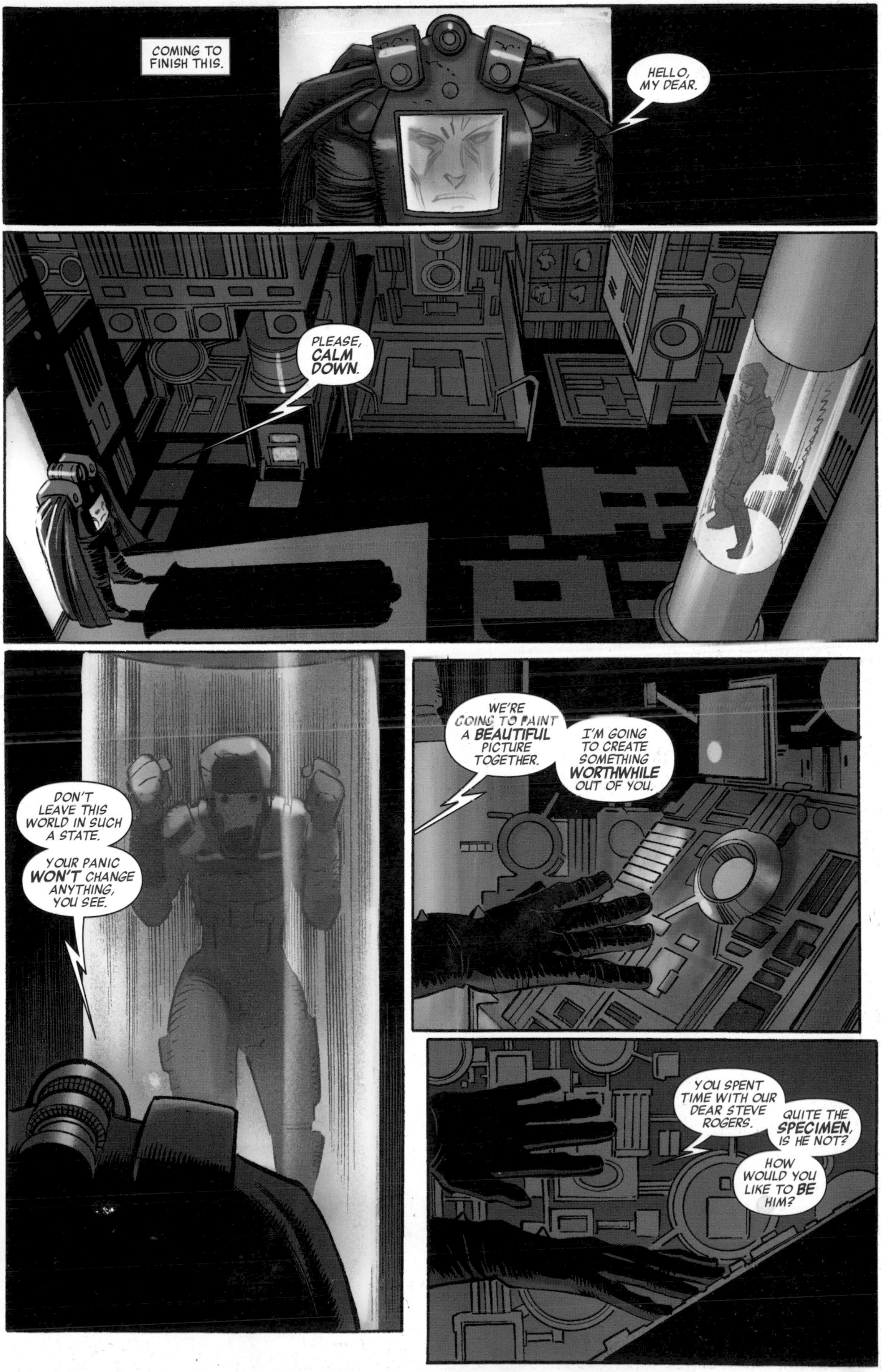
COMING TO FINISH THIS.
HELLO, MY DEAR.
PLEASE, CALM DOWN.
DON'T LEAVE THIS WORLD IN SUCH A STATE.
YOUR PANIC WON'T CHANGE ANYTHING, YOU SEE.
WE'RE GOING TO PAINT A BEAUTIFUL PICTURE TOGETHER.
I'M GOING TO CREATE SOMETHING WORTHWHILE OUT OF YOU.
YOU SPENT TIME WITH OUR DEAR STEVE ROGERS.
QUITE THE SPECIMEN, IS HE NOT?
HOW WOULD YOU LIKE TO BE HIM?

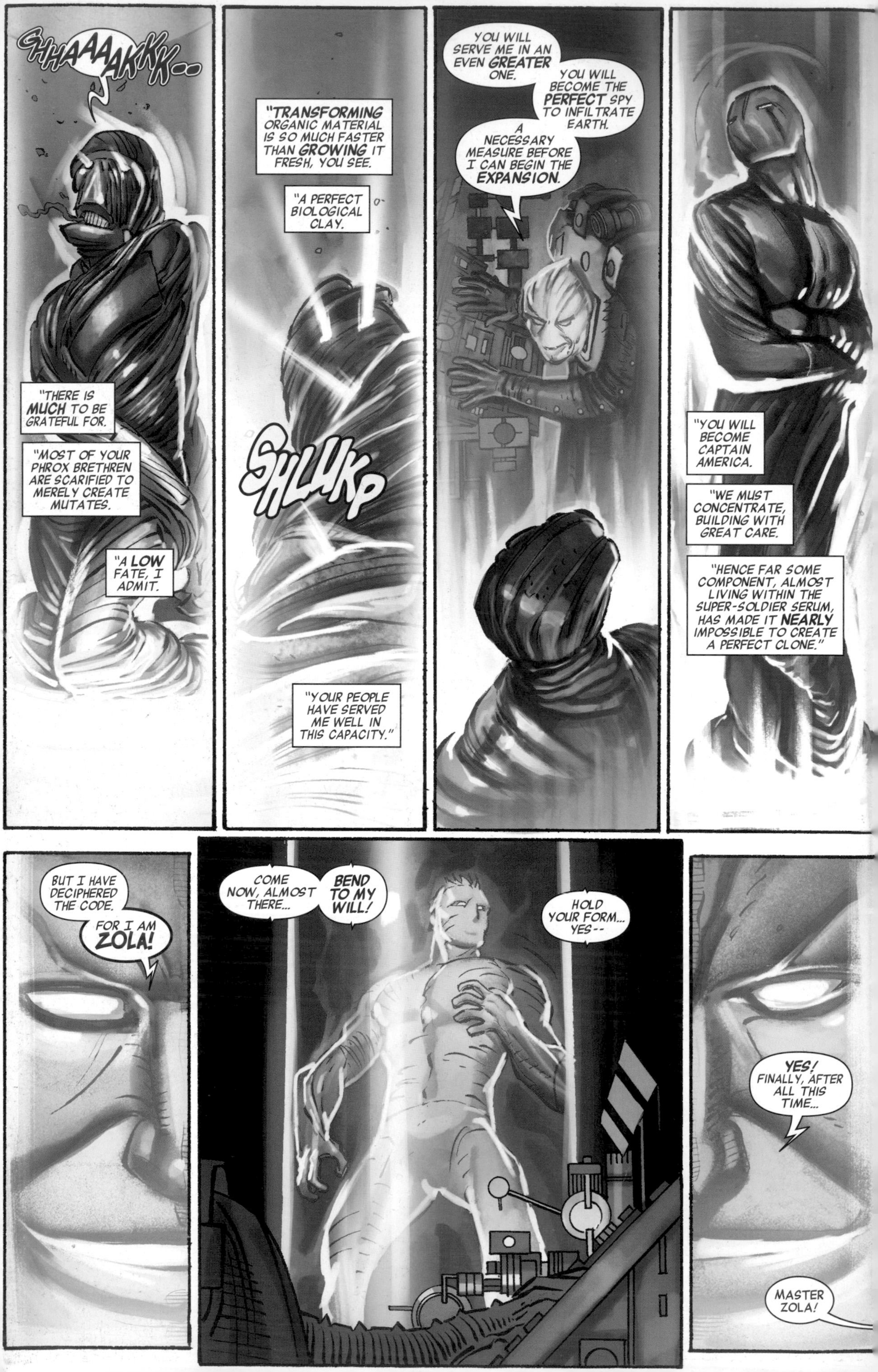
GHHAAAAKKK--
"THERE IS MUCH TO BE GRATEFUL FOR.
"MOST OF YOUR PHROX BRETHREN ARE SCARIFIED TO MERELY CREATE MUTATES.
"A LOW FATE, I ADMIT.
"TRANSFORMING ORGANIC MATERIAL IS SO MUCH FASTER THAN GROWING IT FRESH, YOU SEE.
"A PERFECT BIOLOGICAL CLAY.
SHLUKP
"YOUR PEOPLE HAVE SERVED ME WELL IN THIS CAPACITY."
YOU WILL SERVE ME IN AN EVEN GREATER ONE.
YOU WILL BECOME THE PERFECT SPY TO INFILTRATE EARTH.
A NECESSARY MEASURE BEFORE I CAN BEGIN THE EXPANSION.
"YOU WILL BECOME CAPTAIN AMERICA.
"WE MUST CONCENTRATE, BUILDING WITH GREAT CARE.
"HENCE FAR SOME COMPONENT, ALMOST LIVING WITHIN THE SUPER-SOLDIER SERUM, HAS MADE IT NEARLY IMPOSSIBLE TO CREATE A PERFECT CLONE."
BUT I HAVE DECIPHERED THE CODE.
FOR I AM ZOLA!
COME NOW, ALMOST THERE...
BEND TO MY WILL!
HOLD YOUR FORM... YES--
YES! FINALLY, AFTER ALL THIS TIME...
MASTER ZOLA!

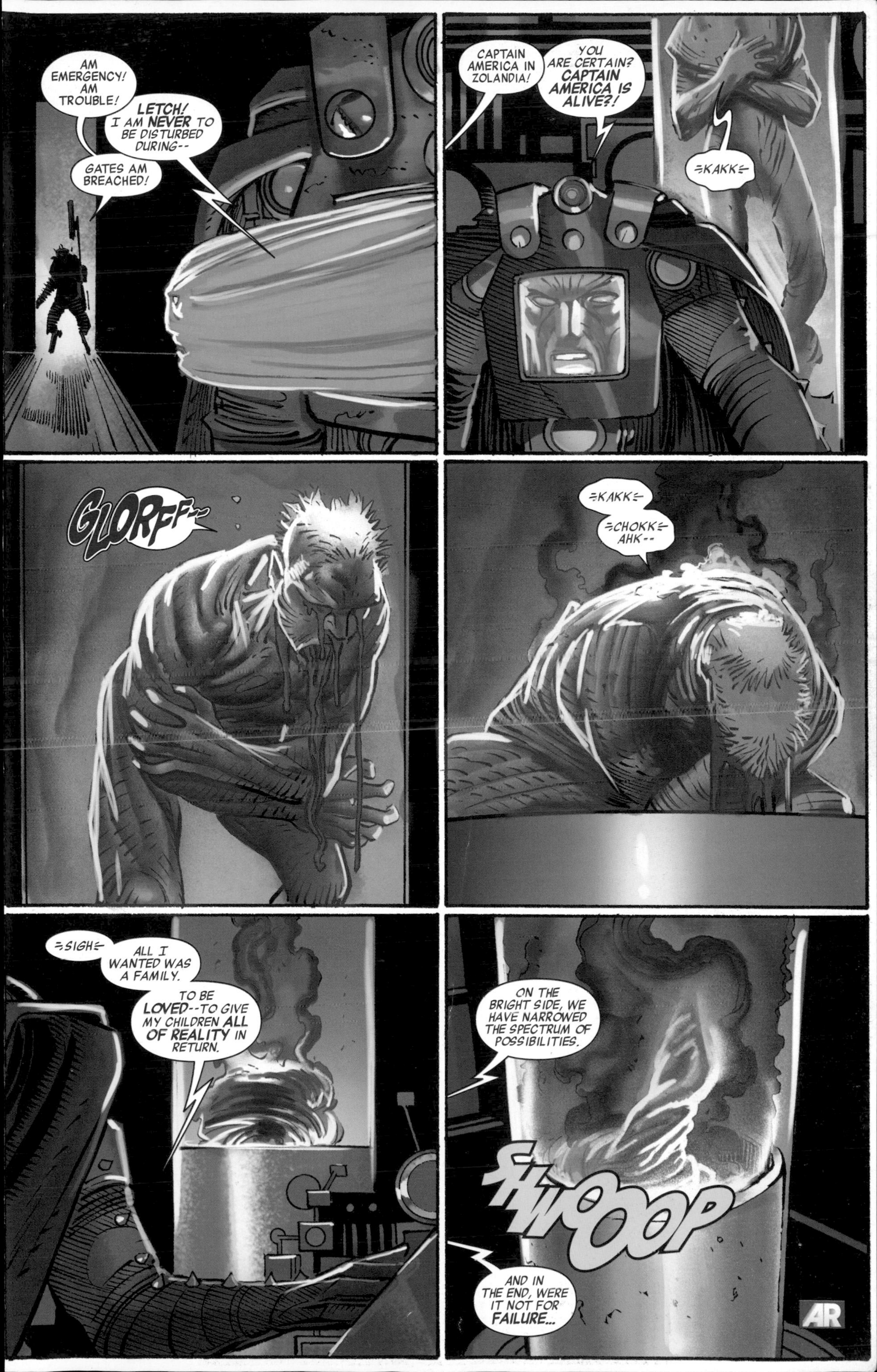
AM EMERGENCY! AM TROUBLE!
LETCH! I AM NEVER TO BE DISTURBED DURING--
GATES AM BREACHED!
CAPTAIN AMERICA IN ZOLANDIA!
YOU ARE CERTAIN? CAPTAIN AMERICA IS ALIVE?!
=KAKK=
GLORFF--
=KAKK=
=CHOKK= AHK--
=SIGH=
ALL I WANTED WAS A FAMILY.
TO BE LOVED--TO GIVE MY CHILDREN ALL OF REALITY IN RETURN.
ON THE BRIGHT SIDE, WE HAVE NARROWED THE SPECTRUM OF POSSIBILITIES.
SHWOOOP
AND IN THE END, WERE IT NOT FOR FAILURE...
AR

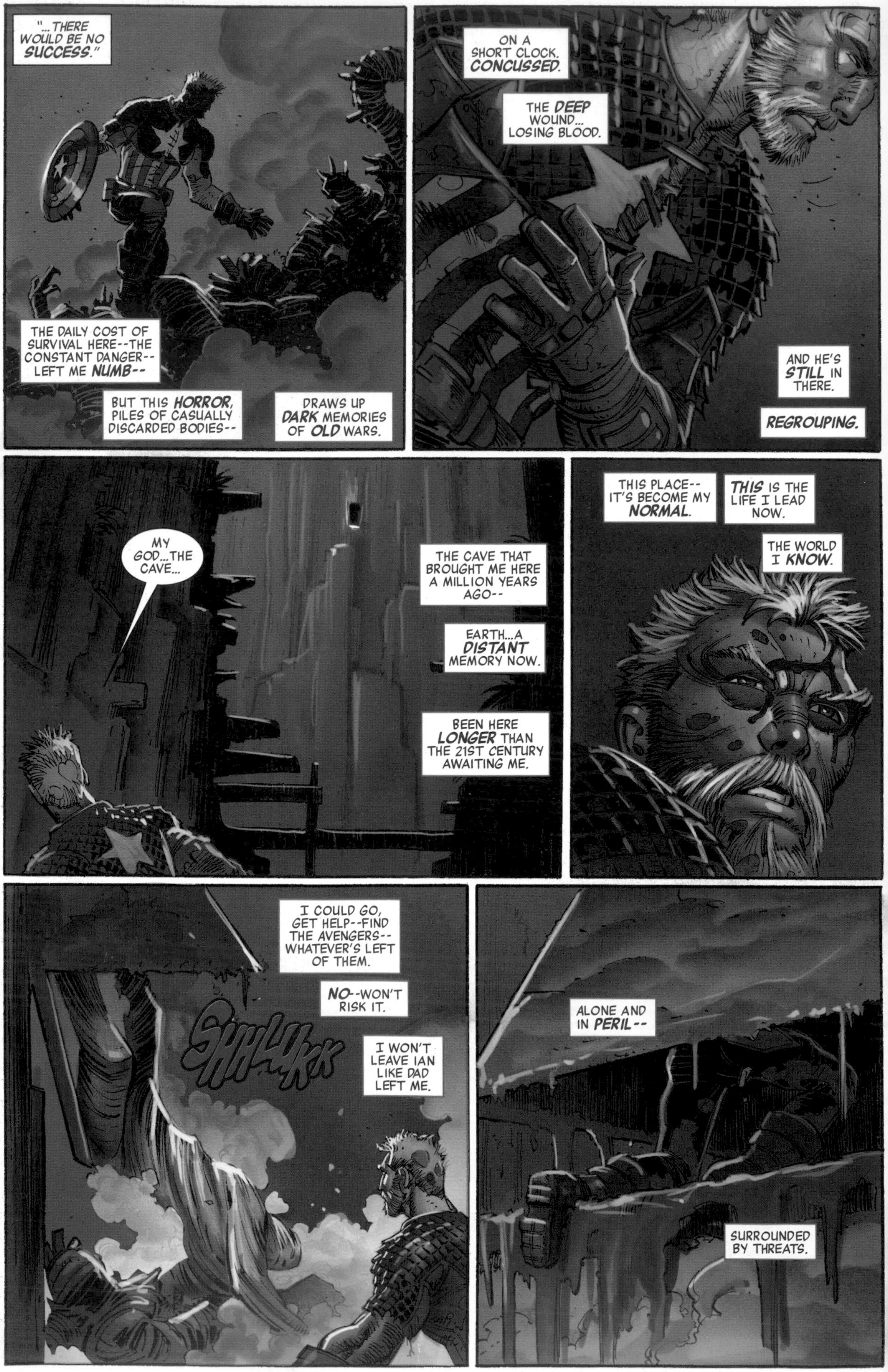
"...THERE WOULD BE NO SUCCESS."
THE DAILY COST OF SURVIVAL HERE--THE CONSTANT DANGER--LEFT ME NUMB--
BUT THIS HORROR, PILES OF CASUALLY DISCARDED BODIES--
DRAWS UP DARK MEMORIES OF OLD WARS.
ON A SHORT CLOCK. CONCUSSED.
THE DEEP WOUND... LOSING BLOOD.
AND HE'S STILL IN THERE.
REGROUPING.
MY GOD...THE CAVE...
THE CAVE THAT BROUGHT ME HERE A MILLION YEARS AGO--
EARTH...A DISTANT MEMORY NOW.
BEEN HERE LONGER THAN THE 21ST CENTURY AWAITING ME.
THIS PLACE--IT'S BECOME MY NORMAL.
THIS IS THE LIFE I LEAD NOW.
THE WORLD I KNOW.
I COULD GO, GET HELP--FIND THE AVENGERS--WHATEVER'S LEFT OF THEM.
NO--WON'T RISK IT.
SHHLUKK
I WON'T LEAVE IAN LIKE DAD LEFT ME.
ALONE AND IN PERIL--
SURROUNDED BY THREATS.

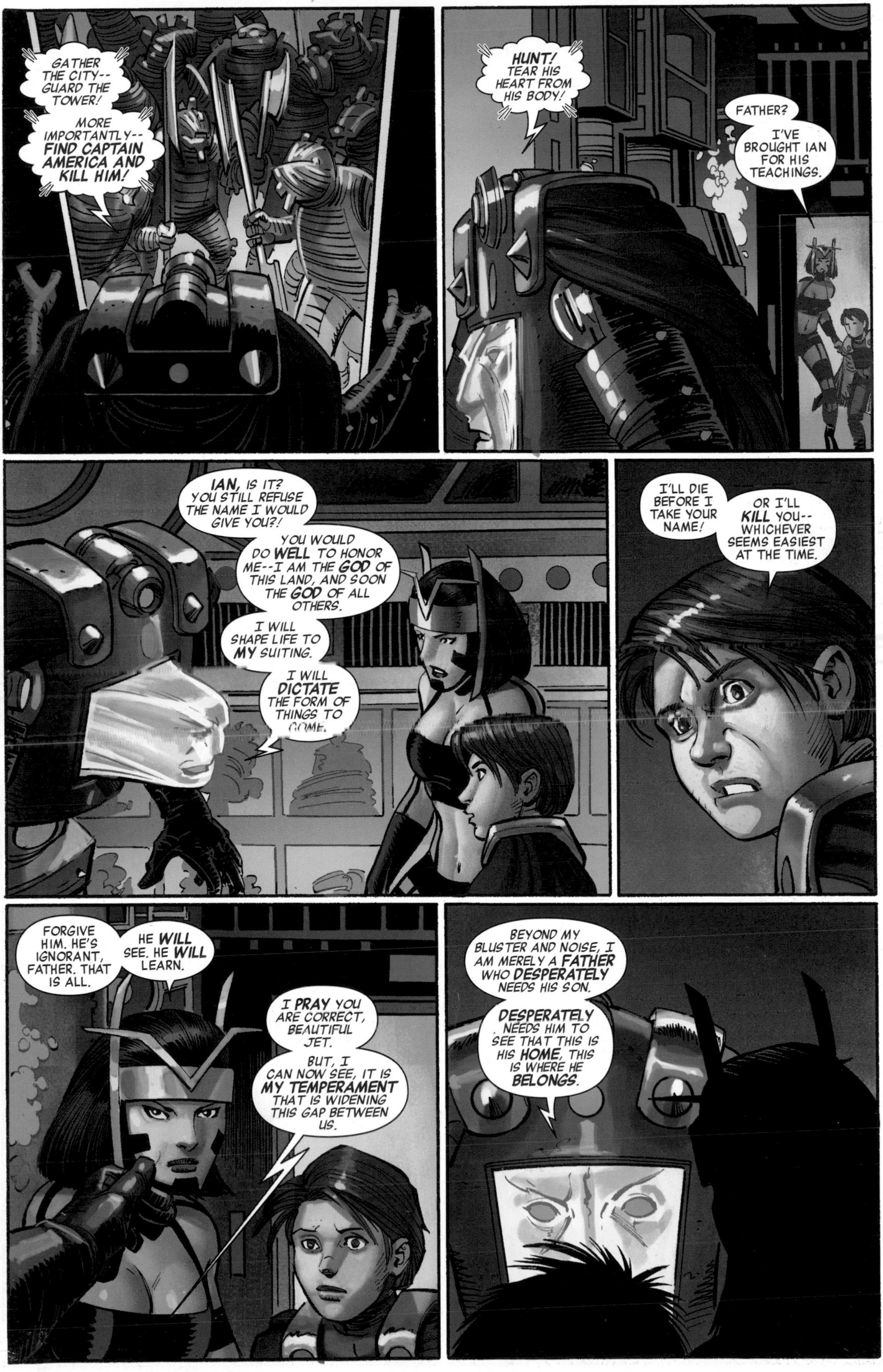
GATHER THE CITY--GUARD THE TOWER!
MORE IMPORTANTLY--FIND CAPTAIN AMERICA AND KILL HIM!
HUNT! TEAR HIS HEART FROM HIS BODY!
FATHER?
I'VE BROUGHT IAN FOR HIS TEACHINGS.
IAN, IS IT? YOU STILL REFUSE THE NAME I WOULD GIVE YOU?!
YOU WOULD DO WELL TO HONOR ME--I AM THE GOD OF THIS LAND, AND SOON THE GOD OF ALL OTHERS.
I WILL SHAPE LIFE TO MY SUITING.
I WILL DICTATE THE FORM OF THINGS TO COME.
I'LL DIE BEFORE I TAKE YOUR NAME!
OR I'LL KILL YOU--WHICHEVER SEEMS EASIEST AT THE TIME.
FORGIVE HIM. HE'S IGNORANT, FATHER. THAT IS ALL.
HE WILL SEE. HE WILL LEARN.
I PRAY YOU ARE CORRECT, BEAUTIFUL JET.
BUT, I CAN NOW SEE, IT IS MY TEMPERAMENT THAT IS WIDENING THIS GAP BETWEEN US.
BEYOND MY BLUSTER AND NOISE, I AM MERELY A FATHER WHO DESPERATELY NEEDS HIS SON.
DESPERATELY NEEDS HIM TO SEE THAT THIS IS HIS HOME, THIS IS WHERE HE BELONGS.

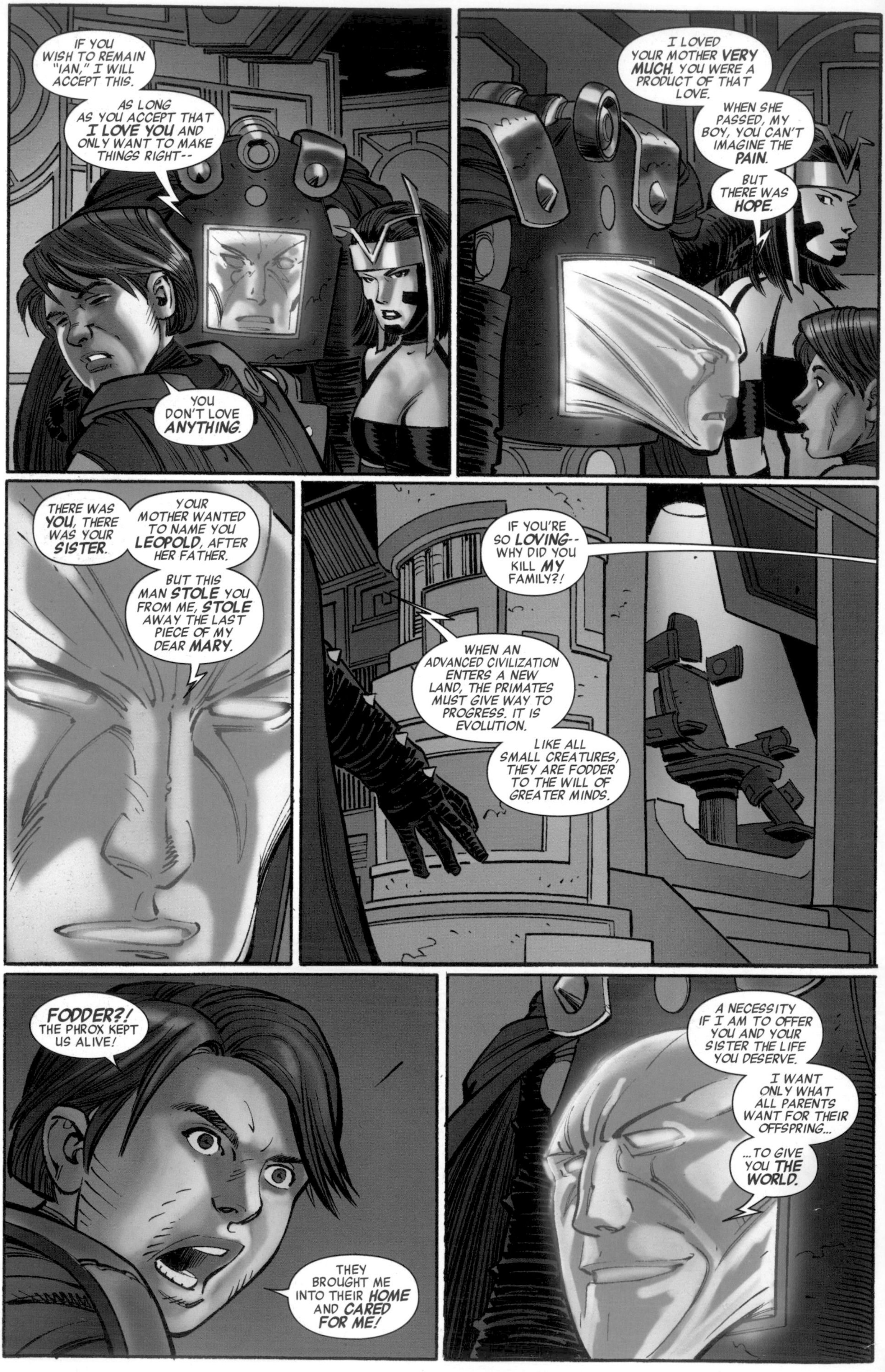
IF YOU WISH TO REMAIN "IAN," I WILL ACCEPT THIS.
AS LONG AS YOU ACCEPT THAT I LOVE YOU AND ONLY WANT TO MAKE THINGS RIGHT--
YOU DON'T LOVE ANYTHING.
I LOVED YOUR MOTHER VERY MUCH. YOU WERE A PRODUCT OF THAT LOVE.
WHEN SHE PASSED, MY BOY, YOU CAN'T IMAGINE THE PAIN.
BUT THERE WAS HOPE.
THERE WAS YOU, THERE WAS YOUR SISTER.
YOUR MOTHER WANTED TO NAME YOU LEOPOLD, AFTER HER FATHER.
BUT THIS MAN STOLE YOU FROM ME, STOLE AWAY THE LAST PIECE OF MY DEAR MARY.
IF YOU'RE SO LOVING--WHY DID YOU KILL MY FAMILY?!
WHEN AN ADVANCED CIVILIZATION ENTERS A NEW LAND, THE PRIMATES MUST GIVE WAY TO PROGRESS. IT IS EVOLUTION.
LIKE ALL SMALL CREATURES, THEY ARE FODDER TO THE WILL OF GREATER MINDS.
FODDER?! THE PHROX KEPT US ALIVE!
THEY BROUGHT ME INTO THEIR HOME AND CARED FOR ME!
A NECESSITY IF I AM TO OFFER YOU AND YOUR SISTER THE LIFE YOU DESERVE.
I WANT ONLY WHAT ALL PARENTS WANT FOR THEIR OFFSPRING...
...TO GIVE YOU THE WORLD.

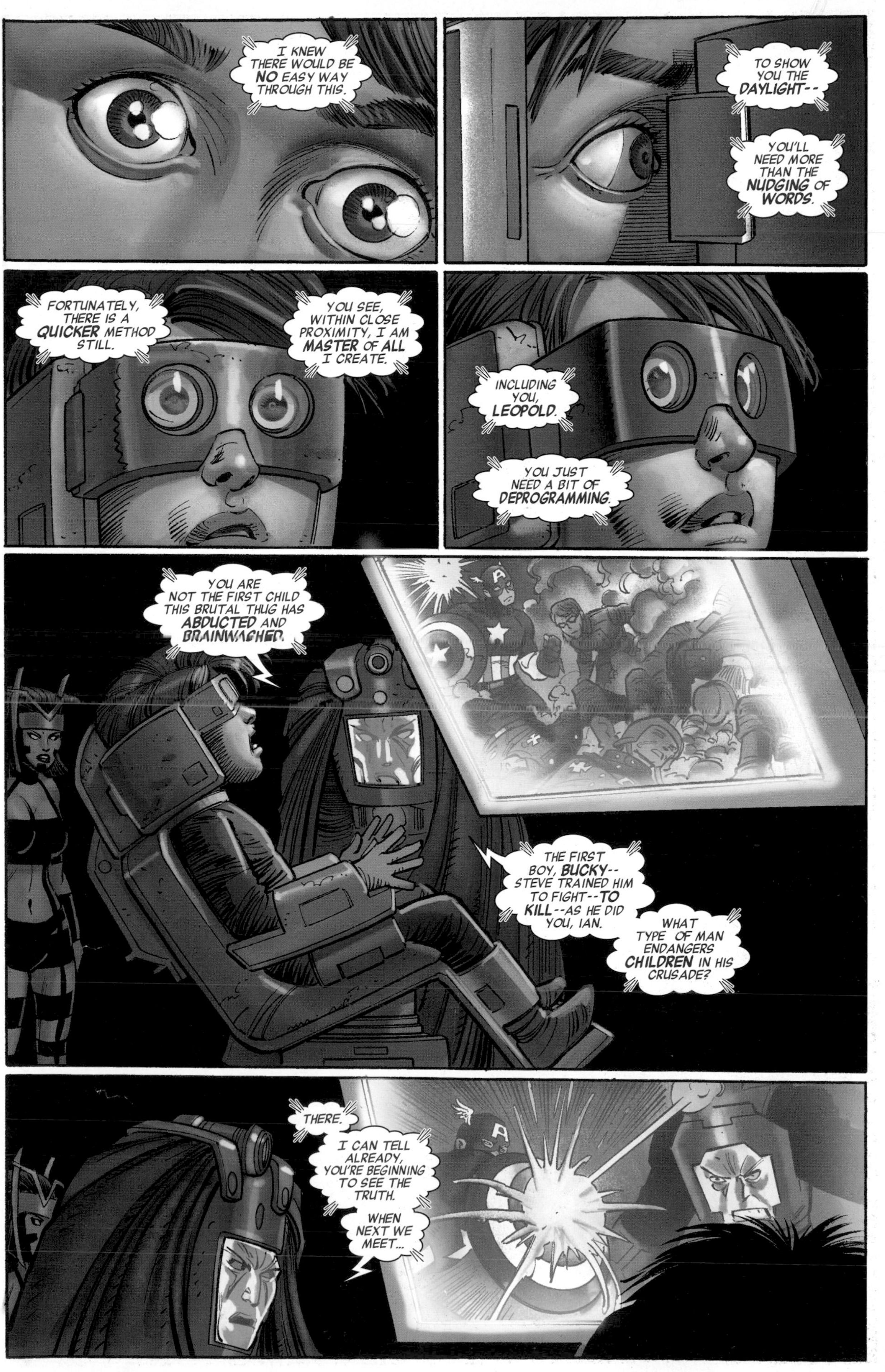
I KNEW THERE WOULD BE NO EASY WAY THROUGH THIS.
TO SHOW YOU THE DAYLIGHT--
YOU'LL NEED MORE THAN THE NUDGING OF WORDS.
FORTUNATELY, THERE IS A QUICKER METHOD STILL.
YOU SEE, WITHIN CLOSE PROXIMITY, I AM MASTER OF ALL I CREATE.
INCLUDING YOU, LEOPOLD.
YOU JUST NEED A BIT OF DEPROGRAMMING.
YOU ARE NOT THE FIRST CHILD THIS BRUTAL THUG HAS ABDUCTED AND BRAINWASHED.
THE FIRST BOY, BUCKY-- STEVE TRAINED HIM TO FIGHT--TO KILL--AS HE DID YOU, IAN.
WHAT TYPE OF MAN ENDANGERS CHILDREN IN HIS CRUSADE?
THERE.
I CAN TELL ALREADY, YOU'RE BEGINNING TO SEE THE TRUTH.
WHEN NEXT WE MEET...

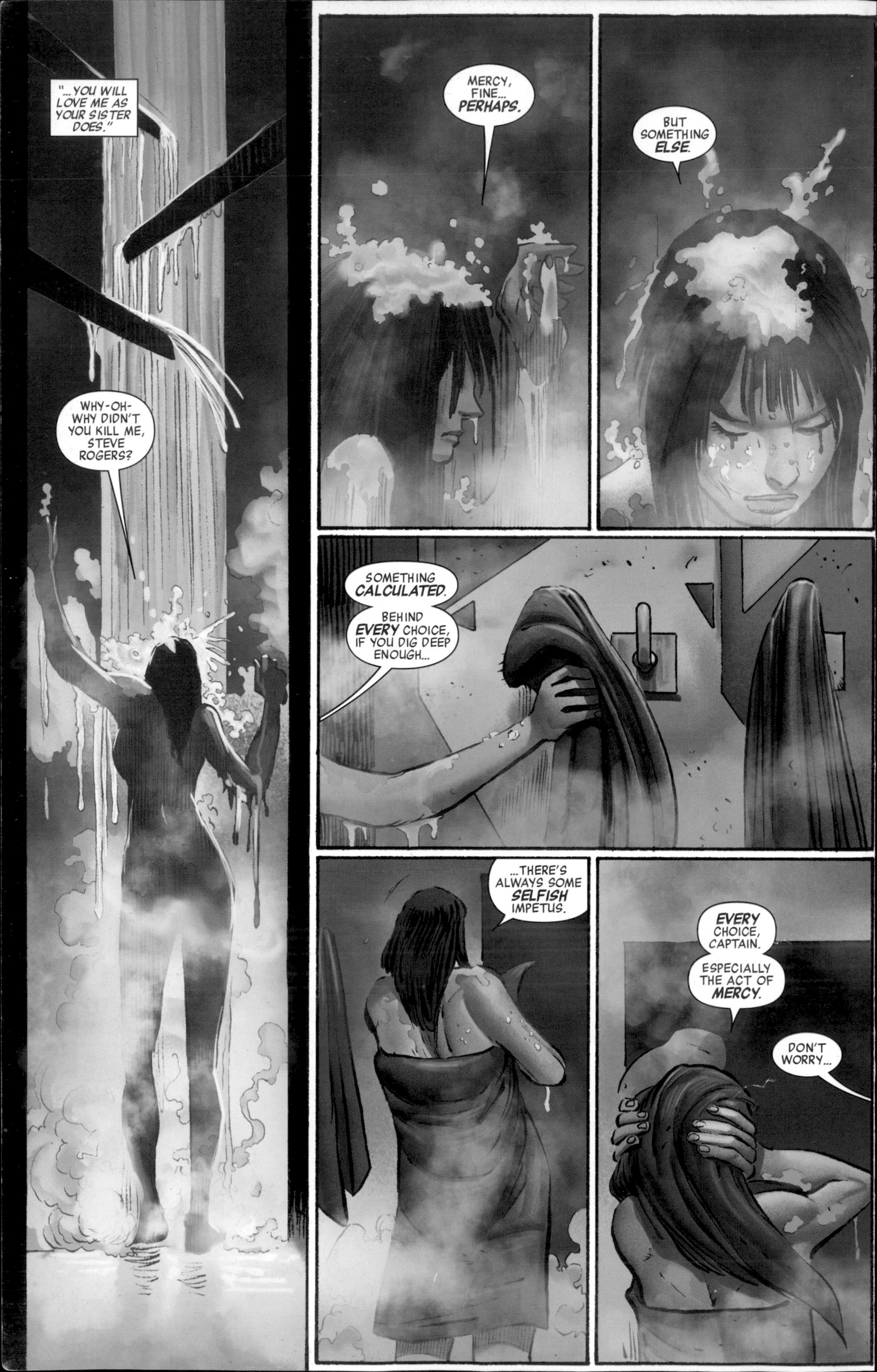
"...YOU WILL LOVE ME AS YOUR SISTER DOES."
WHY-OH-WHY DIDN'T YOU KILL ME, STEVE ROGERS?
MERCY, FINE... PERHAPS.
BUT SOMETHING ELSE.
SOMETHING CALCULATED.
BEHIND EVERY CHOICE, IF YOU DIG DEEP ENOUGH...
...THERE'S ALWAYS SOME SELFISH IMPETUS.
EVERY CHOICE, CAPTAIN.
ESPECIALLY THE ACT OF MERCY.
DON'T WORRY...

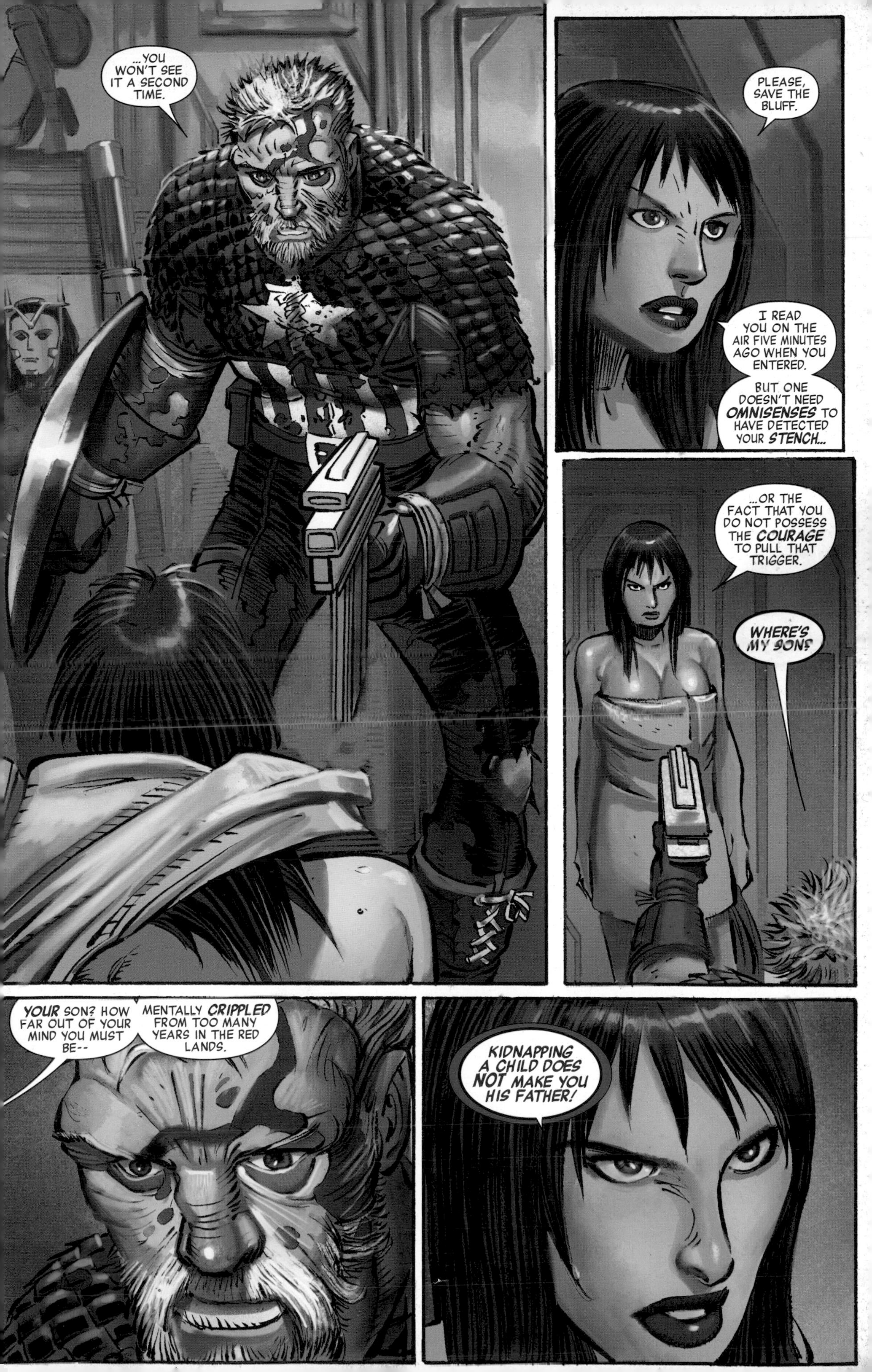
...YOU WON'T SEE IT A SECOND TIME.
PLEASE, SAVE THE BLUFF.
I READ YOU ON THE AIR FIVE MINUTES AGO WHEN YOU ENTERED.
BUT ONE DOESN'T NEED OMNISENSES TO HAVE DETECTED YOUR STENCH...
...OR THE FACT THAT YOU DO NOT POSSESS THE COURAGE TO PULL THAT TRIGGER.
WHERE'S MY SON?
YOUR SON? HOW FAR OUT OF YOUR MIND YOU MUST BE--
MENTALLY CRIPPLED FROM TOO MANY YEARS IN THE RED LANDS.
KIDNAPPING A CHILD DOES NOT MAKE YOU HIS FATHER!

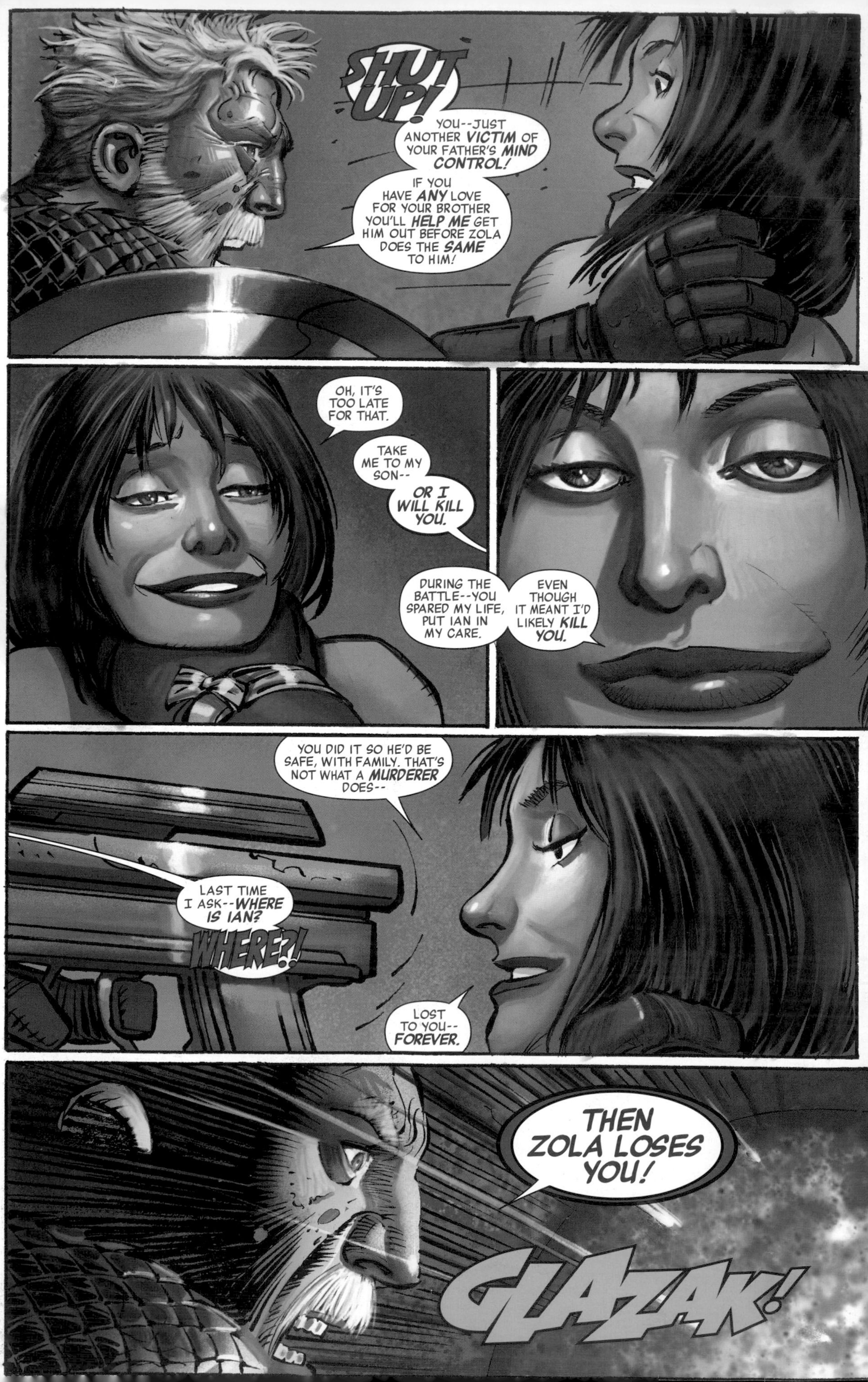
SHUT UP!
YOU--JUST ANOTHER VICTIM OF YOUR FATHER'S MIND CONTROL!
IF YOU HAVE ANY LOVE FOR YOUR BROTHER YOU'LL HELP ME GET HIM OUT BEFORE ZOLA DOES THE SAME TO HIM!
OH, IT'S TOO LATE FOR THAT.
TAKE ME TO MY SON--
OR I WILL KILL YOU.
DURING THE BATTLE--YOU SPARED MY LIFE, PUT IAN IN MY CARE.
EVEN THOUGH IT MEANT I'D LIKELY KILL YOU.
YOU DID IT SO HE'D BE SAFE, WITH FAMILY. THAT'S NOT WHAT A MURDERER DOES--
LAST TIME I ASK--WHERE IS IAN?
WHERE?!
LOST TO YOU--FOREVER.
THEN ZOLA LOSES YOU!
GLAZAK!

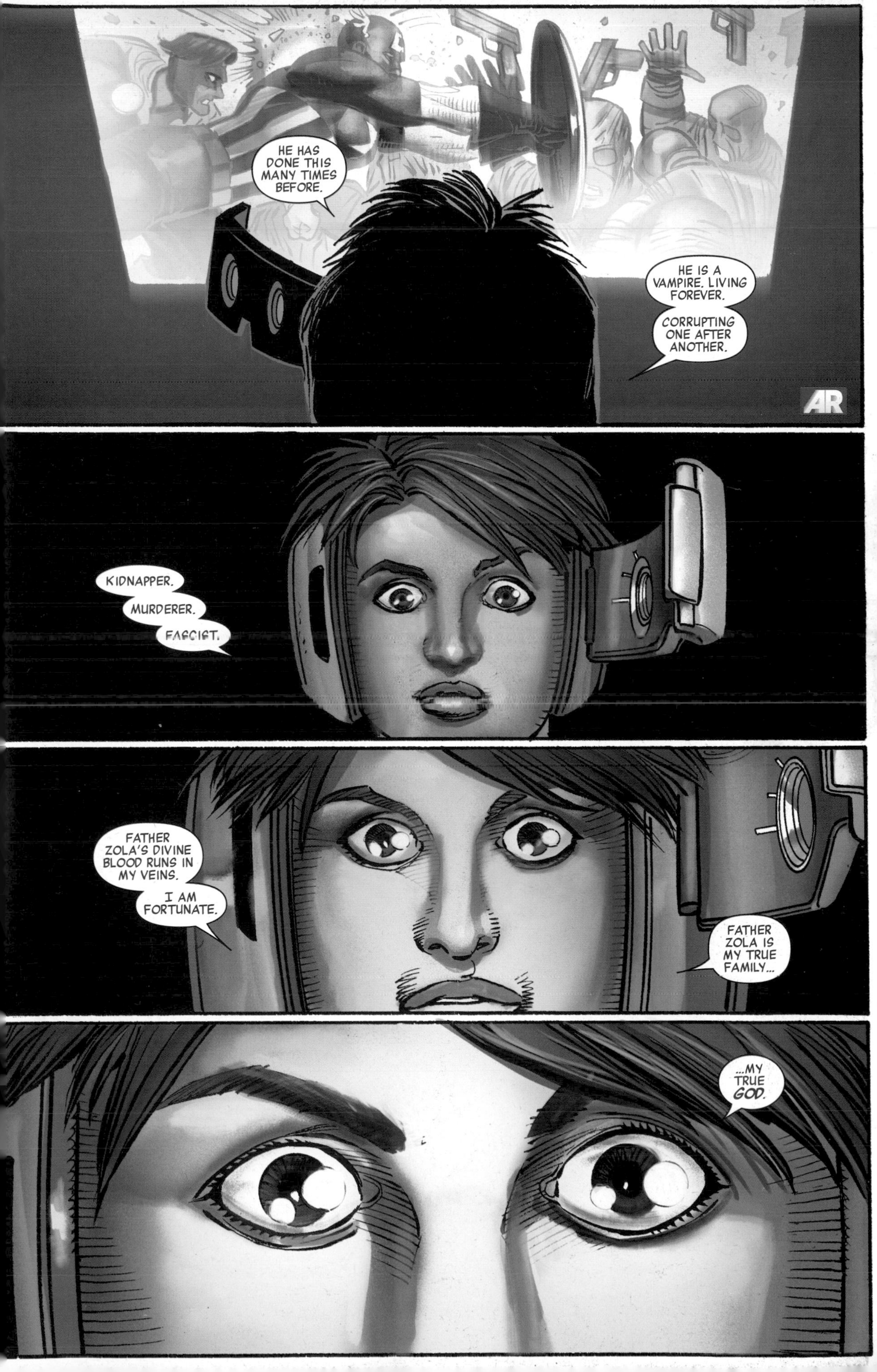
HE HAS DONE THIS MANY TIMES BEFORE.
HE IS A VAMPIRE. LIVING FOREVER.
CORRUPTING ONE AFTER ANOTHER.
AR
KIDNAPPER.
MURDERER.
FASCIST.
FATHER ZOLA'S DIVINE BLOOD RUNS IN MY VEINS.
I AM FORTUNATE.
FATHER ZOLA IS MY TRUE FAMILY...
...MY TRUE GOD.

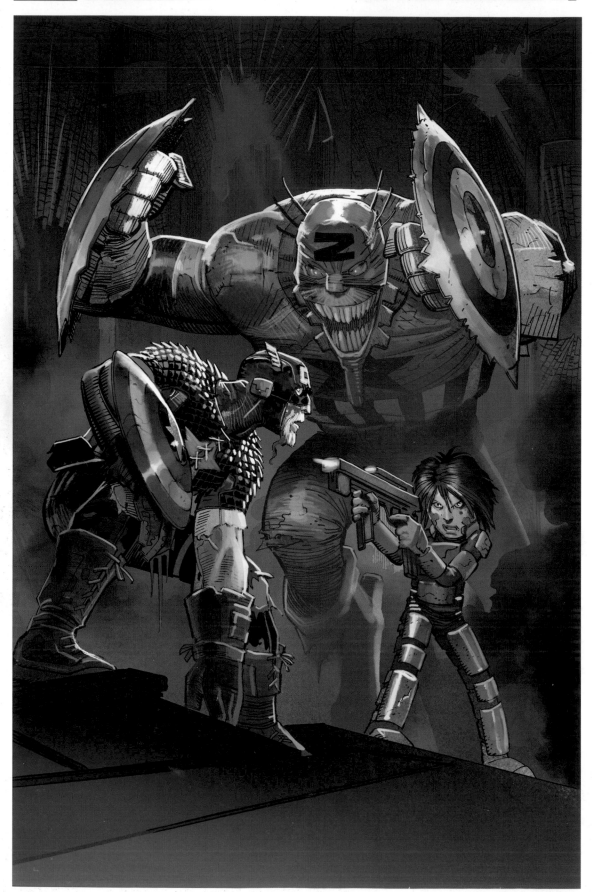

ASHES OF OUR FATHERS

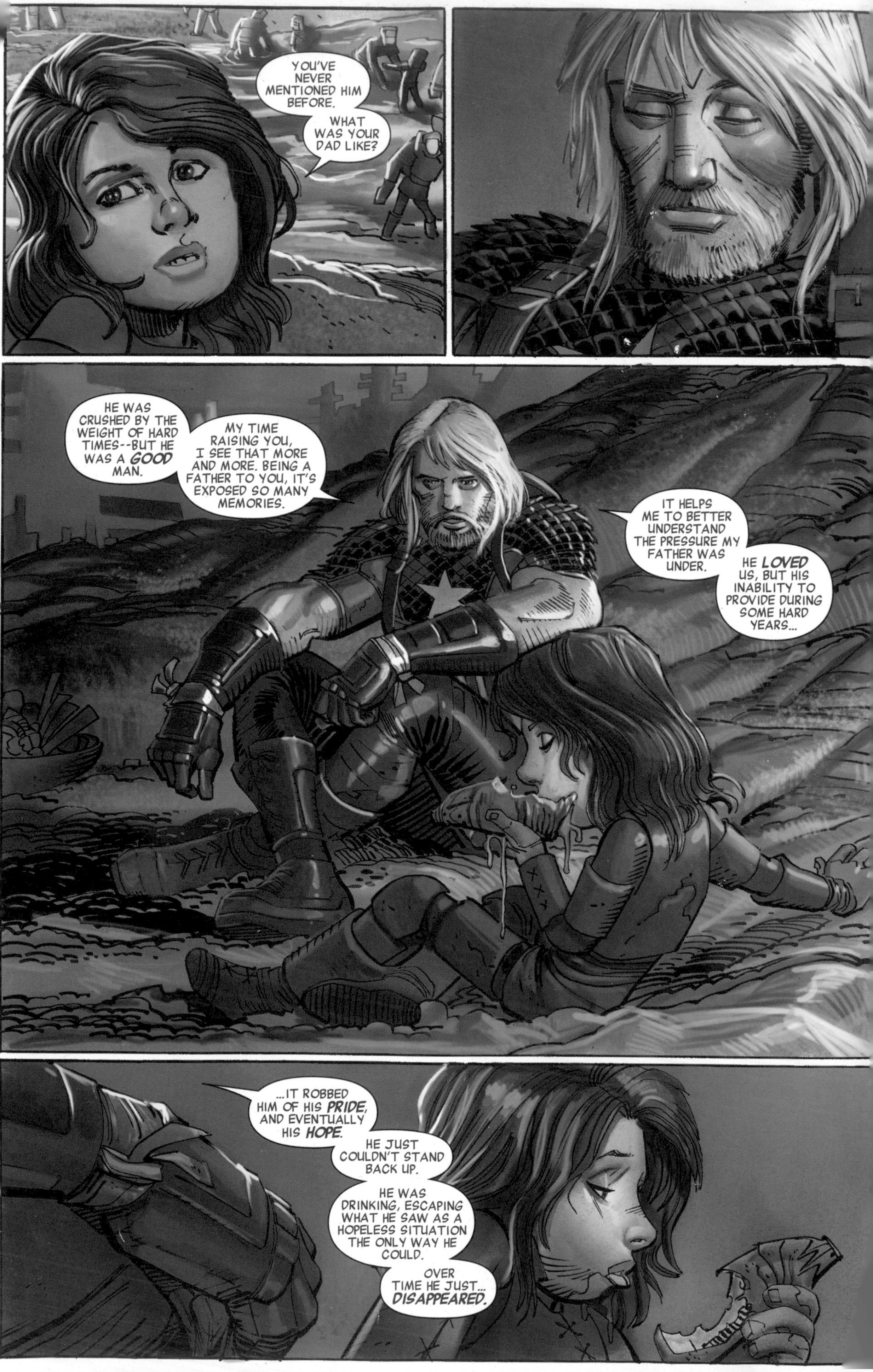
YOU'VE NEVER MENTIONED HIM BEFORE.
WHAT WAS YOUR DAD LIKE?
HE WAS CRUSHED BY THE WEIGHT OF HARD TIMES--BUT HE WAS A GOOD MAN.
MY TIME RAISING YOU, I SEE THAT MORE AND MORE. BEING A FATHER TO YOU, IT'S EXPOSED SO MANY MEMORIES.
IT HELPS ME TO BETTER UNDERSTAND THE PRESSURE MY FATHER WAS UNDER.
HE LOVED US, BUT HIS INABILITY TO PROVIDE DURING SOME HARD YEARS...
...IT ROBBED HIM OF HIS PRIDE, AND EVENTUALLY HIS HOPE.
HE JUST COULDN'T STAND BACK UP.
HE WAS DRINKING, ESCAPING WHAT HE SAW AS A HOPELESS SITUATION THE ONLY WAY HE COULD.
OVER TIME HE JUST... DISAPPEARED.

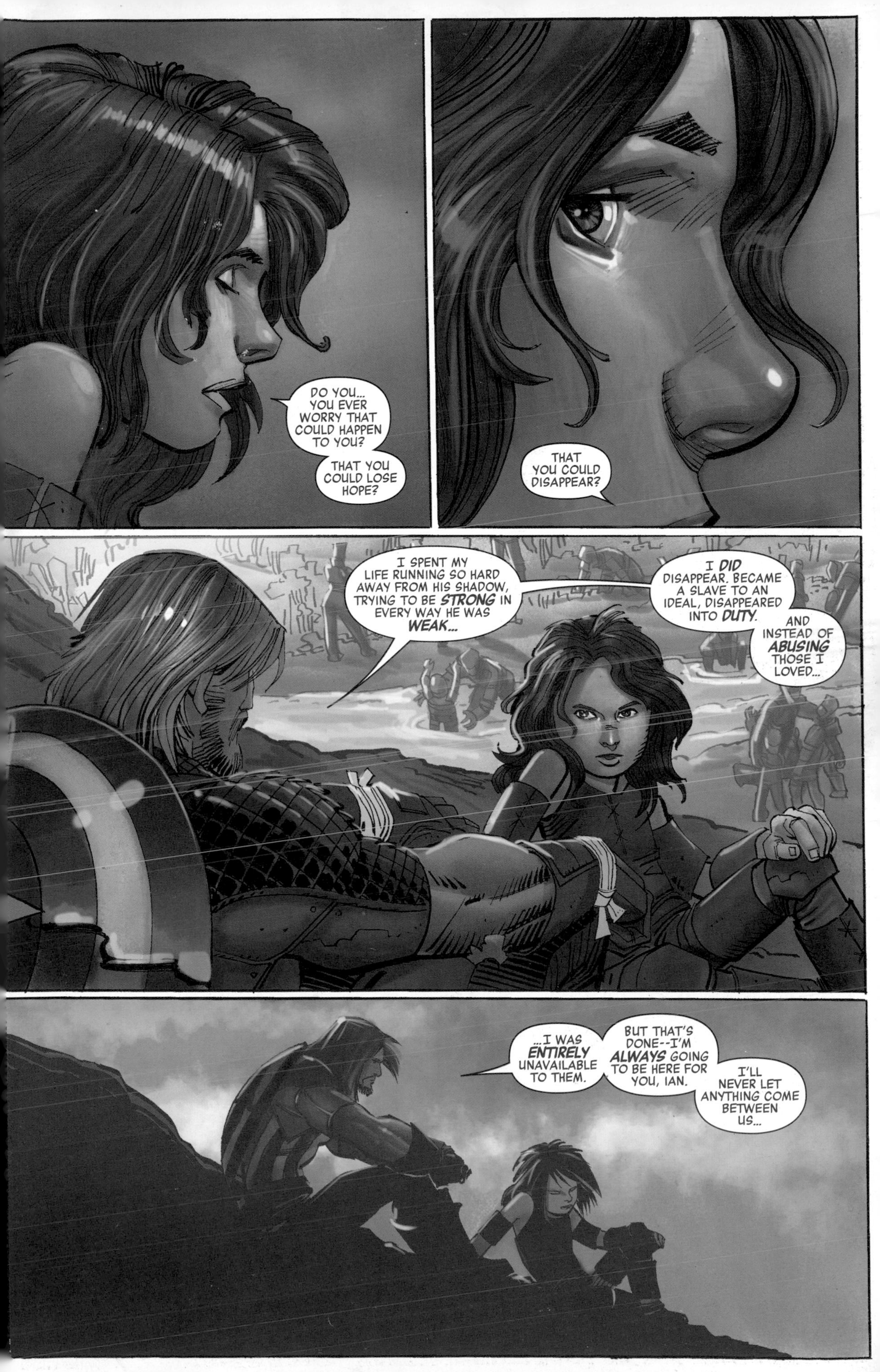
DO YOU... YOU EVER WORRY THAT COULD HAPPEN TO YOU?
THAT YOU COULD LOSE HOPE?
THAT YOU COULD DISAPPEAR?
I SPENT MY LIFE RUNNING SO HARD AWAY FROM HIS SHADOW, TRYING TO BE STRONG IN EVERY WAY HE WAS WEAK...
I DID DISAPPEAR. BECAME A SLAVE TO AN IDEAL, DISAPPEARED INTO DUTY.
AND INSTEAD OF ABUSING THOSE I LOVED...
...I WAS ENTIRELY UNAVAILABLE TO THEM.
BUT THAT'S DONE--I'M ALWAYS GOING TO BE HERE FOR YOU, IAN.
I'LL NEVER LET ANYTHING COME BETWEEN US...

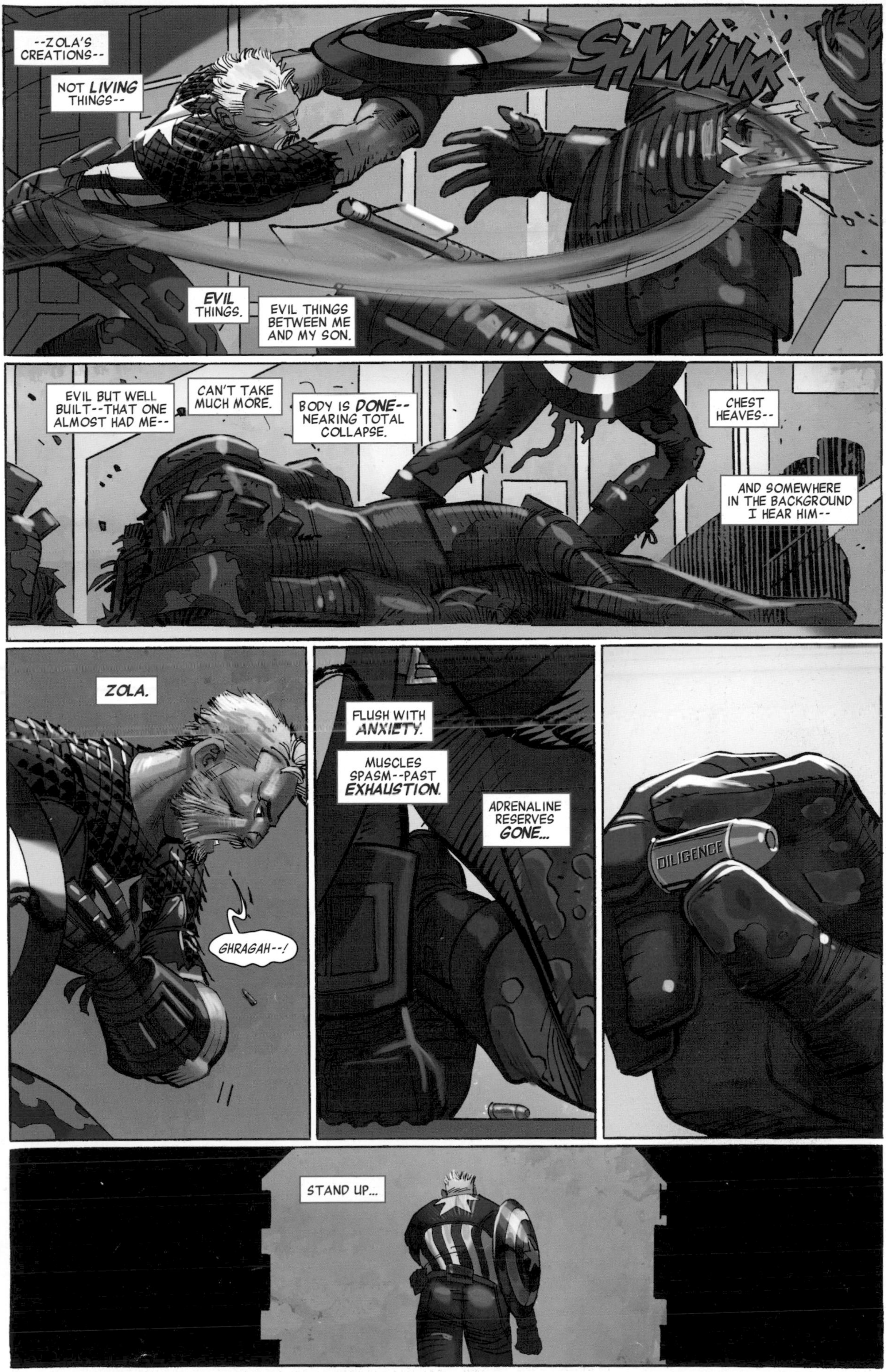
--ZOLA'S CREATIONS--
NOT LIVING THINGS--
SHVUNKK
EVIL THINGS.
EVIL THINGS BETWEEN ME AND MY SON.
EVIL BUT WELL BUILT--THAT ONE ALMOST HAD ME--
CAN'T TAKE MUCH MORE.
BODY IS DONE--NEARING TOTAL COLLAPSE.
CHEST HEAVES--
AND SOMEWHERE IN THE BACKGROUND I HEAR HIM--
ZOLA.
GHRAGAH--!
FLUSH WITH ANXIETY.
MUSCLES SPASM--PAST EXHAUSTION.
ADRENALINE RESERVES GONE...
DILIGENCE
STAND UP...

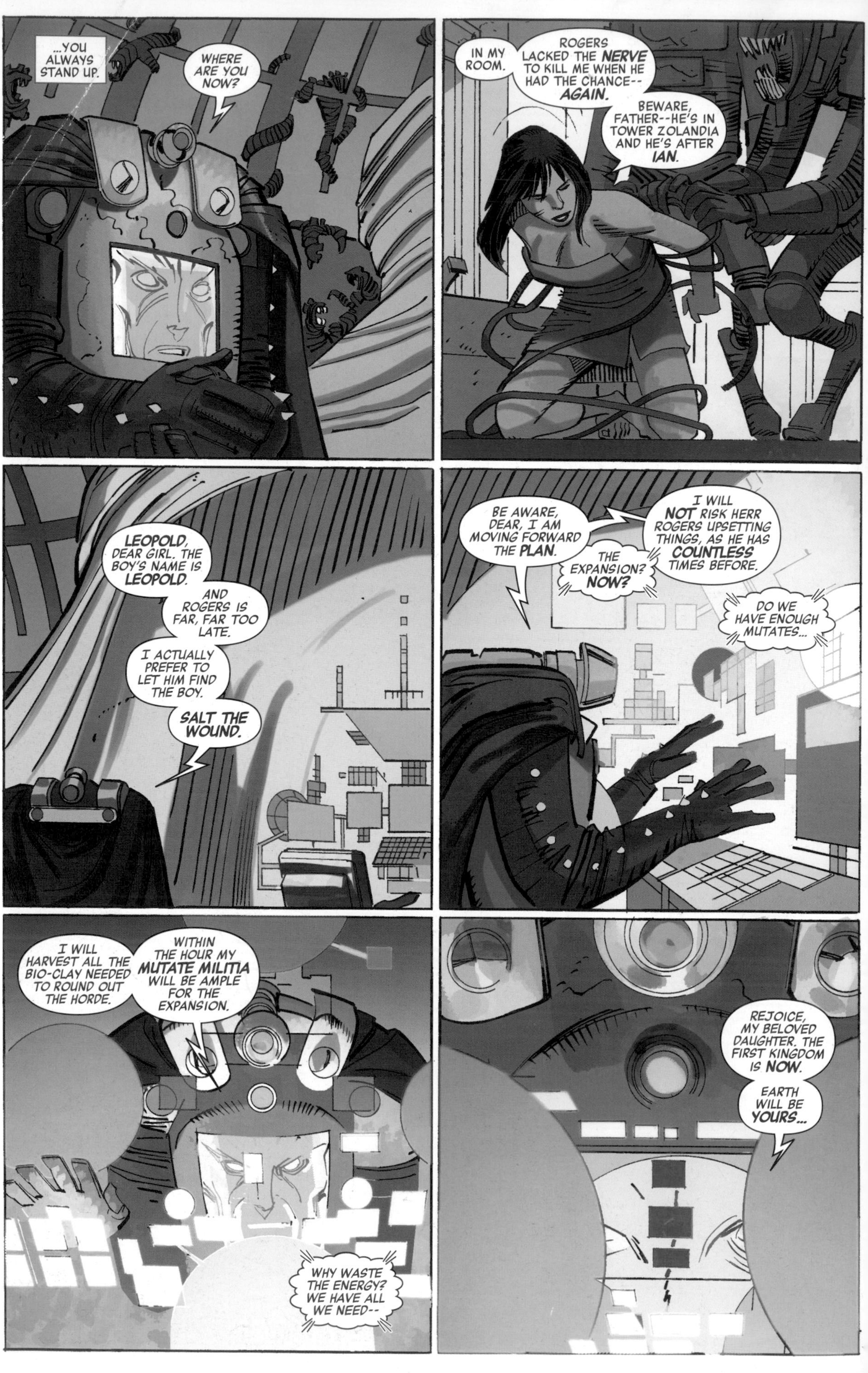
...YOU ALWAYS STAND UP.
WHERE ARE YOU NOW?
IN MY ROOM.
ROGERS LACKED THE NERVE TO KILL ME WHEN HE HAD THE CHANCE-- AGAIN.
BEWARE, FATHER--HE'S IN TOWER ZOLANDIA AND HE'S AFTER IAN.
LEOPOLD, DEAR GIRL. THE BOY'S NAME IS LEOPOLD.
AND ROGERS IS FAR, FAR TOO LATE.
I ACTUALLY PREFER TO LET HIM FIND THE BOY.
SALT THE WOUND.
BE AWARE, DEAR, I AM MOVING FORWARD THE PLAN.
THE EXPANSION? NOW?
I WILL NOT RISK HERR ROGERS UPSETTING THINGS, AS HE HAS COUNTLESS TIMES BEFORE.
DO WE HAVE ENOUGH MUTATES...
I WILL HARVEST ALL THE BIO-CLAY NEEDED TO ROUND OUT THE HORDE.
WITHIN THE HOUR MY MUTATE MILITIA WILL BE AMPLE FOR THE EXPANSION.
WHY WASTE THE ENERGY? WE HAVE ALL WE NEED--
REJOICE, MY BELOVED DAUGHTER. THE FIRST KINGDOM IS NOW.
EARTH WILL BE YOURS...

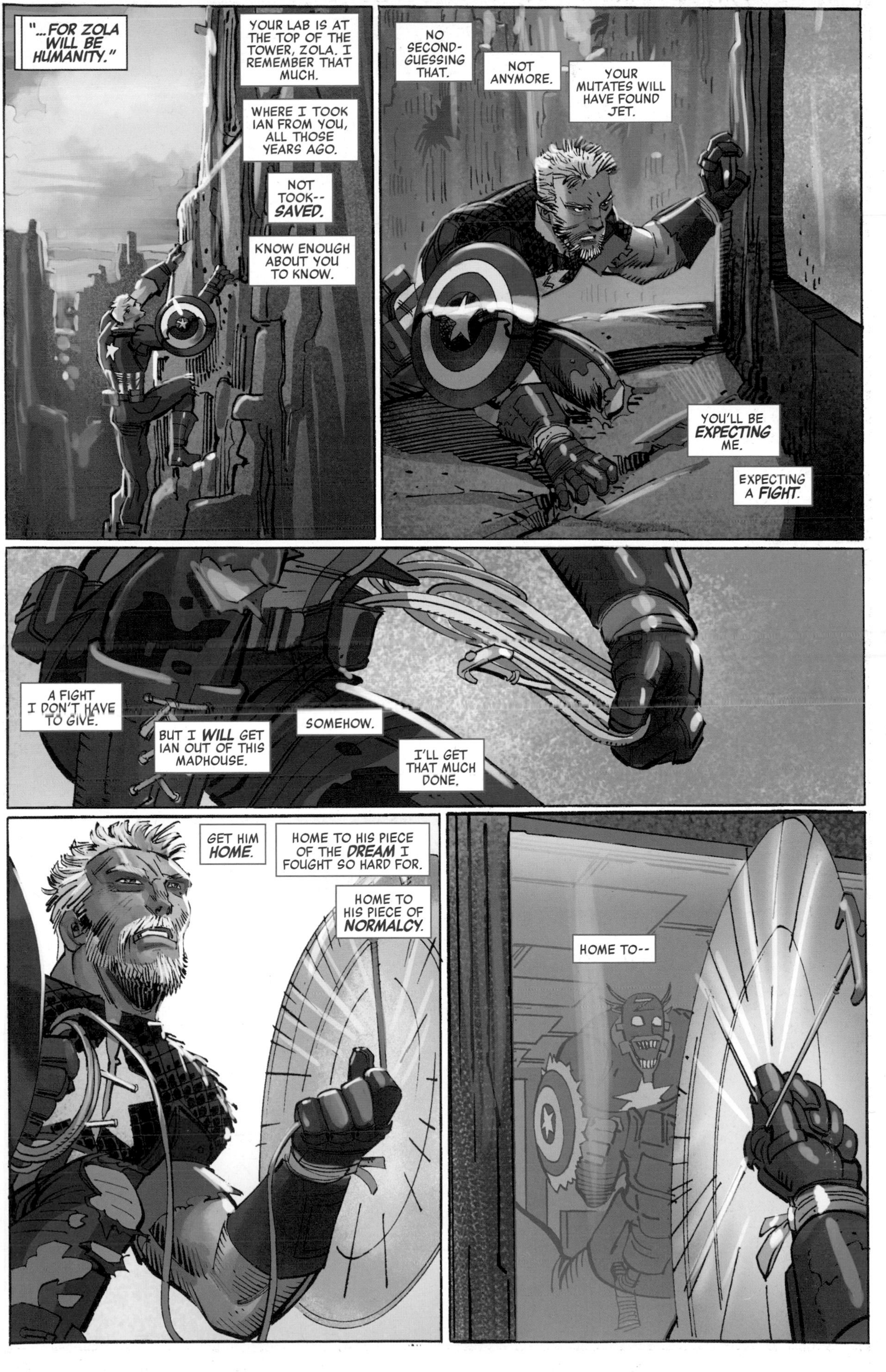
"...FOR ZOLA WILL BE HUMANITY."
YOUR LAB IS AT THE TOP OF THE TOWER, ZOLA. I REMEMBER THAT MUCH.
WHERE I TOOK IAN FROM YOU, ALL THOSE YEARS AGO.
NOT TOOK-- SAVED.
KNOW ENOUGH ABOUT YOU TO KNOW.
NO SECOND-GUESSING THAT.
NOT ANYMORE.
YOUR MUTATES WILL HAVE FOUND JET.
YOU'LL BE EXPECTING ME.
EXPECTING A FIGHT.
A FIGHT I DON'T HAVE TO GIVE.
BUT I WILL GET IAN OUT OF THIS MADHOUSE.
SOMEHOW.
I'LL GET THAT MUCH DONE.
GET HIM HOME.
HOME TO HIS PIECE OF THE DREAM I FOUGHT SO HARD FOR.
HOME TO HIS PIECE OF NORMALCY.
HOME TO--

OOF--!

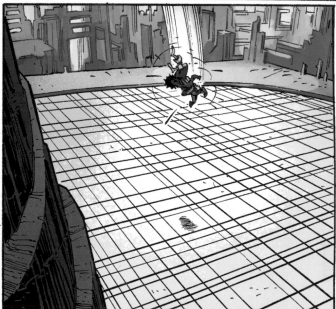

SON OF A--

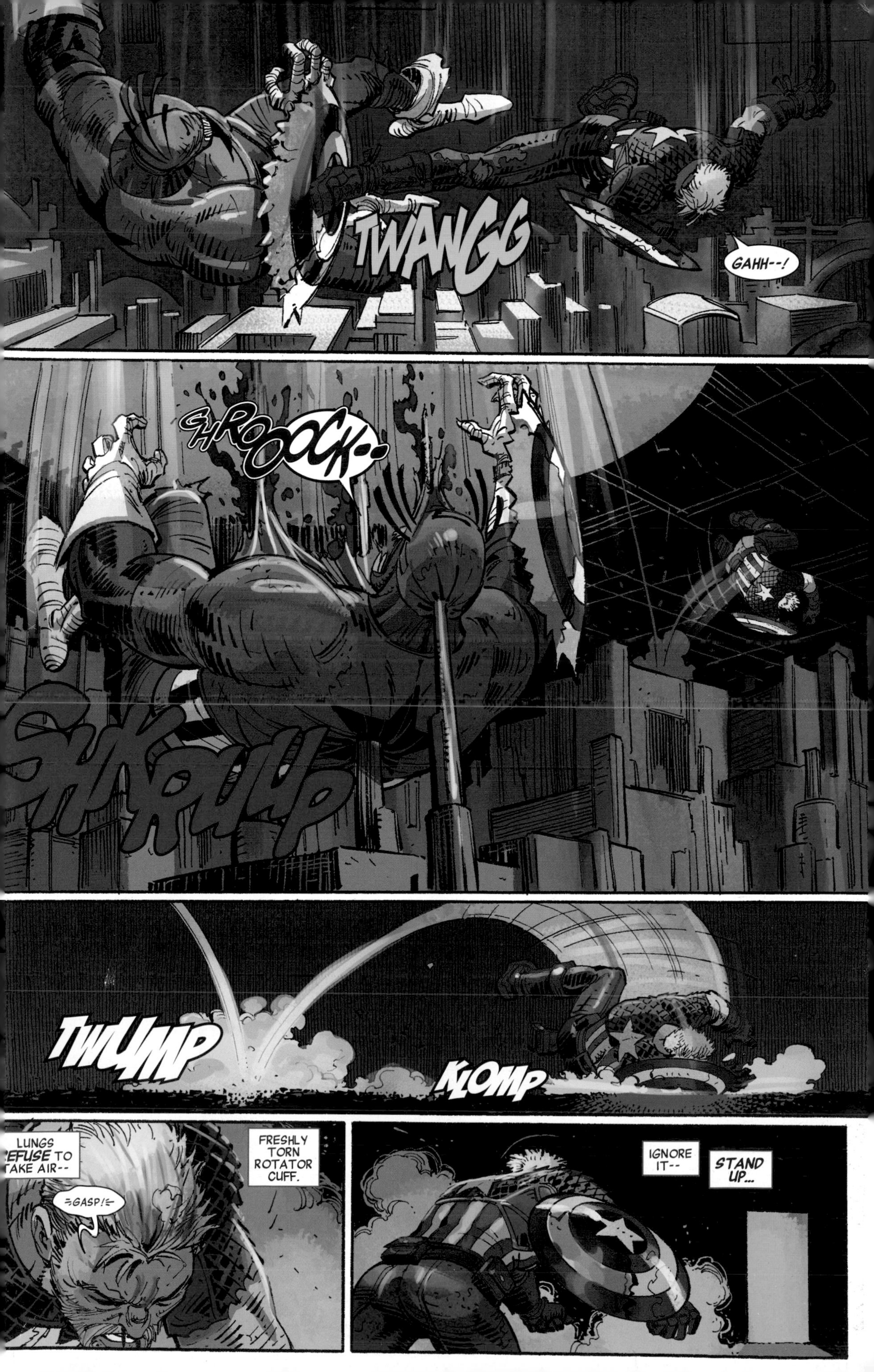

TWANGG
GAHH--!
CHROOOCK--
SHKRUMP
TWUMP
KLOMP
LUNGS REFUSE TO TAKE AIR--
FRESHLY TORN ROTATOR CUFF.
=GASP!=
IGNORE IT--
STAND UP...

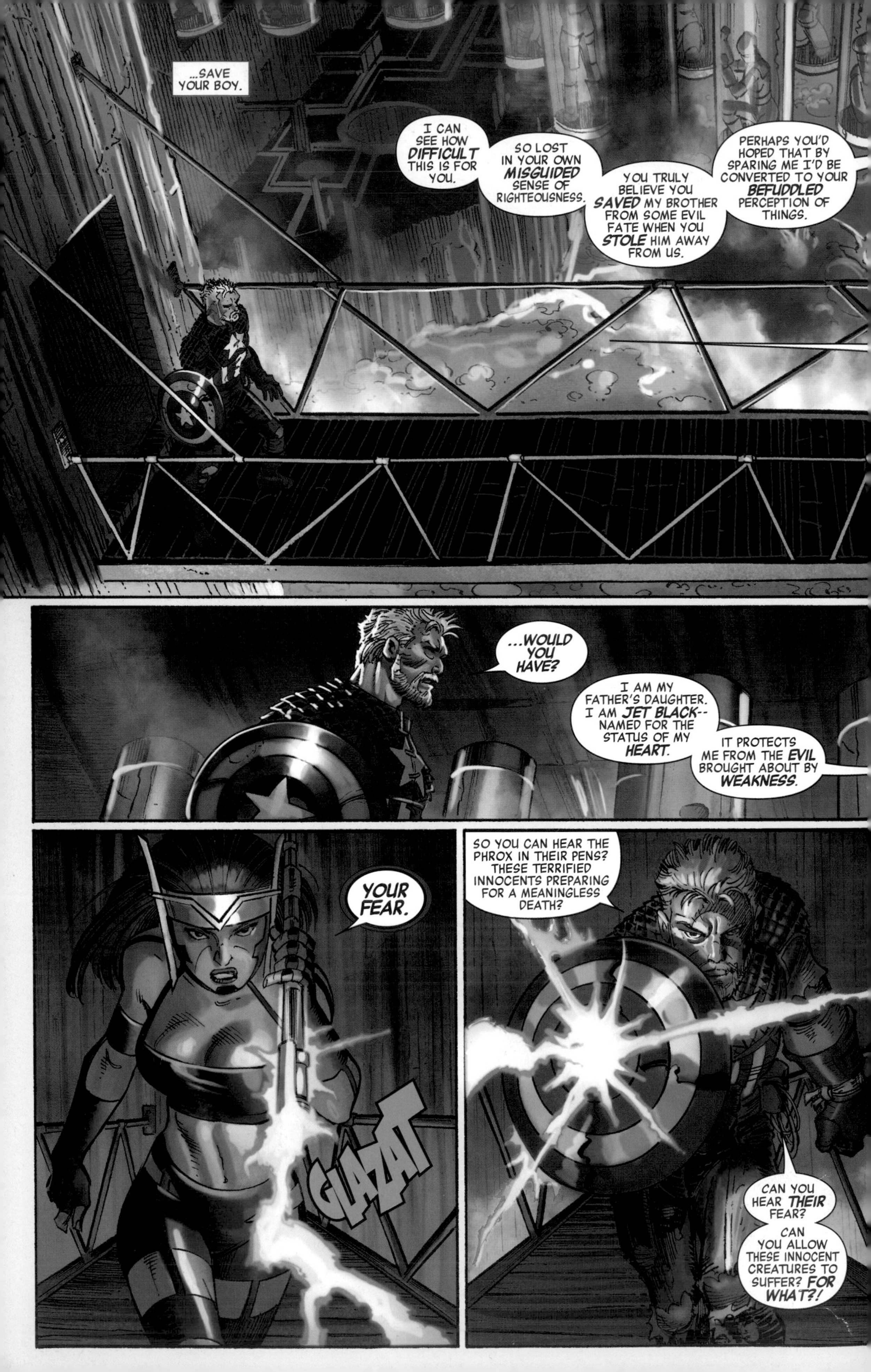
...SAVE YOUR BOY.
I CAN SEE HOW DIFFICULT THIS IS FOR YOU.
SO LOST IN YOUR OWN MISGUIDED SENSE OF RIGHTEOUSNESS.
YOU TRULY BELIEVE YOU SAVED MY BROTHER FROM SOME EVIL FATE WHEN YOU STOLE HIM AWAY FROM US.
PERHAPS YOU'D HOPED THAT BY SPARING ME I'D BE CONVERTED TO YOUR BEFUDDLED PERCEPTION OF THINGS.
...WOULD YOU HAVE?
I AM MY FATHER'S DAUGHTER. I AM JET BLACK-- NAMED FOR THE STATUS OF MY HEART.
IT PROTECTS ME FROM THE EVIL BROUGHT ABOUT BY WEAKNESS.
YOUR FEAR.
GLAZAT
SO YOU CAN HEAR THE PHROX IN THEIR PENS? THESE TERRIFIED INNOCENTS PREPARING FOR A MEANINGLESS DEATH?
CAN YOU HEAR THEIR FEAR?
CAN YOU ALLOW THESE INNOCENT CREATURES TO SUFFER? FOR WHAT?!

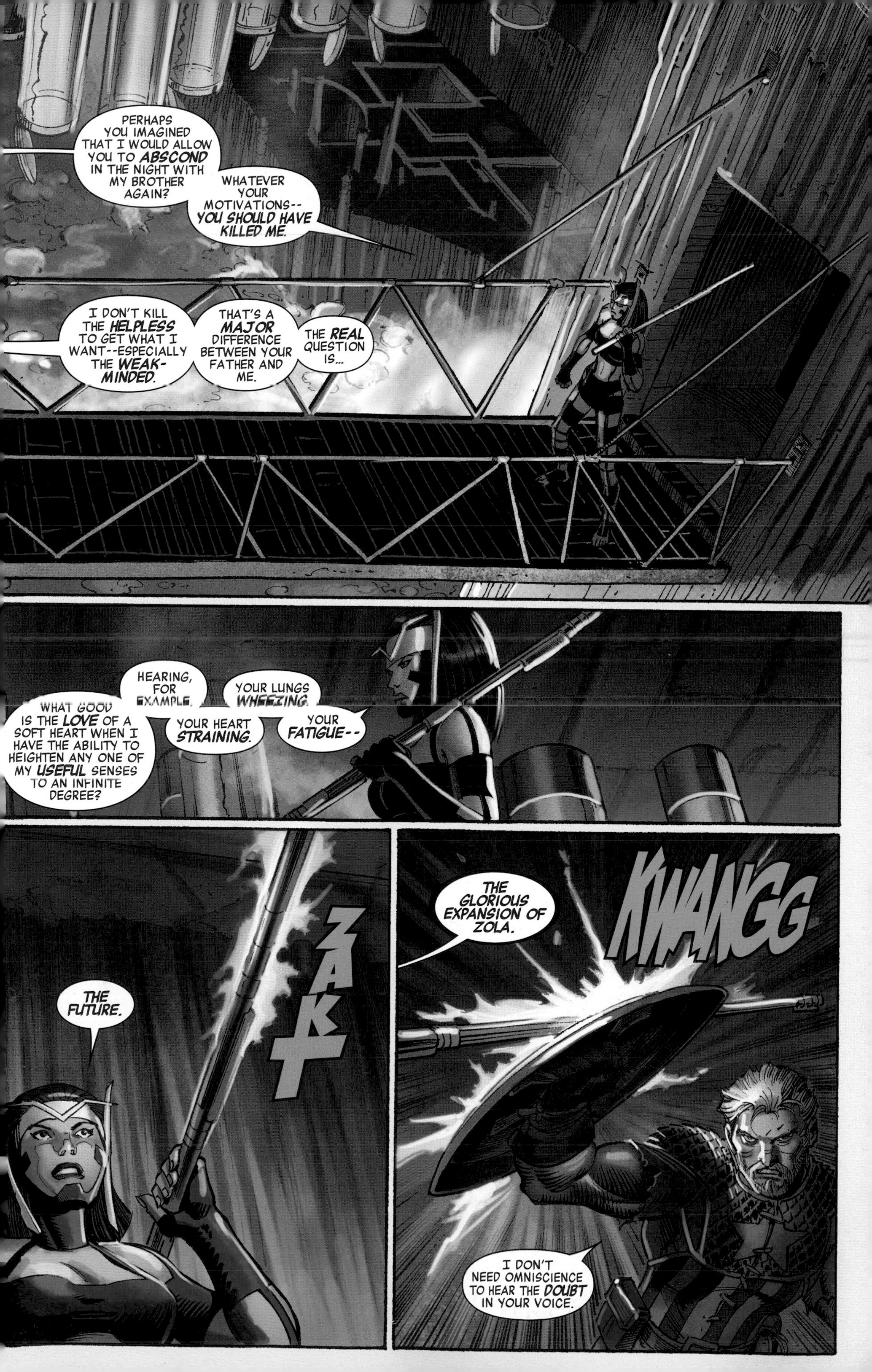

PERHAPS YOU IMAGINED THAT I WOULD ALLOW YOU TO ABSCOND IN THE NIGHT WITH MY BROTHER AGAIN?
WHATEVER YOUR MOTIVATIONS-- YOU SHOULD HAVE KILLED ME.
I DON'T KILL THE HELPLESS TO GET WHAT I WANT--ESPECIALLY THE WEAK-MINDED.
THAT'S A MAJOR DIFFERENCE BETWEEN YOUR FATHER AND ME.
THE REAL QUESTION IS...
WHAT GOOD IS THE LOVE OF A SOFT HEART WHEN I HAVE THE ABILITY TO HEIGHTEN ANY ONE OF MY USEFUL SENSES TO AN INFINITE DEGREE?
HEARING, FOR EXAMPLE.
YOUR HEART STRAINING.
YOUR LUNGS WHEEZING.
YOUR FATIGUE--
THE FUTURE.
ZAKT
THE GLORIOUS EXPANSION OF ZOLA.
KWANGG
I DON'T NEED OMNISCIENCE TO HEAR THE DOUBT IN YOUR VOICE.

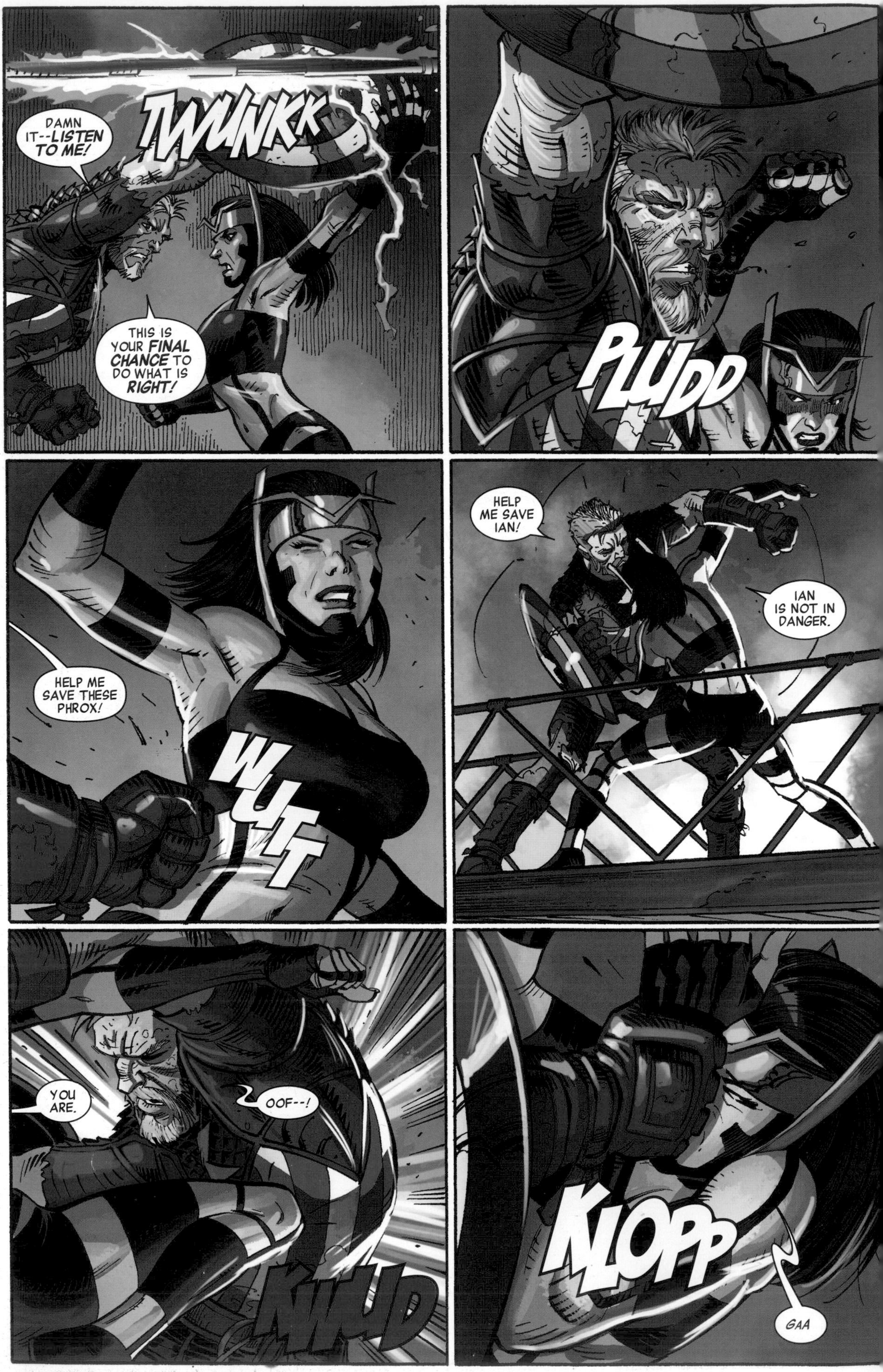

DAMN IT--LISTEN TO ME!
TWUNKK
THIS IS YOUR FINAL CHANCE TO DO WHAT IS RIGHT!
PLUDD
HELP ME SAVE THESE PHROX!
WUTT
HELP ME SAVE IAN!
IAN IS NOT IN DANGER.
YOU ARE.
OOF--!
NNUD
KLOPP
GAA

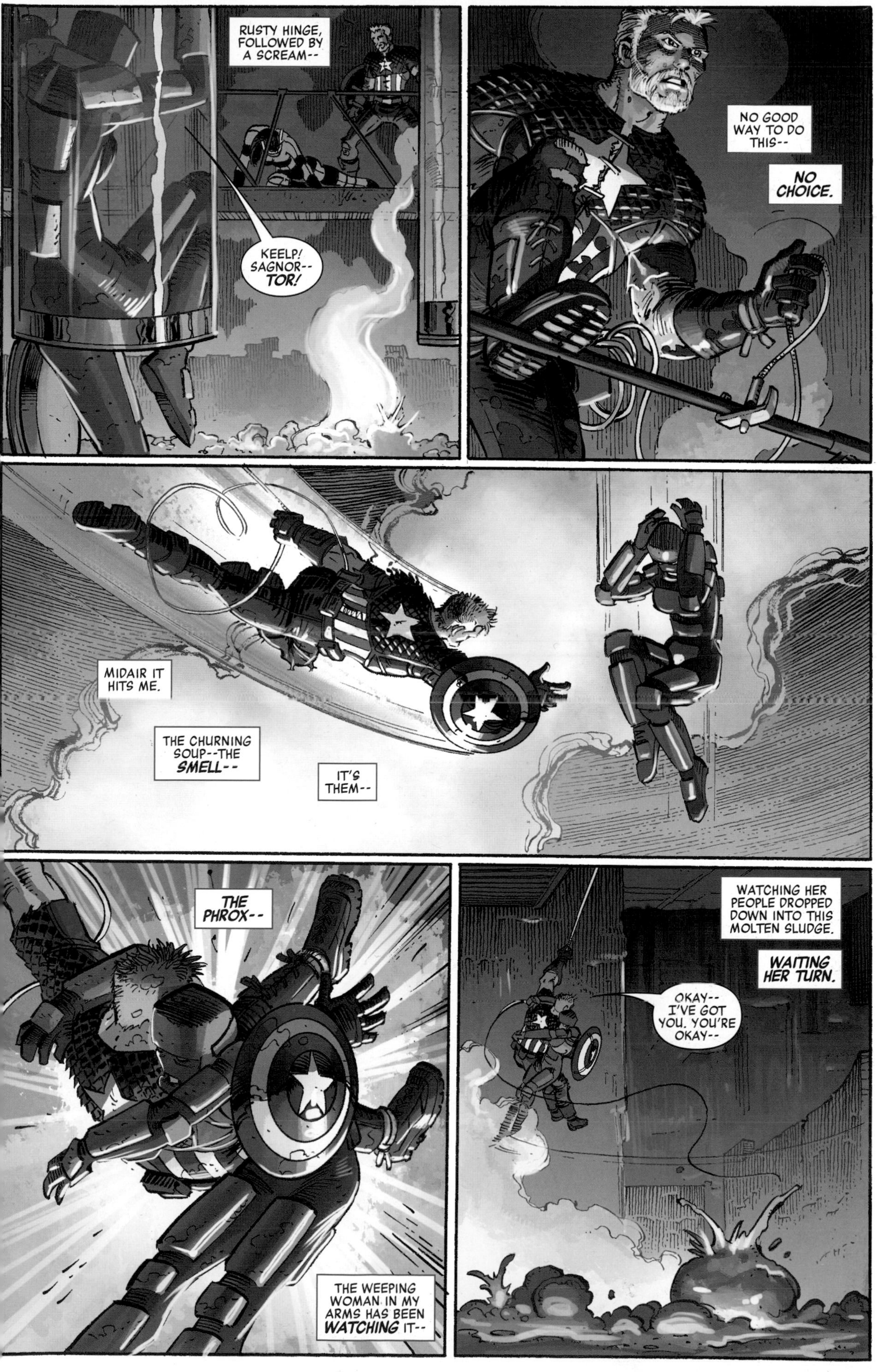
RUSTY HINGE, FOLLOWED BY A SCREAM--
KEELP! SAGNOR--TOR!
NO GOOD WAY TO DO THIS--
NO CHOICE.
MIDAIR IT HITS ME.
THE CHURNING SOUP--THE SMELL--
IT'S THEM--
THE PHROX--
THE WEEPING WOMAN IN MY ARMS HAS BEEN WATCHING IT--
WATCHING HER PEOPLE DROPPED DOWN INTO THIS MOLTEN SLUDGE.
WAITING HER TURN.
OKAY-- I'VE GOT YOU. YOU'RE OKAY--

PULL
US UP!

BEFORE
ANOTHER
ONE IS DROPPED
IN--*BEFORE
ANOTHER
DIES!*

FOOL,
WHY SHOULD
I LISTEN FOR
A SINGLE
MOMENT?

YOUR FATHER
KEPT YOU HERE
SO YOU NEVER HAD
A CHANCE TO SEE
COMPASSION--

IT'S *NOT
YOUR FAULT
WHAT HE'S
DONE--NONE
OF IT!*

THE NAUSEA,
THE TIGHTNESS IN
YOUR CHEST, THE
SLEEPLESS NIGHTS--
*YOU KNOW THIS
IS WRONG!*

IF
YOU STAND
BY AND DO
NOTHING--YOU
*SHARE THE
GUILT!*

YOU'VE
SEEN BOTH
OPTIONS, JET,
SO PICK--

WHAT
SIDE DO YOU
CHOOSE?

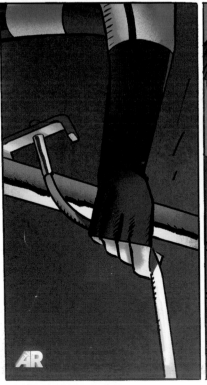

FATHER,
FORGIVE
ME...

AR

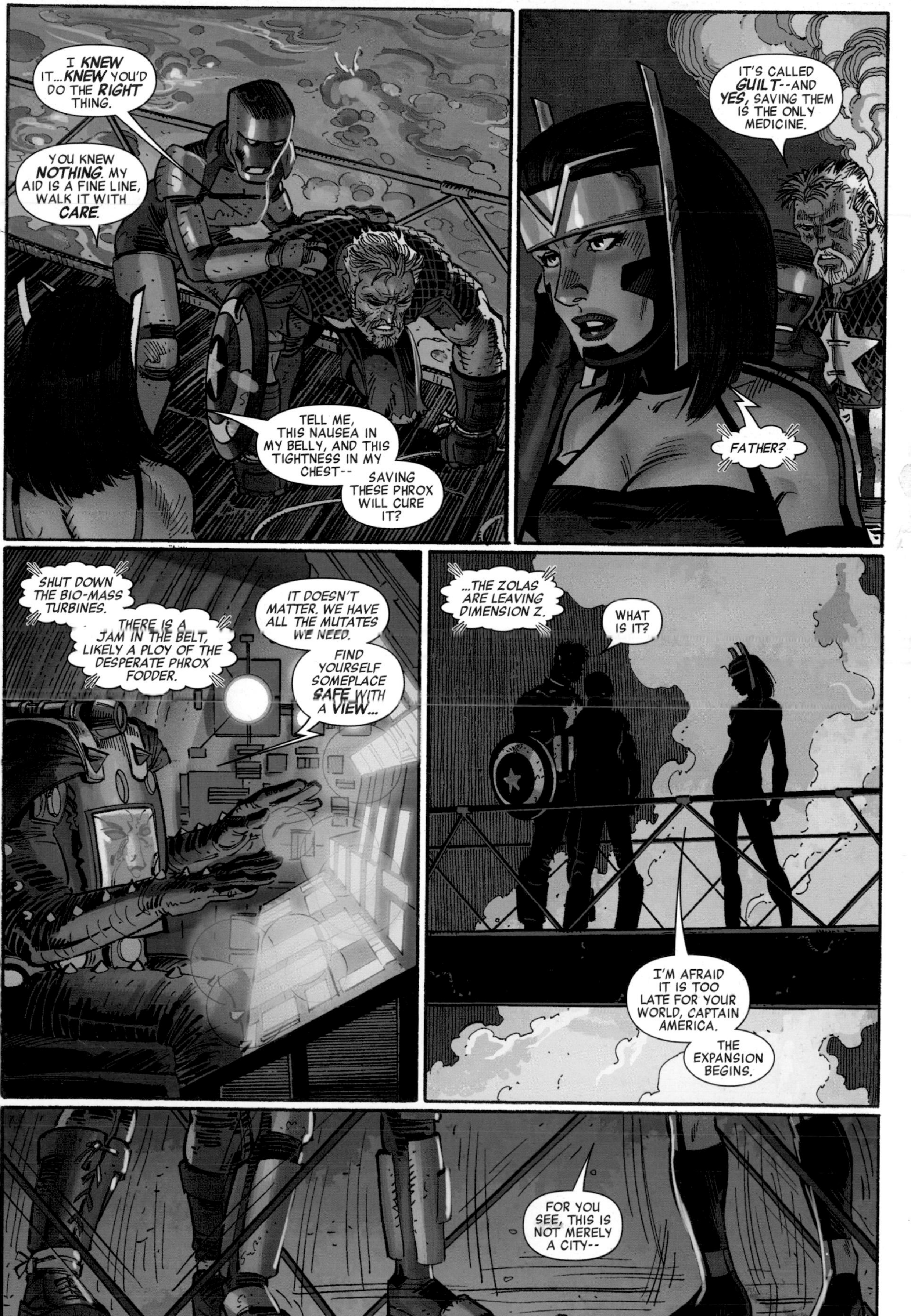
I KNEW IT...KNEW YOU'D DO THE RIGHT THING.
YOU KNEW NOTHING. MY AID IS A FINE LINE, WALK IT WITH CARE.
TELL ME, THIS NAUSEA IN MY BELLY, AND THIS TIGHTNESS IN MY CHEST--
SAVING THESE PHROX WILL CURE IT?
IT'S CALLED GUILT--AND YES, SAVING THEM IS THE ONLY MEDICINE.
FATHER?
SHUT DOWN THE BIO-MASS TURBINES.
THERE IS A JAM IN THE BELT, LIKELY A PLOY OF THE DESPERATE PHROX FODDER.
IT DOESN'T MATTER. WE HAVE ALL THE MUTATES WE NEED.
FIND YOURSELF SOMEPLACE SAFE WITH A VIEW...
...THE ZOLAS ARE LEAVING DIMENSION Z.
WHAT IS IT?
I'M AFRAID IT IS TOO LATE FOR YOUR WORLD, CAPTAIN AMERICA.
THE EXPANSION BEGINS.
FOR YOU SEE, THIS IS NOT MERELY A CITY--

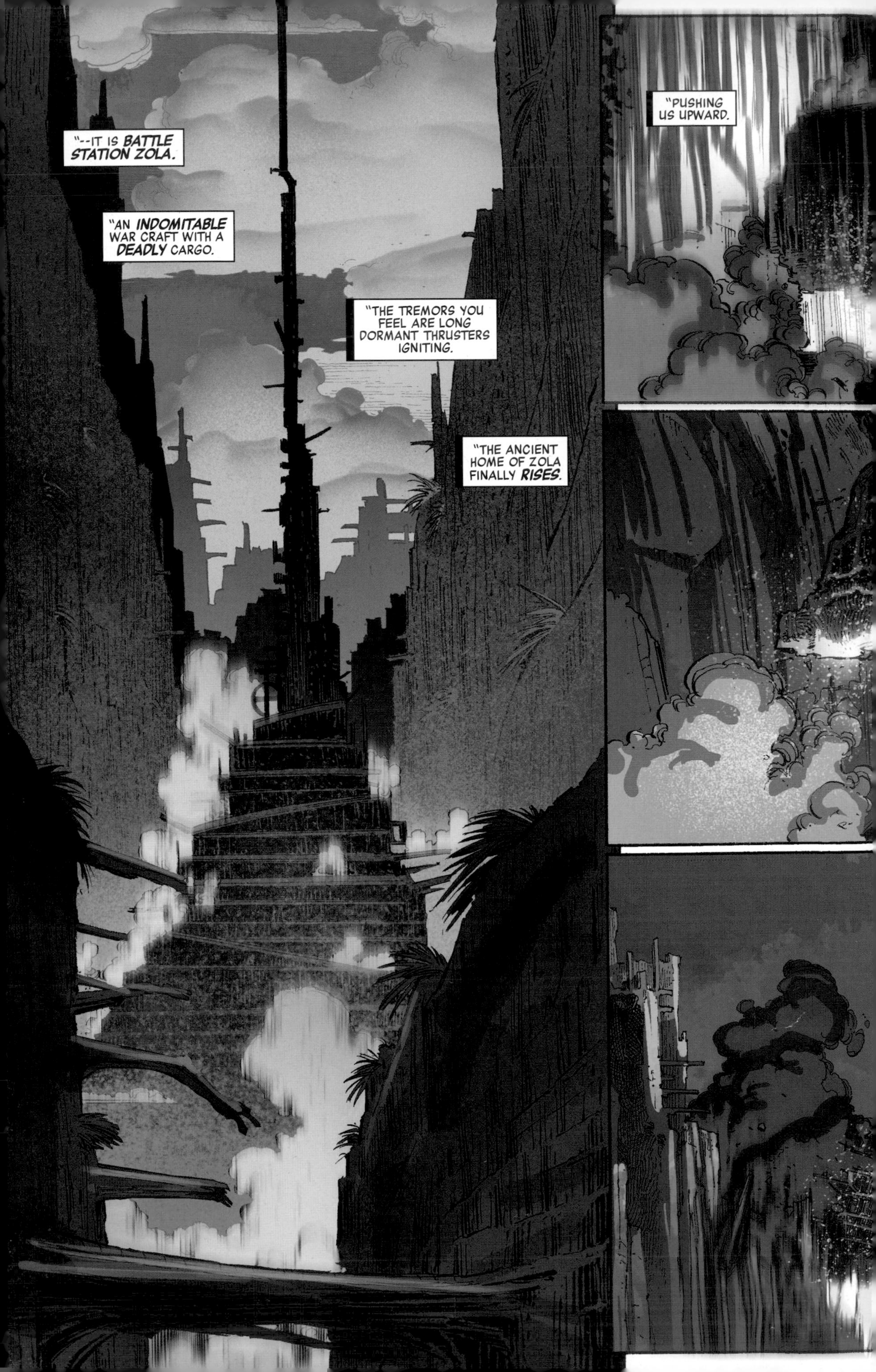

"--IT IS BATTLE STATION ZOLA.
"AN INDOMITABLE WAR CRAFT WITH A DEADLY CARGO.
"THE TREMORS YOU FEEL ARE LONG DORMANT THRUSTERS IGNITING.
"THE ANCIENT HOME OF ZOLA FINALLY RISES.
"PUSHING US UPWARD.

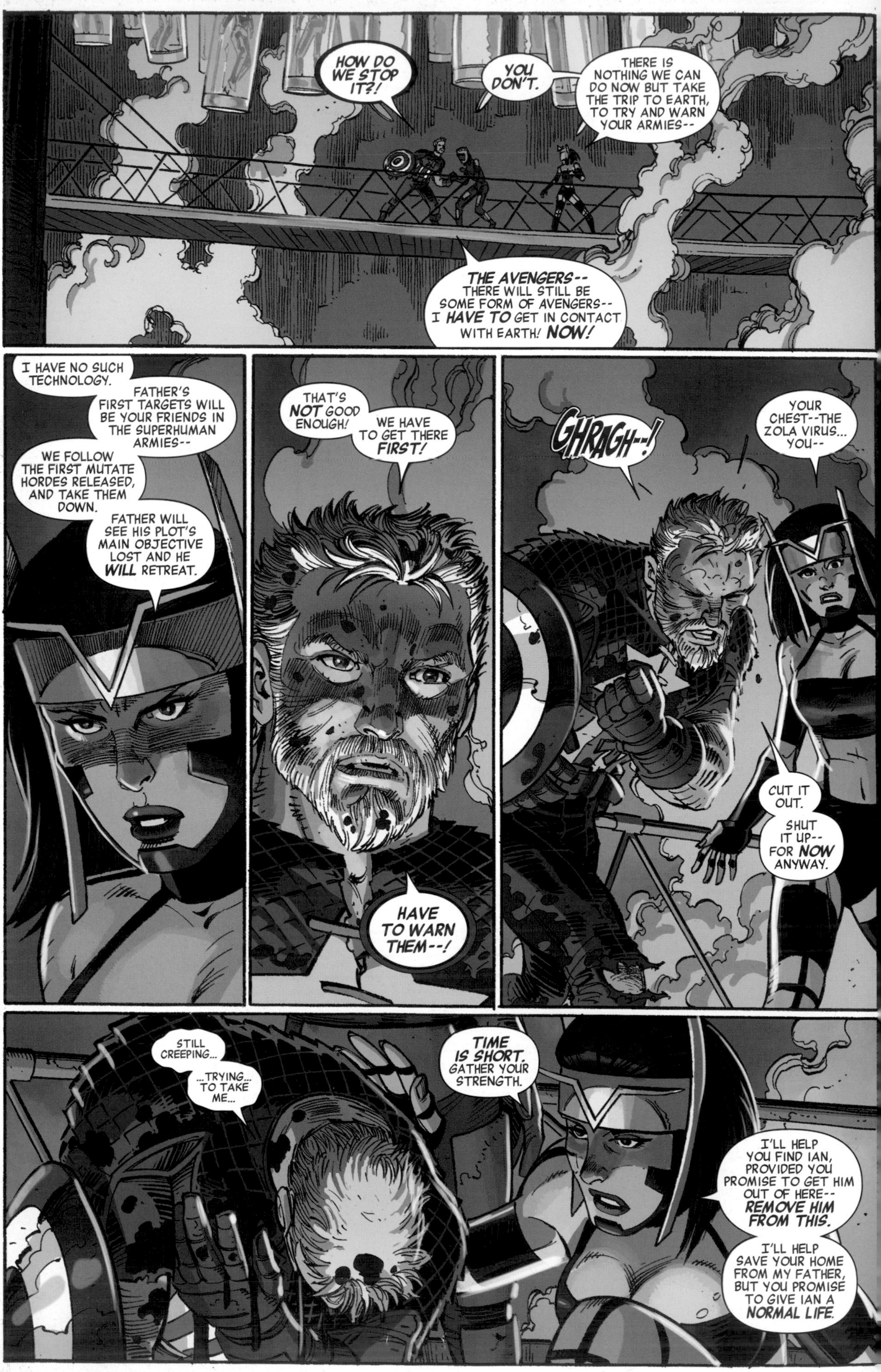
HOW DO WE STOP IT?!
YOU DON'T.
THERE IS NOTHING WE CAN DO NOW BUT TAKE THE TRIP TO EARTH, TO TRY AND WARN YOUR ARMIES--
THE AVENGERS-- THERE WILL STILL BE SOME FORM OF AVENGERS-- I HAVE TO GET IN CONTACT WITH EARTH! NOW!
I HAVE NO SUCH TECHNOLOGY.
FATHER'S FIRST TARGETS WILL BE YOUR FRIENDS IN THE SUPERHUMAN ARMIES--
WE FOLLOW THE FIRST MUTATE HORDES RELEASED, AND TAKE THEM DOWN.
FATHER WILL SEE HIS PLOT'S MAIN OBJECTIVE LOST AND HE WILL RETREAT.
THAT'S NOT GOOD ENOUGH!
WE HAVE TO GET THERE FIRST!
HAVE TO WARN THEM--!
GHRAGH--!
YOUR CHEST--THE ZOLA VIRUS... YOU--
CUT IT OUT.
SHUT IT UP-- FOR NOW ANYWAY.
STILL CREEPING...
...TRYING... TO TAKE ME...
TIME IS SHORT. GATHER YOUR STRENGTH.
I'LL HELP YOU FIND IAN, PROVIDED YOU PROMISE TO GET HIM OUT OF HERE-- REMOVE HIM FROM THIS.
I'LL HELP SAVE YOUR HOME FROM MY FATHER, BUT YOU PROMISE TO GIVE IAN A NORMAL LIFE.

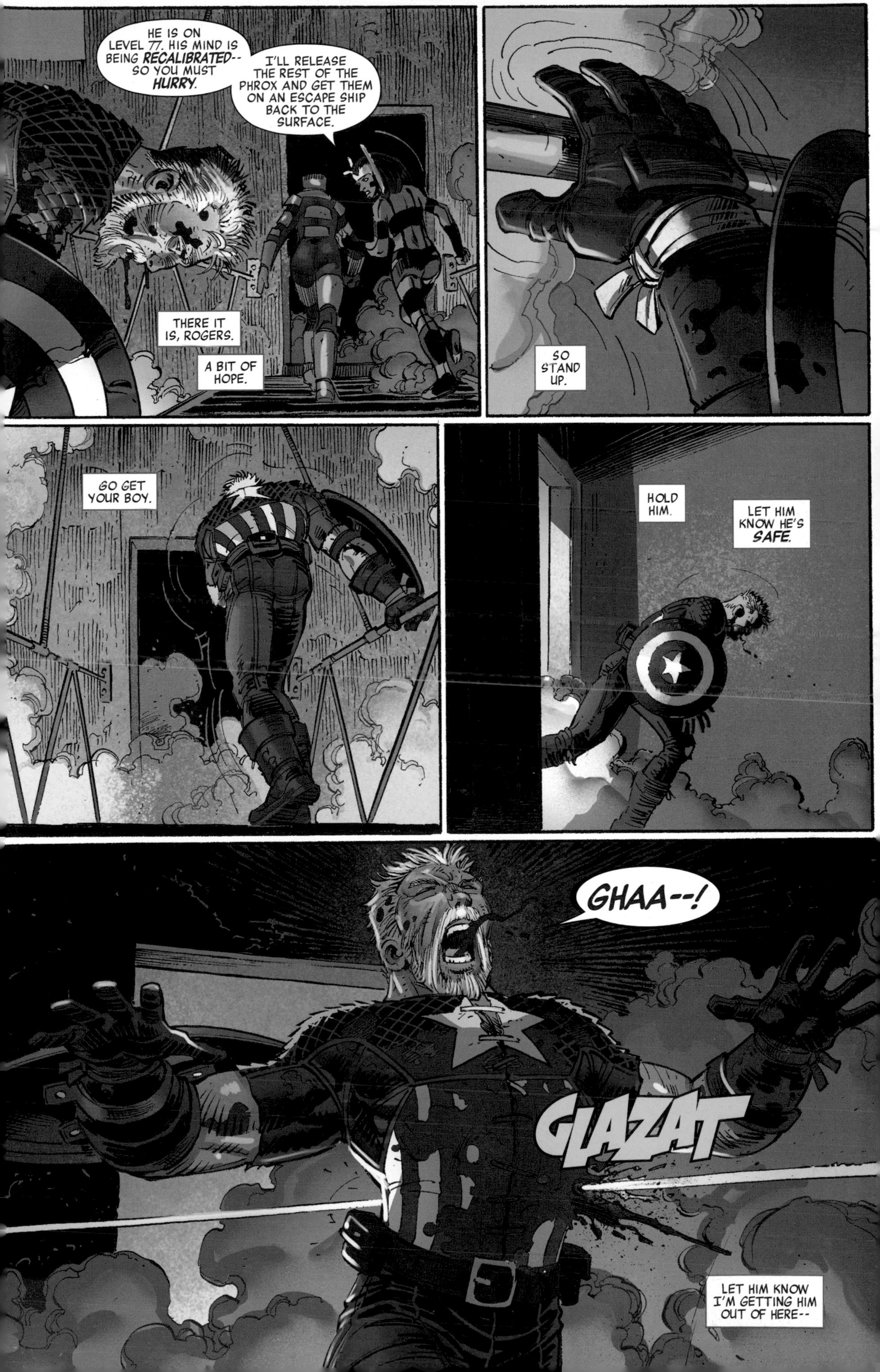
HE IS ON LEVEL 77. HIS MIND IS BEING RECALIBRATED-- SO YOU MUST HURRY.
I'LL RELEASE THE REST OF THE PHROX AND GET THEM ON AN ESCAPE SHIP BACK TO THE SURFACE.
THERE IT IS, ROGERS.
A BIT OF HOPE.
SO STAND UP.
GO GET YOUR BOY.
HOLD HIM.
LET HIM KNOW HE'S SAFE.
GHAA--!
GLAZAT
LET HIM KNOW I'M GETTING HIM OUT OF HERE--

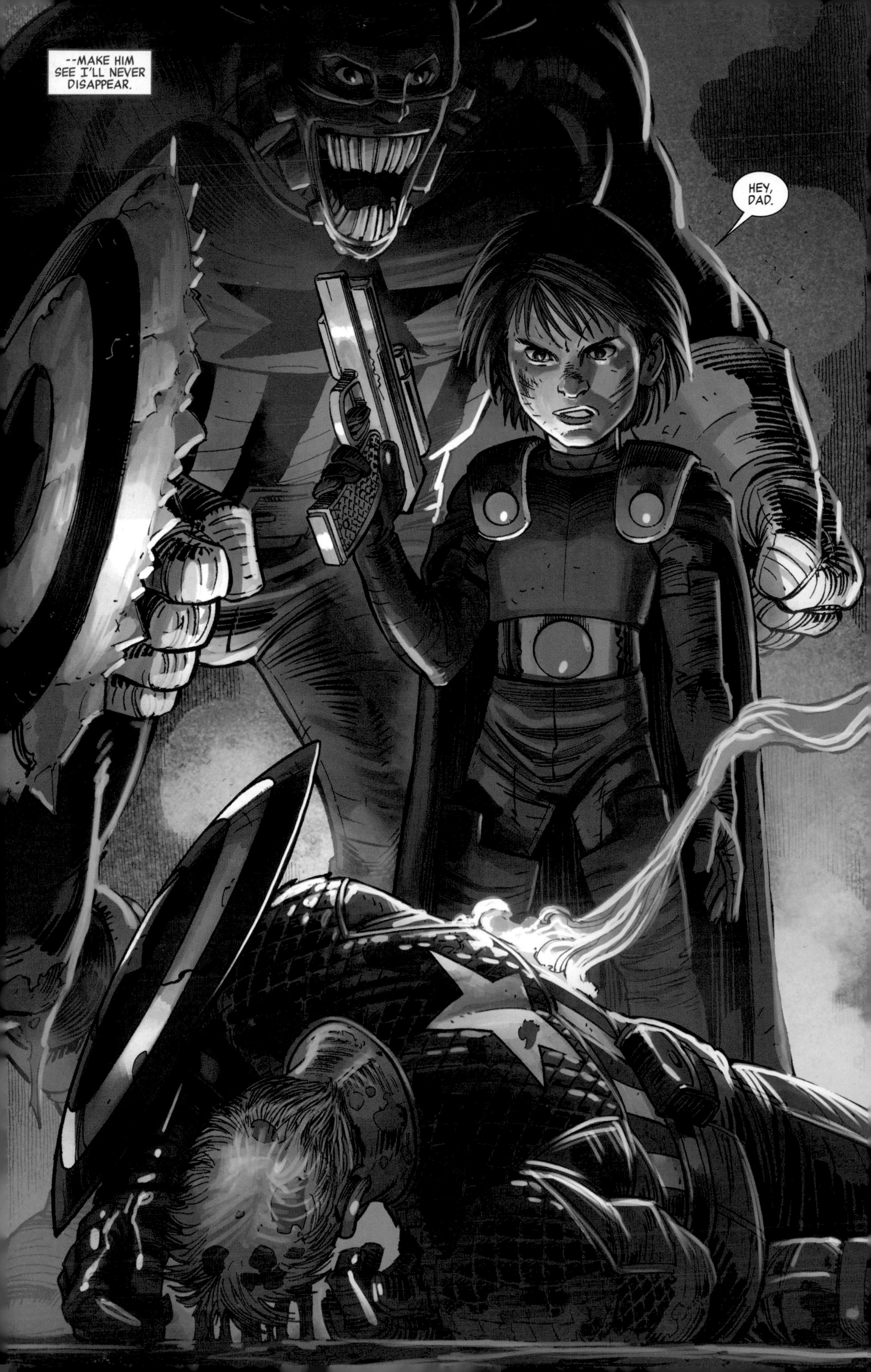
--MAKE HIM SEE I'LL NEVER DISAPPEAR.
HEY, DAD.

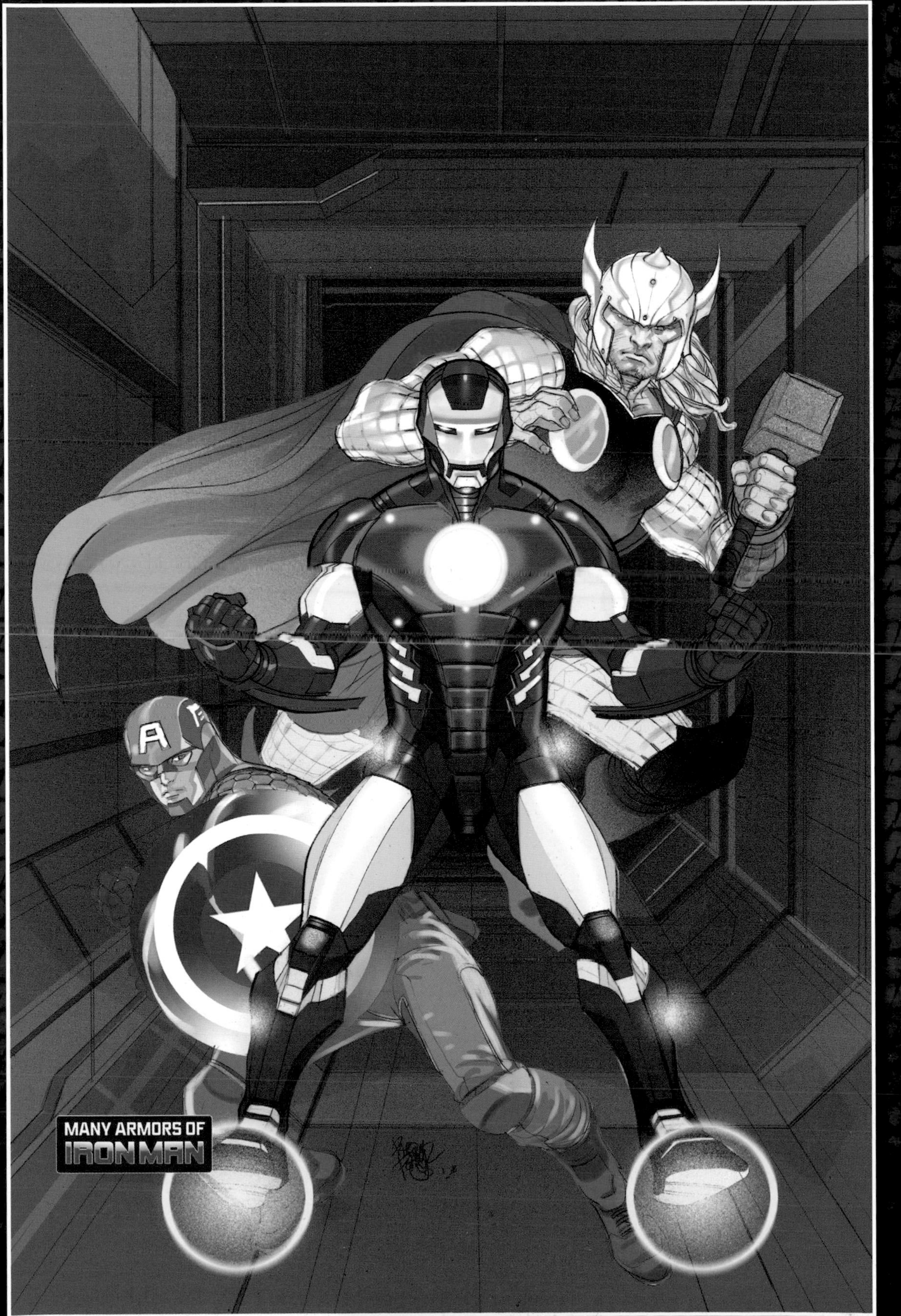
MANY ARMORS OF
IRON MAN

Captain America #6 by Pasqual Ferry.

CAPTAIN AMERICA #8

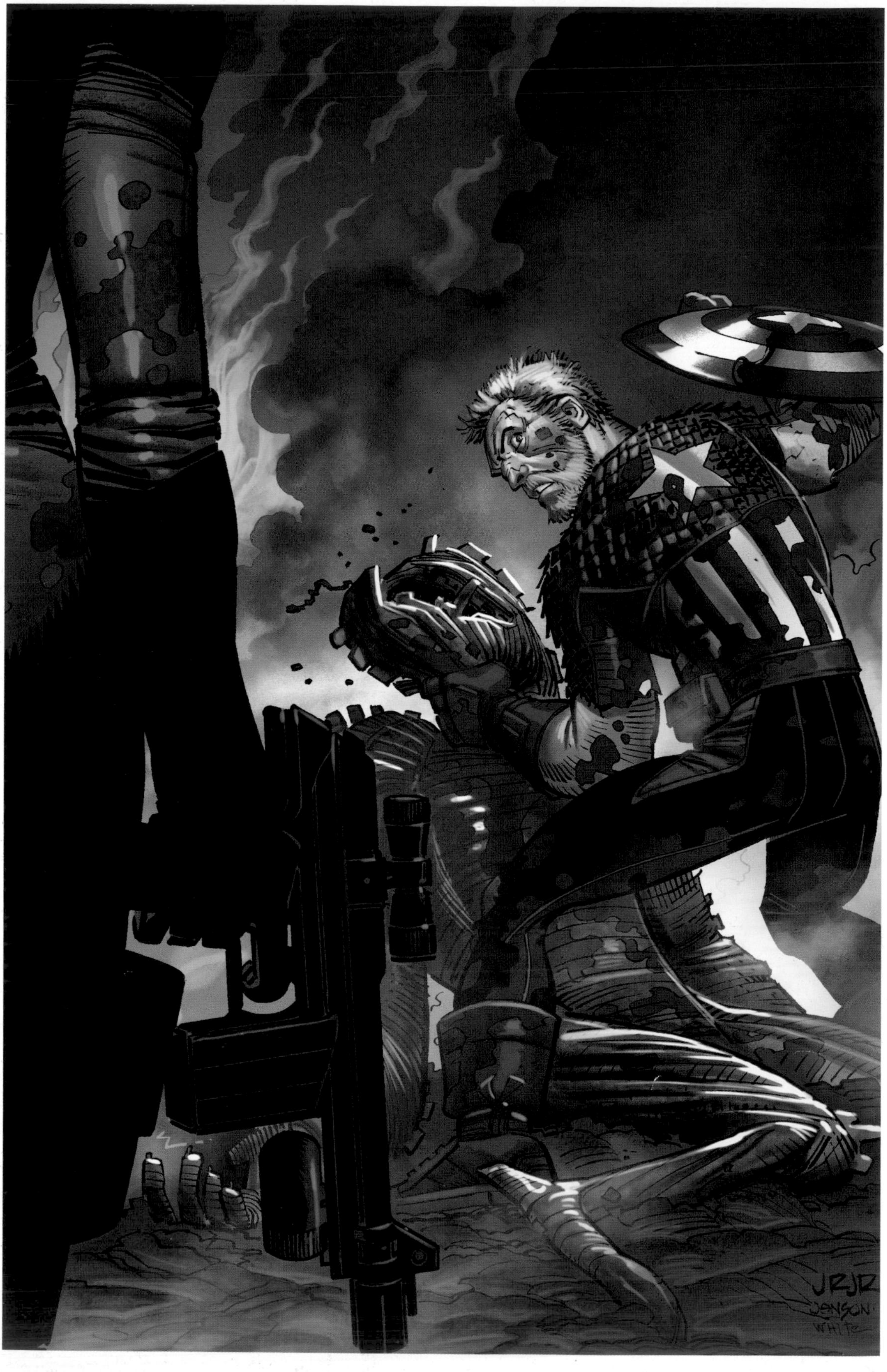
JRJR
JANSON
WHITE

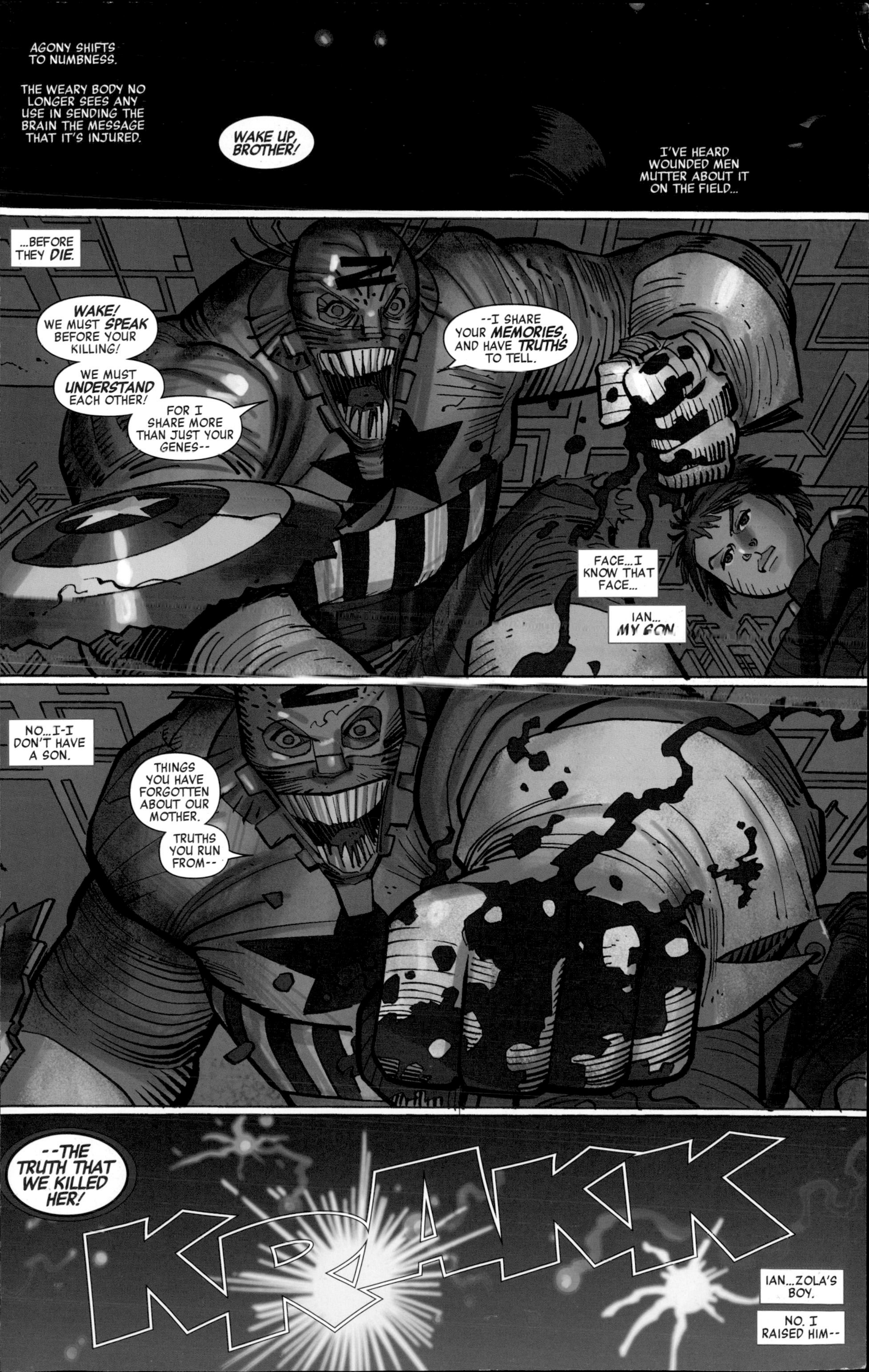
AGONY SHIFTS TO NUMBNESS.
THE WEARY BODY NO LONGER SEES ANY USE IN SENDING THE BRAIN THE MESSAGE THAT IT'S INJURED.
WAKE UP, BROTHER!
I'VE HEARD WOUNDED MEN MUTTER ABOUT IT ON THE FIELD...
...BEFORE THEY DIE.
WAKE! WE MUST SPEAK BEFORE YOUR KILLING!
WE MUST UNDERSTAND EACH OTHER!
FOR I SHARE MORE THAN JUST YOUR GENES--
--I SHARE YOUR MEMORIES, AND HAVE TRUTHS TO TELL.
FACE...I KNOW THAT FACE...
IAN... MY SON.
NO...I-I DON'T HAVE A SON.
THINGS YOU HAVE FORGOTTEN ABOUT OUR MOTHER.
TRUTHS YOU RUN FROM--
--THE TRUTH THAT WE KILLED HER!
KRAKK
IAN...ZOLA'S BOY.
NO. I RAISED HIM--

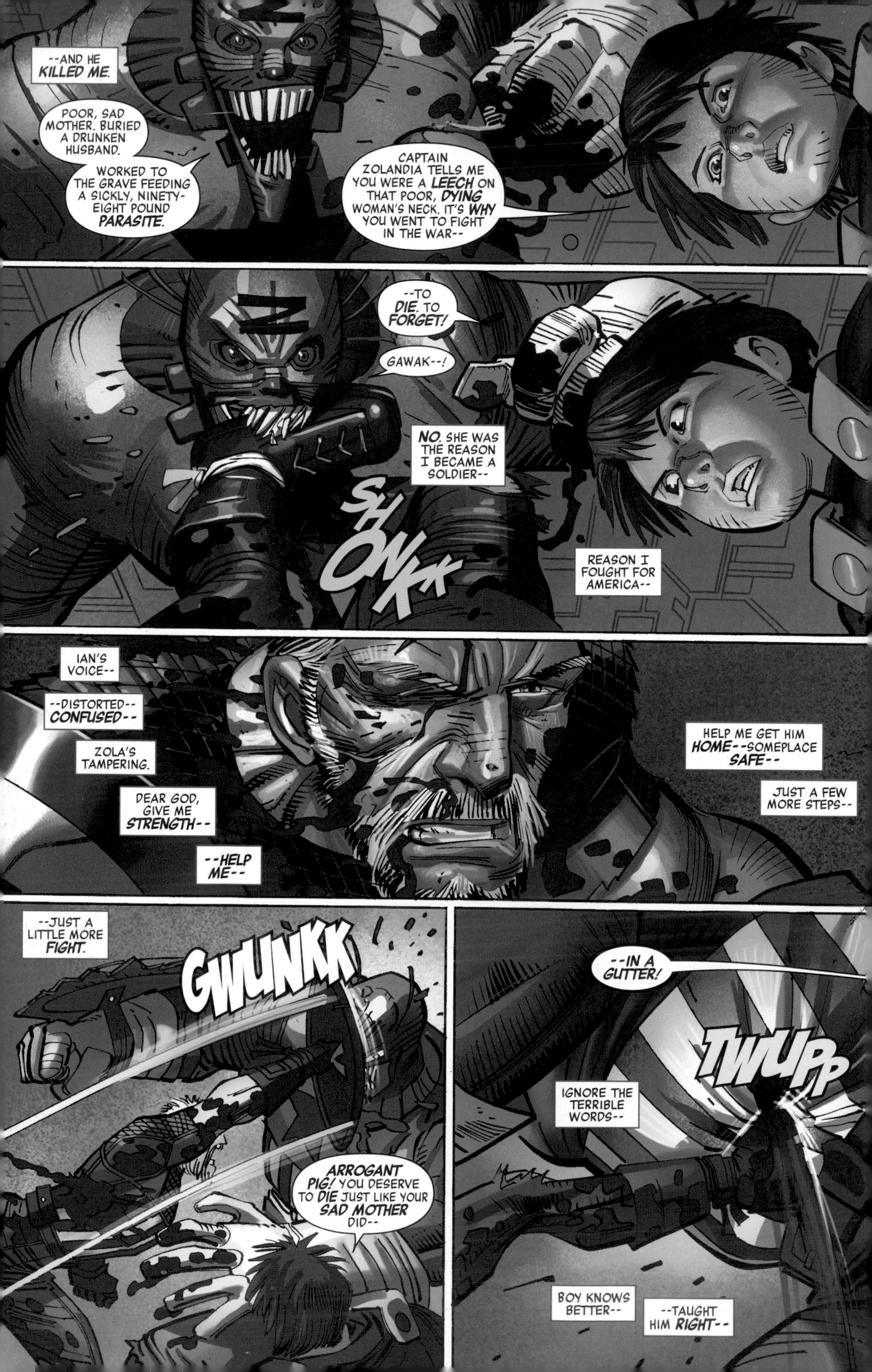
--AND HE KILLED ME.
POOR, SAD MOTHER. BURIED A DRUNKEN HUSBAND.
WORKED TO THE GRAVE FEEDING A SICKLY, NINETY-EIGHT POUND PARASITE.
CAPTAIN ZOLANDIA TELLS ME YOU WERE A LEECH ON THAT POOR, DYING WOMAN'S NECK. IT'S WHY YOU WENT TO FIGHT IN THE WAR--
--TO DIE. TO FORGET!
GAWAK--!
NO. SHE WAS THE REASON I BECAME A SOLDIER--
SHONKK
REASON I FOUGHT FOR AMERICA--
IAN'S VOICE--
--DISTORTED--CONFUSED--
ZOLA'S TAMPERING.
DEAR GOD, GIVE ME STRENGTH--
--HELP ME--
HELP ME GET HIM HOME--SOMEPLACE SAFE--
JUST A FEW MORE STEPS--
--JUST A LITTLE MORE FIGHT.
GWUNKK
ARROGANT PIG! YOU DESERVE TO DIE JUST LIKE YOUR SAD MOTHER DID--
--IN A GUTTER!
TWUPP
IGNORE THE TERRIBLE WORDS--
BOY KNOWS BETTER--
--TAUGHT HIM RIGHT--

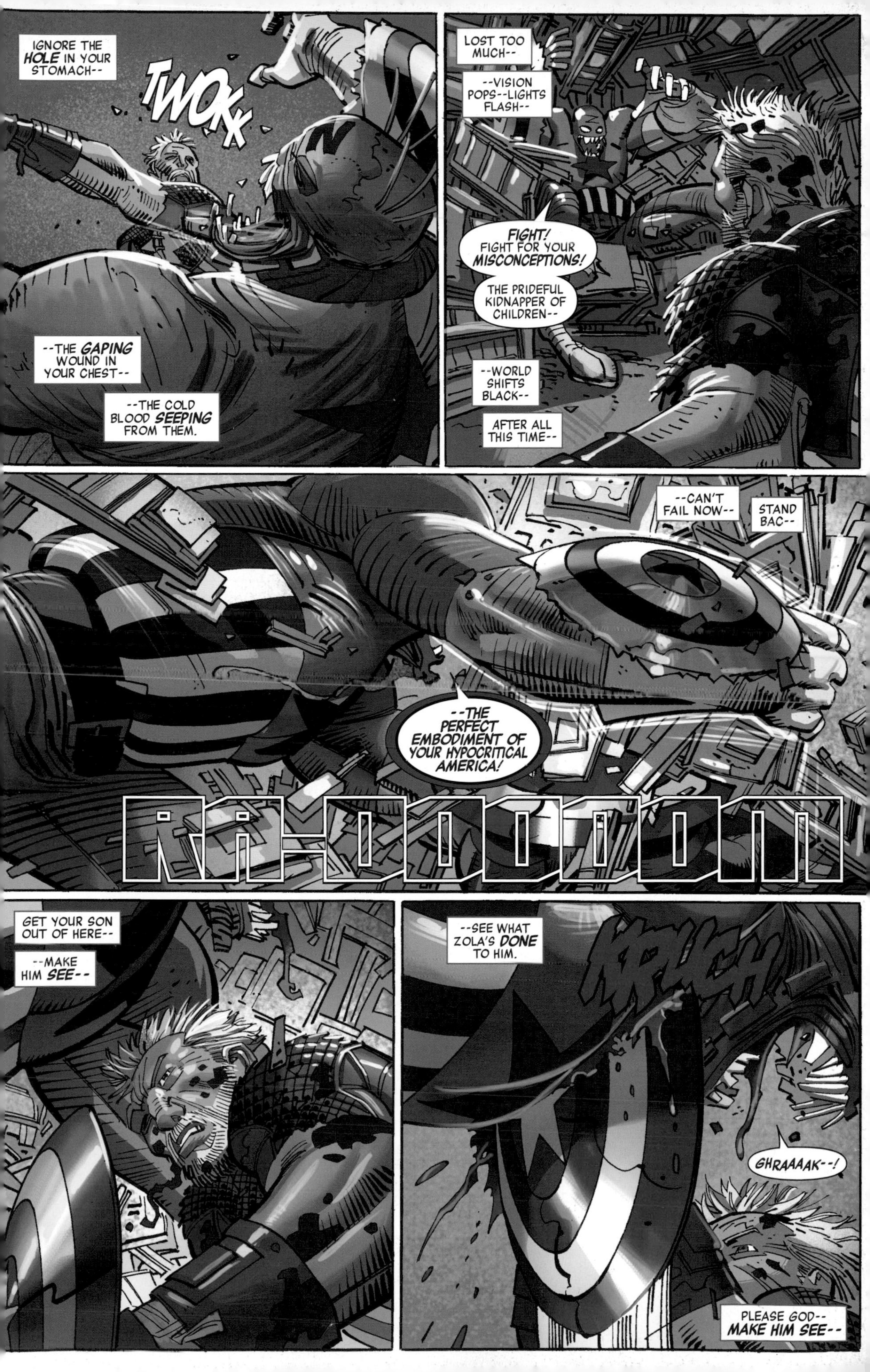
IGNORE THE HOLE IN YOUR STOMACH--
TWOKK
--THE GAPING WOUND IN YOUR CHEST--
--THE COLD BLOOD SEEPING FROM THEM.
LOST TOO MUCH--
--VISION POPS--LIGHTS FLASH--
FIGHT! FIGHT FOR YOUR MISCONCEPTIONS!
THE PRIDEFUL KIDNAPPER OF CHILDREN--
--WORLD SHIFTS BLACK--
AFTER ALL THIS TIME--
--CAN'T FAIL NOW--
STAND BAC--
--THE PERFECT EMBODIMENT OF YOUR HYPOCRITICAL AMERICA!
KA-BOOOOM
GET YOUR SON OUT OF HERE--
--MAKE HIM SEE--
--SEE WHAT ZOLA'S DONE TO HIM.
GHRAAAAK--!
PLEASE GOD-- MAKE HIM SEE--

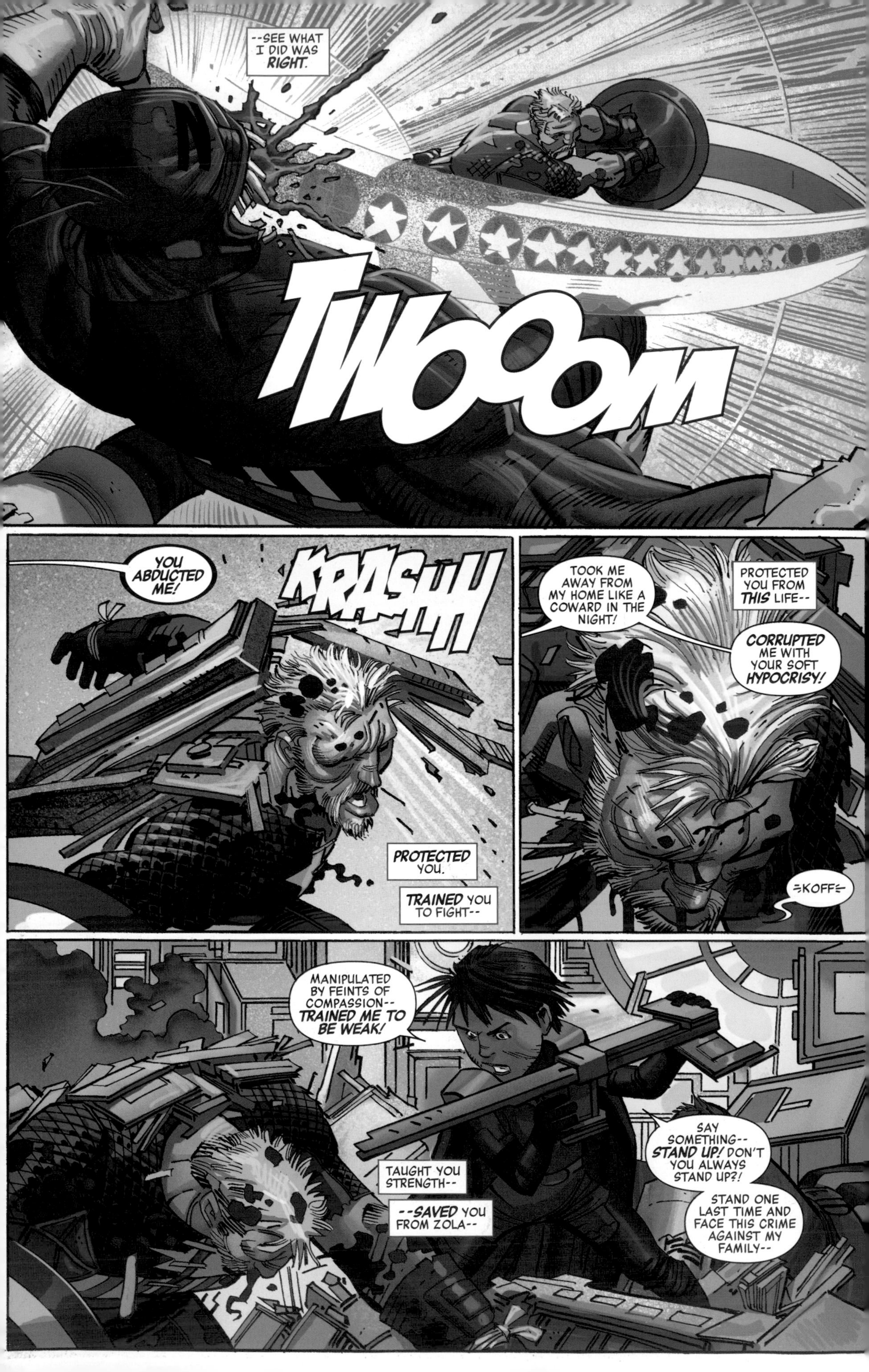
--SEE WHAT I DID WAS RIGHT.
TWOOOM
YOU ABDUCTED ME!
KRASHH
PROTECTED YOU.
TRAINED YOU TO FIGHT--
TOOK ME AWAY FROM MY HOME LIKE A COWARD IN THE NIGHT!
PROTECTED YOU FROM THIS LIFE--
CORRUPTED ME WITH YOUR SOFT HYPOCRISY!
=KOFF=
MANIPULATED BY FEINTS OF COMPASSION-- TRAINED ME TO BE WEAK!
TAUGHT YOU STRENGTH--
--SAVED YOU FROM ZOLA--
SAY SOMETHING-- STAND UP! DON'T YOU ALWAYS STAND UP?!
STAND ONE LAST TIME AND FACE THIS CRIME AGAINST MY FAMILY--

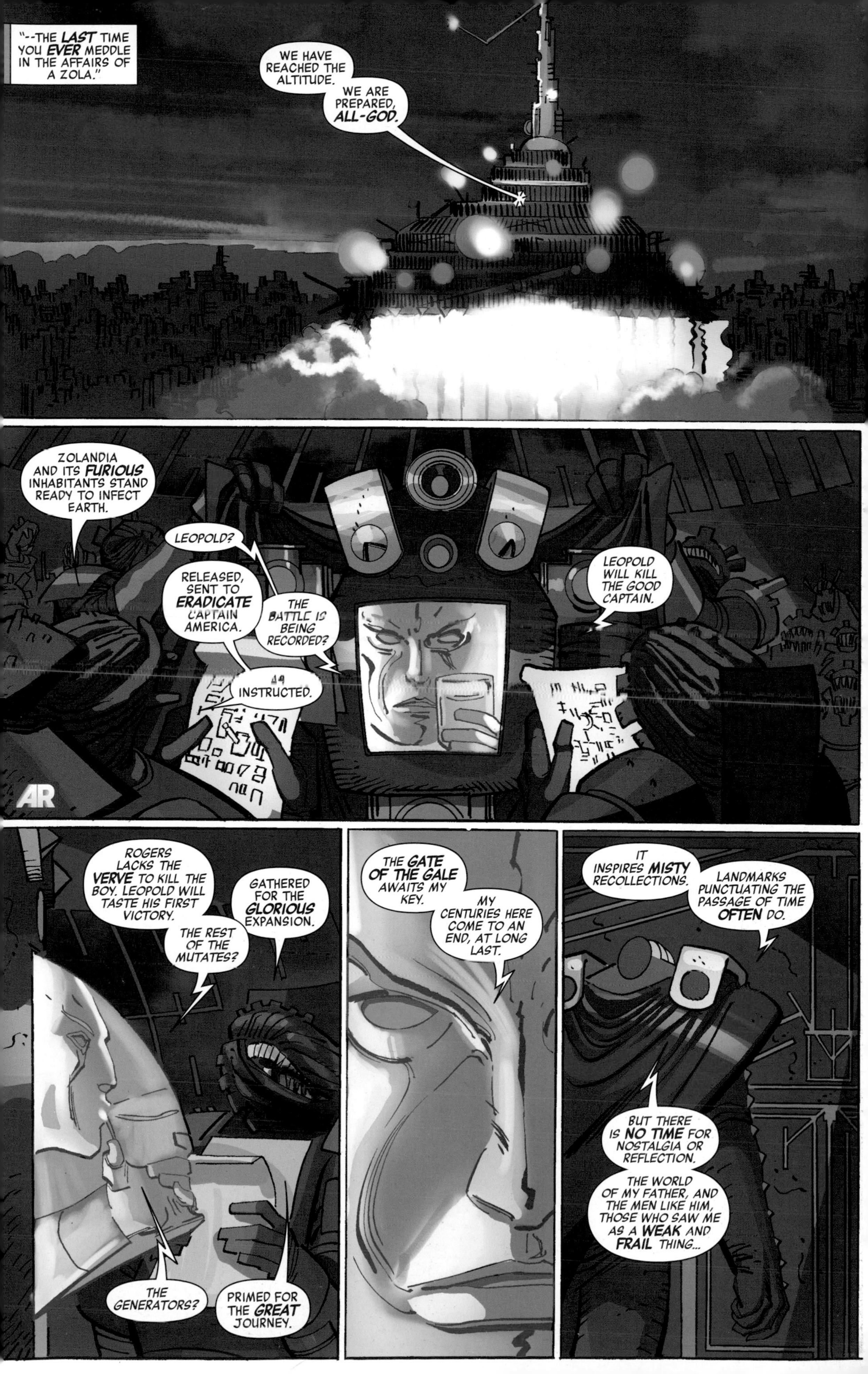
"--THE LAST TIME YOU EVER MEDDLE IN THE AFFAIRS OF A ZOLA."
WE HAVE REACHED THE ALTITUDE.
WE ARE PREPARED, ALL-GOD.
ZOLANDIA AND ITS FURIOUS INHABITANTS STAND READY TO INFECT EARTH.
LEOPOLD?
RELEASED, SENT TO ERADICATE CAPTAIN AMERICA.
THE BATTLE IS BEING RECORDED?
AS INSTRUCTED.
LEOPOLD WILL KILL THE GOOD CAPTAIN.
ROGERS LACKS THE VERVE TO KILL THE BOY. LEOPOLD WILL TASTE HIS FIRST VICTORY.
THE REST OF THE MUTATES?
GATHERED FOR THE GLORIOUS EXPANSION.
THE GENERATORS?
PRIMED FOR THE GREAT JOURNEY.
THE GATE OF THE GALE AWAITS MY KEY.
MY CENTURIES HERE COME TO AN END, AT LONG LAST.
IT INSPIRES MISTY RECOLLECTIONS.
LANDMARKS PUNCTUATING THE PASSAGE OF TIME OFTEN DO.
BUT THERE IS NO TIME FOR NOSTALGIA OR REFLECTION.
THE WORLD OF MY FATHER, AND THE MEN LIKE HIM, THOSE WHO SAW ME AS A WEAK AND FRAIL THING...

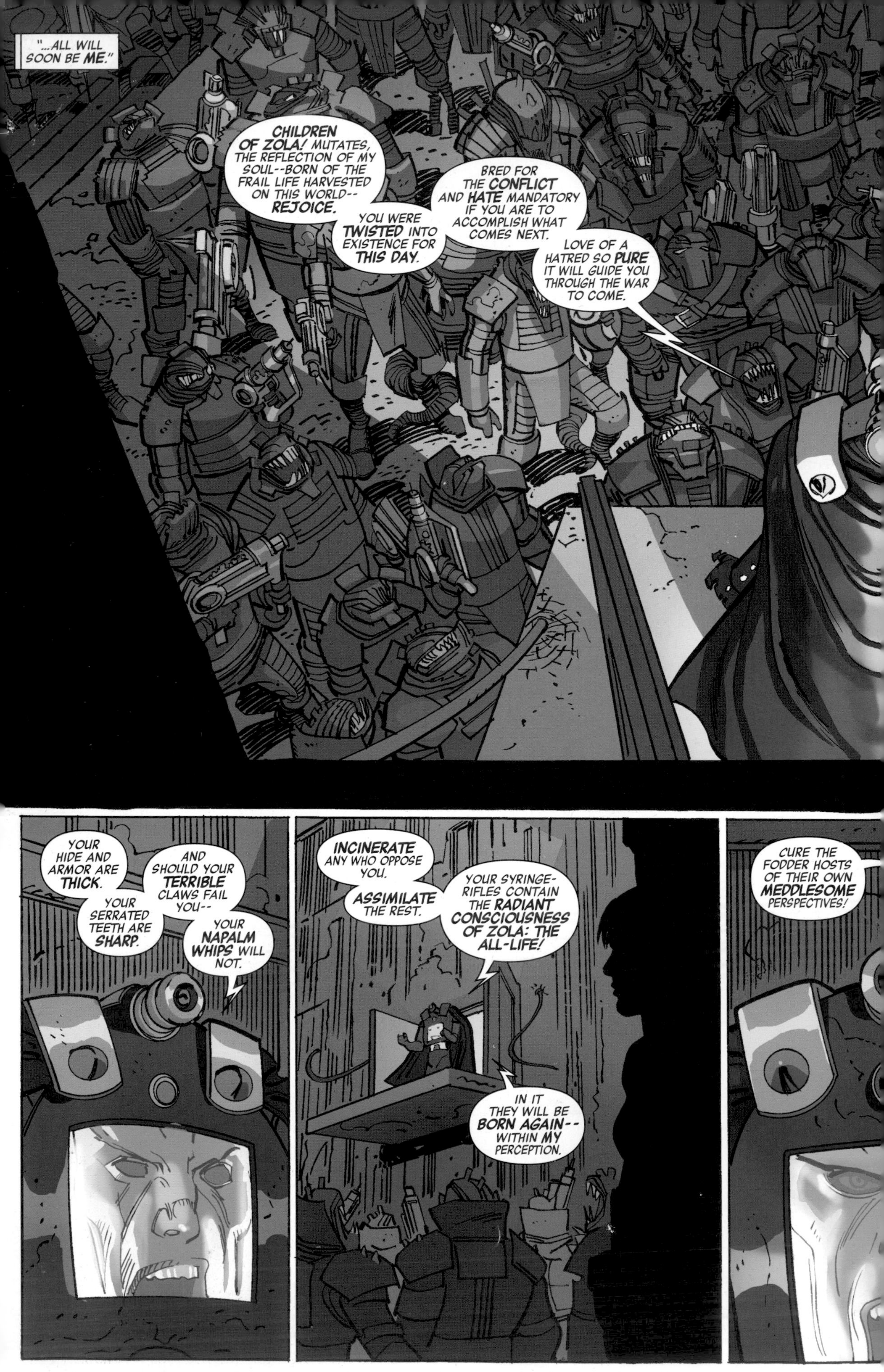
"...ALL WILL SOON BE ME."
CHILDREN OF ZOLA! MUTATES, THE REFLECTION OF MY SOUL--BORN OF THE FRAIL LIFE HARVESTED ON THIS WORLD-- REJOICE.
YOU WERE TWISTED INTO EXISTENCE FOR THIS DAY.
BRED FOR THE CONFLICT AND HATE MANDATORY IF YOU ARE TO ACCOMPLISH WHAT COMES NEXT.
LOVE OF A HATRED SO PURE IT WILL GUIDE YOU THROUGH THE WAR TO COME.
YOUR HIDE AND ARMOR ARE THICK.
YOUR SERRATED TEETH ARE SHARP.
AND SHOULD YOUR TERRIBLE CLAWS FAIL YOU--
YOUR NAPALM WHIPS WILL NOT.
INCINERATE ANY WHO OPPOSE YOU.
ASSIMILATE THE REST.
YOUR SYRINGE-RIFLES CONTAIN THE RADIANT CONSCIOUSNESS OF ZOLA: THE ALL-LIFE!
IN IT THEY WILL BE BORN AGAIN-- WITHIN MY PERCEPTION.
CURE THE FODDER HOSTS OF THEIR OWN MEDDLESOME PERSPECTIVES!

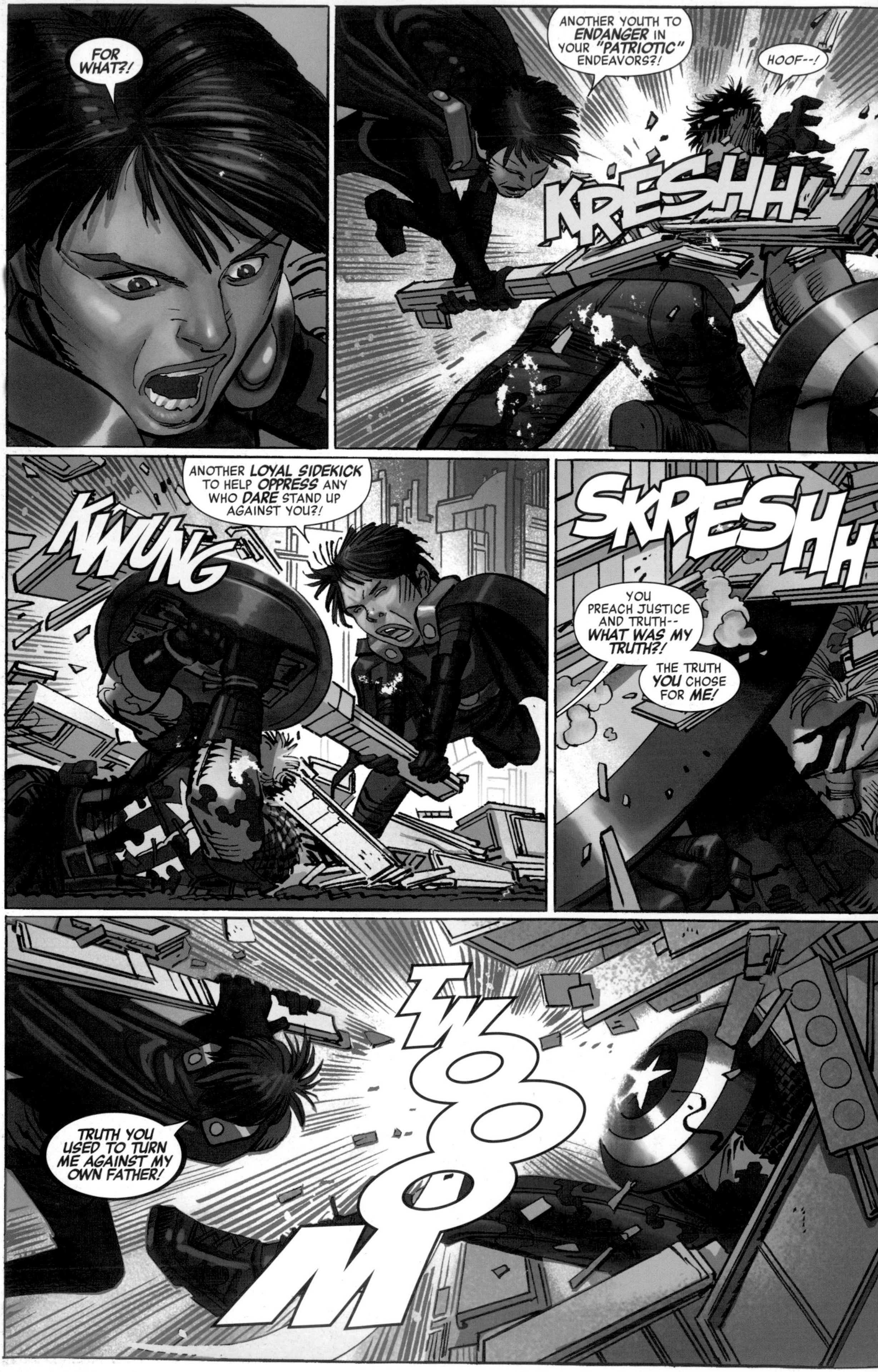

FOR WHAT?!
ANOTHER YOUTH TO ENDANGER IN YOUR "PATRIOTIC" ENDEAVORS?!
HOOF--!
KRESHH
ANOTHER LOYAL SIDEKICK TO HELP OPPRESS ANY WHO DARE STAND UP AGAINST YOU?!
KWUNG
SKRESHH
YOU PREACH JUSTICE AND TRUTH-- WHAT WAS MY TRUTH?!
THE TRUTH YOU CHOSE FOR ME!
TRUTH YOU USED TO TURN ME AGAINST MY OWN FATHER!
TWOOOM

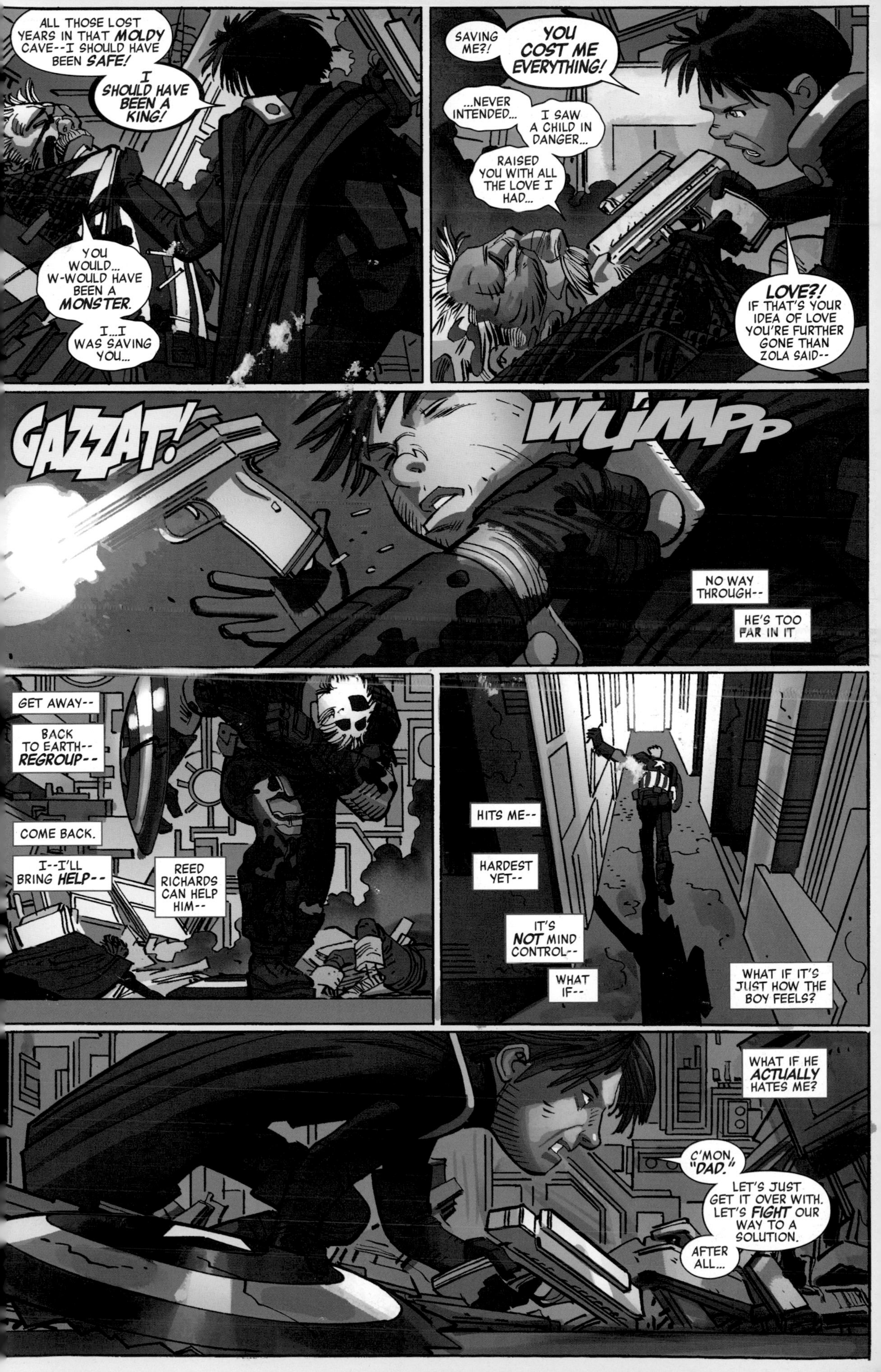

ALL THOSE LOST YEARS IN THAT MOLDY CAVE--I SHOULD HAVE BEEN SAFE!
I SHOULD HAVE BEEN A KING!
YOU WOULD... W-WOULD HAVE BEEN A MONSTER.
I...I WAS SAVING YOU...
SAVING ME?!
YOU COST ME EVERYTHING!
...NEVER INTENDED...
I SAW A CHILD IN DANGER...
RAISED YOU WITH ALL THE LOVE I HAD...
LOVE?! IF THAT'S YOUR IDEA OF LOVE YOU'RE FURTHER GONE THAN ZOLA SAID--
GAZZAT!
WUMPP
NO WAY THROUGH--
HE'S TOO FAR IN IT
GET AWAY--
BACK TO EARTH-- REGROUP--
COME BACK.
I--I'LL BRING HELP--
REED RICHARDS CAN HELP HIM--
HITS ME--
HARDEST YET--
IT'S NOT MIND CONTROL--
WHAT IF--
WHAT IF IT'S JUST HOW THE BOY FEELS?
WHAT IF HE ACTUALLY HATES ME?
C'MON, "DAD."
LET'S JUST GET IT OVER WITH. LET'S FIGHT OUR WAY TO A SOLUTION.
AFTER ALL...

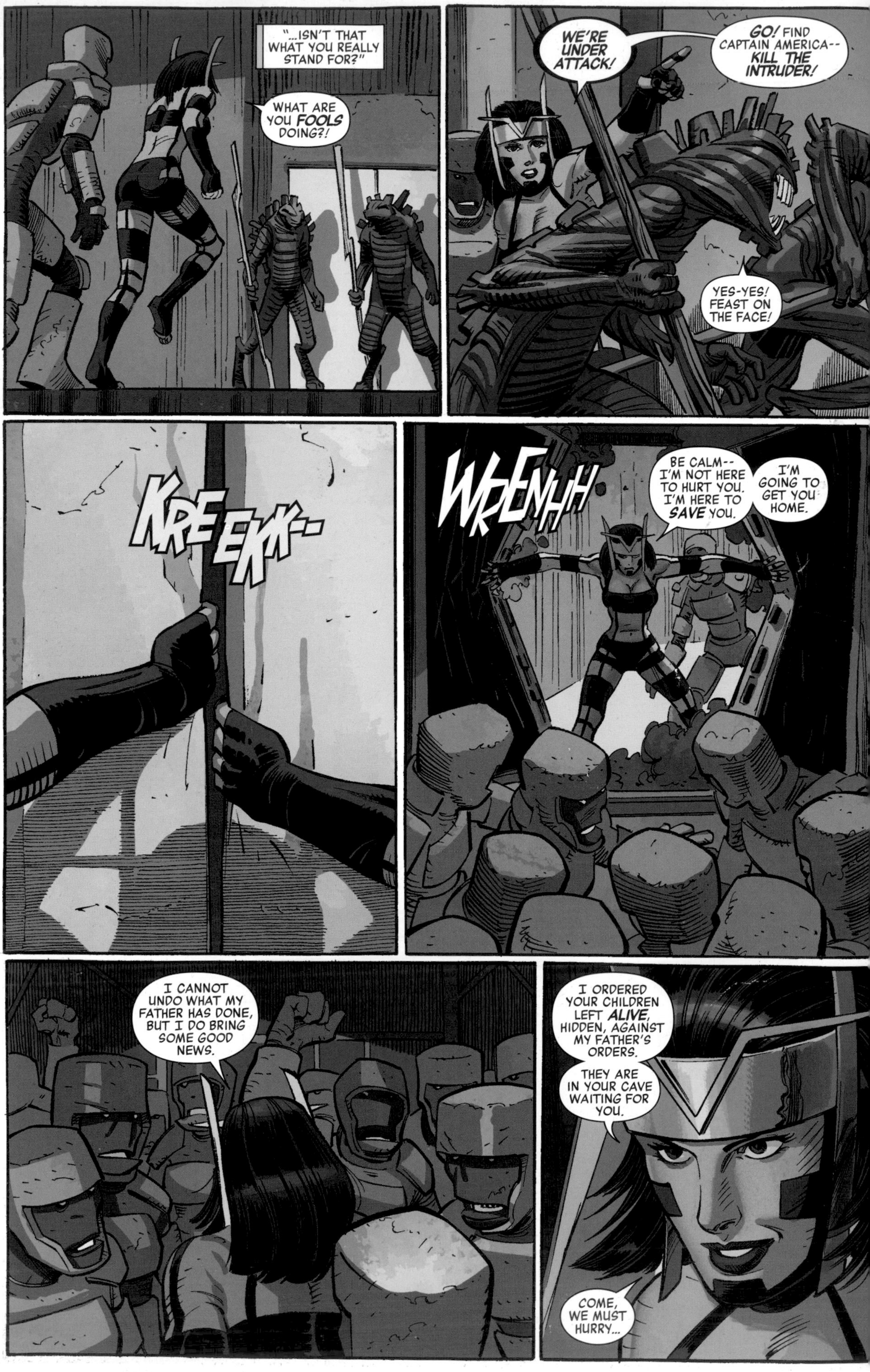
"...ISN'T THAT WHAT YOU REALLY STAND FOR?"
WHAT ARE YOU FOOLS DOING?!
WE'RE UNDER ATTACK!
GO! FIND CAPTAIN AMERICA-- KILL THE INTRUDER!
YES-YES! FEAST ON THE FACE!
KREEKK--
WRENHH
BE CALM-- I'M NOT HERE TO HURT YOU. I'M HERE TO SAVE YOU.
I'M GOING TO GET YOU HOME.
I CANNOT UNDO WHAT MY FATHER HAS DONE, BUT I DO BRING SOME GOOD NEWS.
I ORDERED YOUR CHILDREN LEFT ALIVE, HIDDEN, AGAINST MY FATHER'S ORDERS.
THEY ARE IN YOUR CAVE WAITING FOR YOU.
COME, WE MUST HURRY...

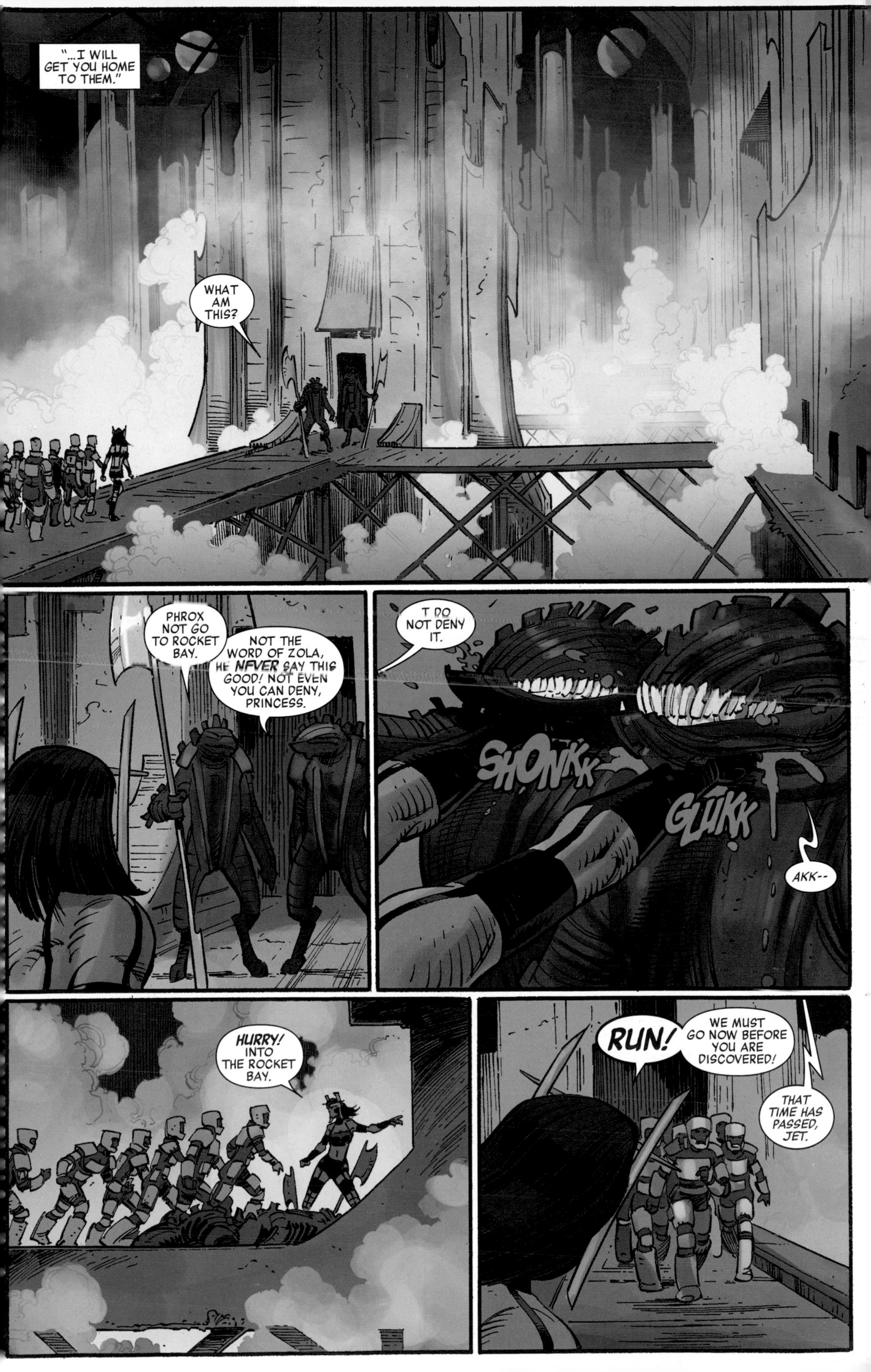
"...I WILL GET YOU HOME TO THEM."
WHAT AM THIS?
PHROX NOT GO TO ROCKET BAY.
NOT THE WORD OF ZOLA, HE NEVER SAY THIS GOOD! NOT EVEN YOU CAN DENY, PRINCESS.
I DO NOT DENY IT.
SHONKK
GLUKK
AKK--
HURRY! INTO THE ROCKET BAY.
RUN!
WE MUST GO NOW BEFORE YOU ARE DISCOVERED!
THAT TIME HAS PASSED, JET.

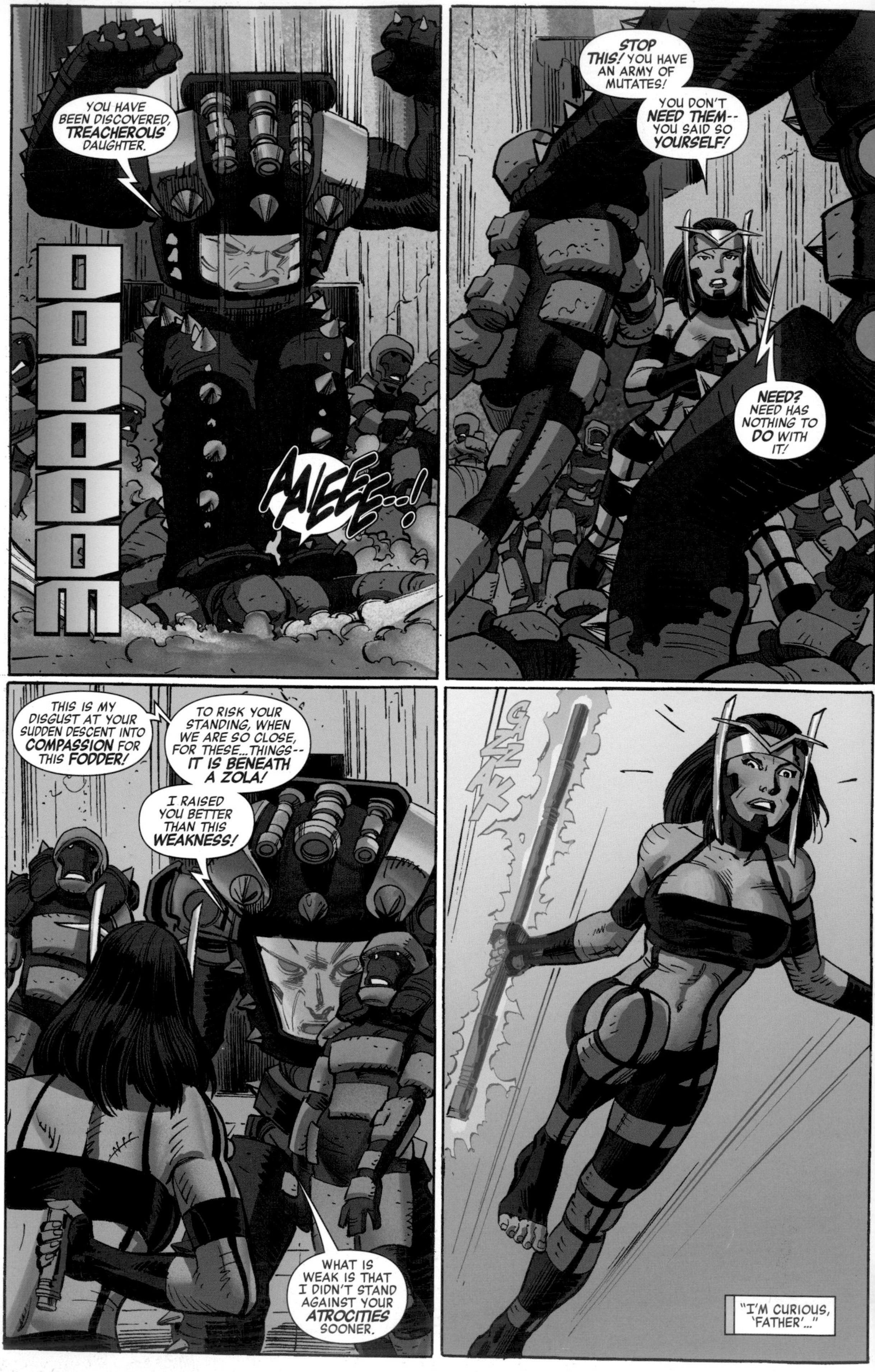
YOU HAVE BEEN DISCOVERED, TREACHEROUS DAUGHTER.
DOOOOOM
AAIEEE..!
STOP THIS! YOU HAVE AN ARMY OF MUTATES!
YOU DON'T NEED THEM-- YOU SAID SO YOURSELF!
NEED? NEED HAS NOTHING TO DO WITH IT!
THIS IS MY DISGUST AT YOUR SUDDEN DESCENT INTO COMPASSION FOR THIS FODDER!
TO RISK YOUR STANDING, WHEN WE ARE SO CLOSE, FOR THESE...THINGS-- IT IS BENEATH A ZOLA!
I RAISED YOU BETTER THAN THIS WEAKNESS!
WHAT IS WEAK IS THAT I DIDN'T STAND AGAINST YOUR ATROCITIES SOONER.
GZZAK
"I'M CURIOUS, 'FATHER'..."

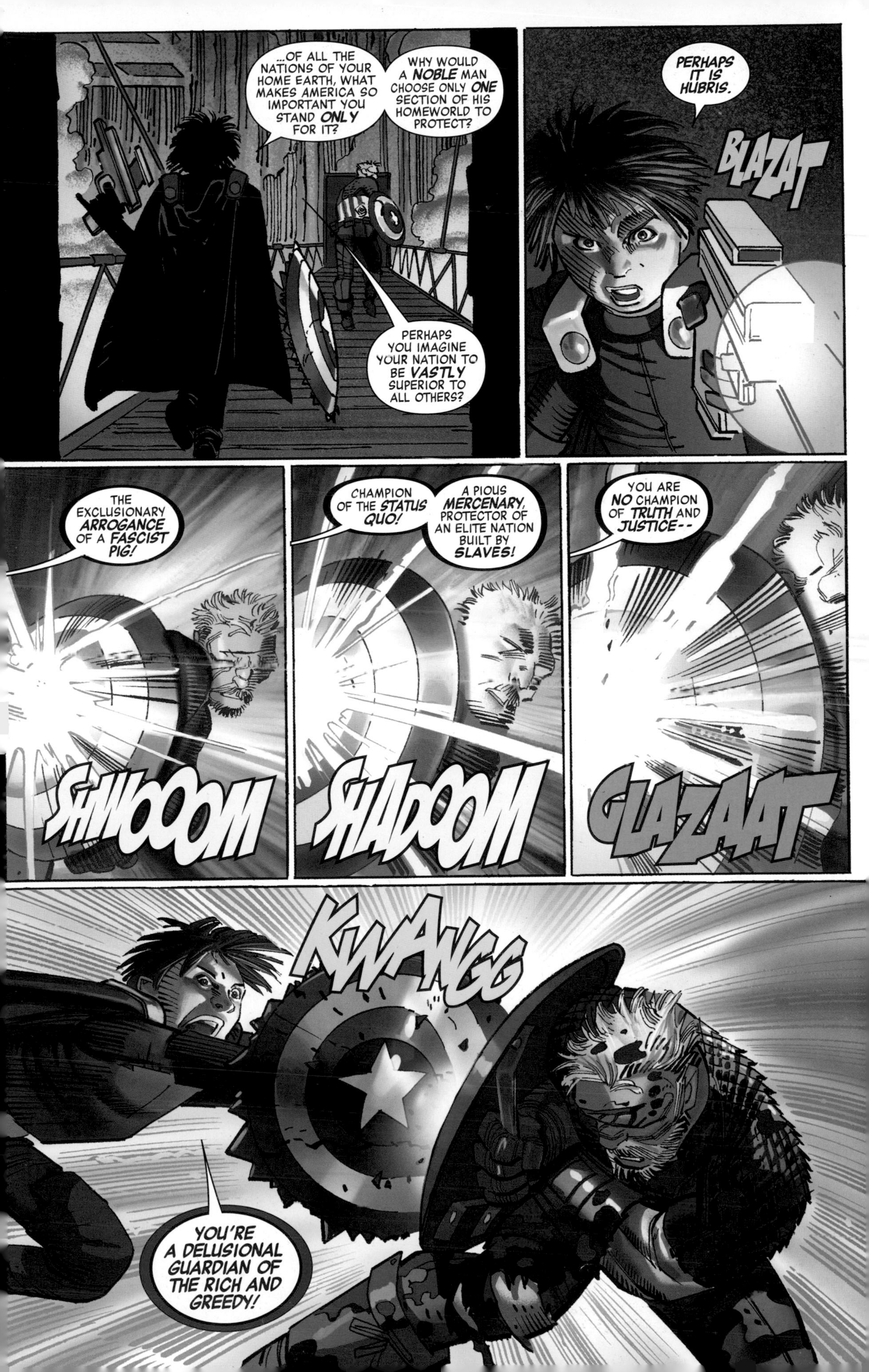

...OF ALL THE NATIONS OF YOUR HOME EARTH, WHAT MAKES AMERICA SO IMPORTANT YOU STAND ONLY FOR IT?
WHY WOULD A NOBLE MAN CHOOSE ONLY ONE SECTION OF HIS HOMEWORLD TO PROTECT?
PERHAPS YOU IMAGINE YOUR NATION TO BE VASTLY SUPERIOR TO ALL OTHERS?
PERHAPS IT IS HUBRIS.
BLAZAT
THE EXCLUSIONARY ARROGANCE OF A FASCIST PIG!
SHWOOOM
CHAMPION OF THE STATUS QUO!
A PIOUS MERCENARY, PROTECTOR OF AN ELITE NATION BUILT BY SLAVES!
SHADOOM
YOU ARE NO CHAMPION OF TRUTH AND JUSTICE--
GLAZAAT
KWANGG
YOU'RE A DELUSIONAL GUARDIAN OF THE RICH AND GREEDY!

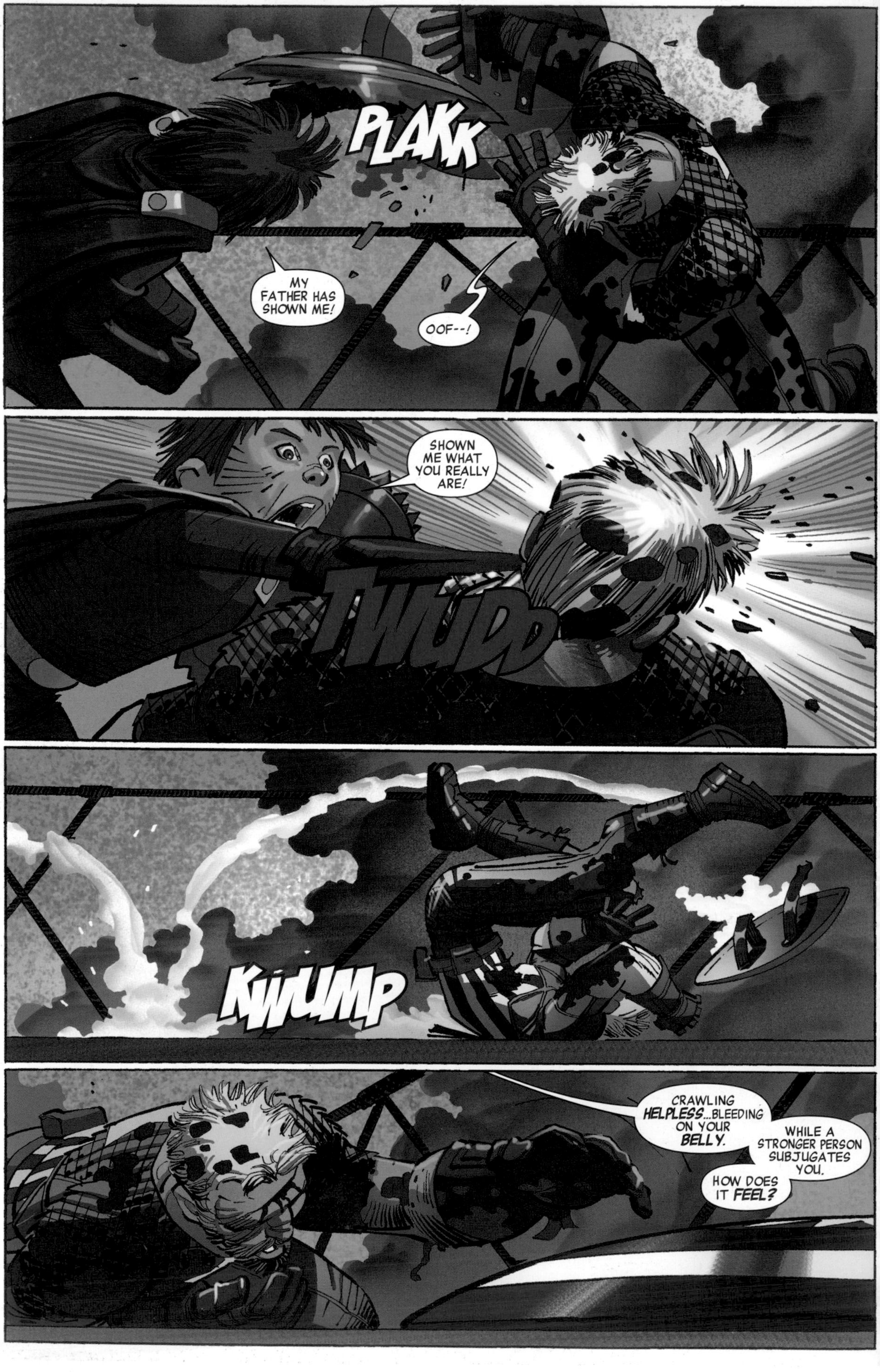
PLAKK
MY FATHER HAS SHOWN ME!
OOF--!
SHOWN ME WHAT YOU REALLY ARE!
TWUDD
KWUMP
CRAWLING HELPLESS...BLEEDING ON YOUR BELLY.
WHILE A STRONGER PERSON SUBJUGATES YOU.
HOW DOES IT FEEL?

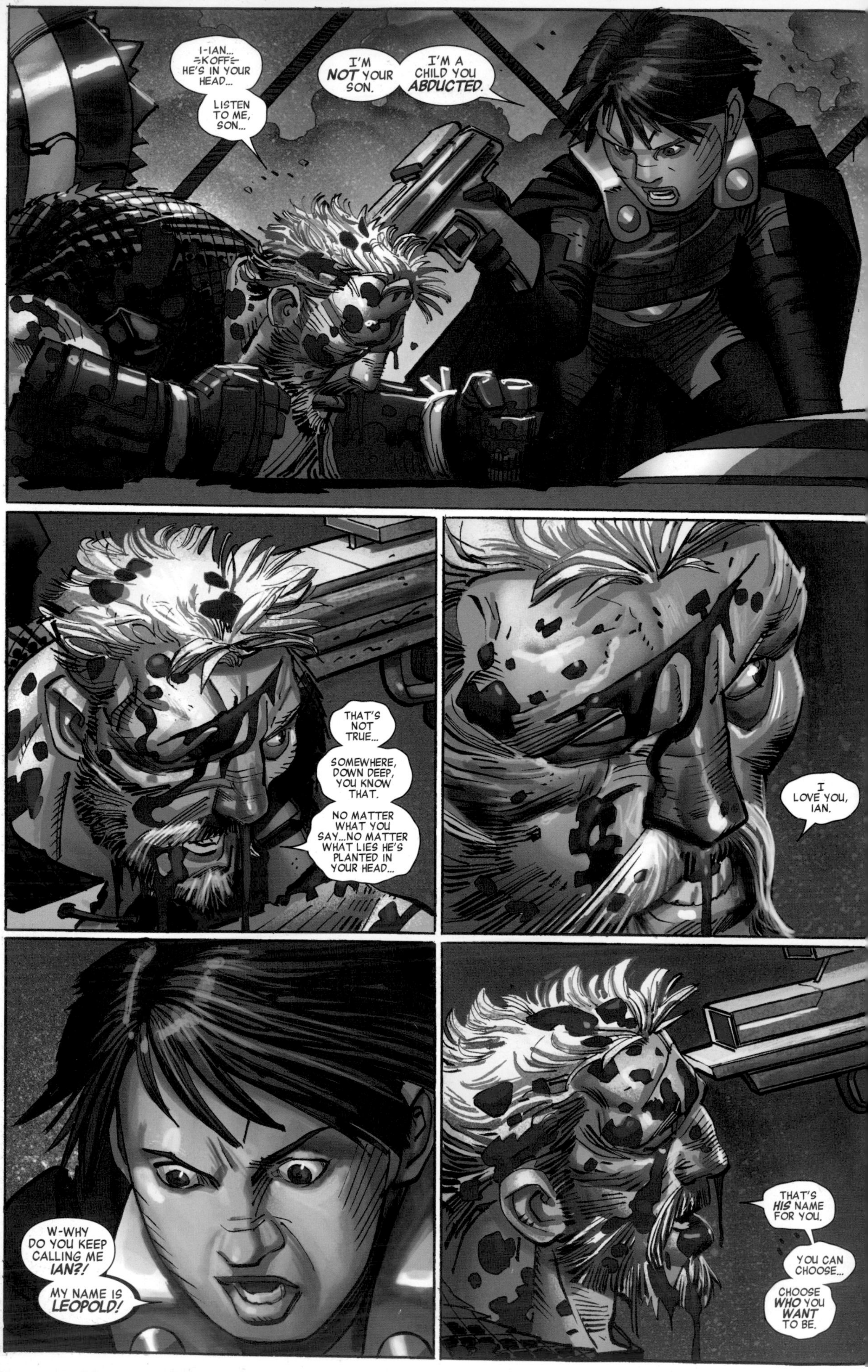

I-IAN... =KOFF= HE'S IN YOUR HEAD...
LISTEN TO ME, SON...
I'M NOT YOUR SON.
I'M A CHILD YOU ABDUCTED.
THAT'S NOT TRUE...
SOMEWHERE, DOWN DEEP, YOU KNOW THAT.
NO MATTER WHAT YOU SAY...NO MATTER WHAT LIES HE'S PLANTED IN YOUR HEAD...
I LOVE YOU, IAN.
W-WHY DO YOU KEEP CALLING ME IAN?!
MY NAME IS LEOPOLD!
THAT'S HIS NAME FOR YOU.
YOU CAN CHOOSE...
CHOOSE WHO YOU WANT TO BE.

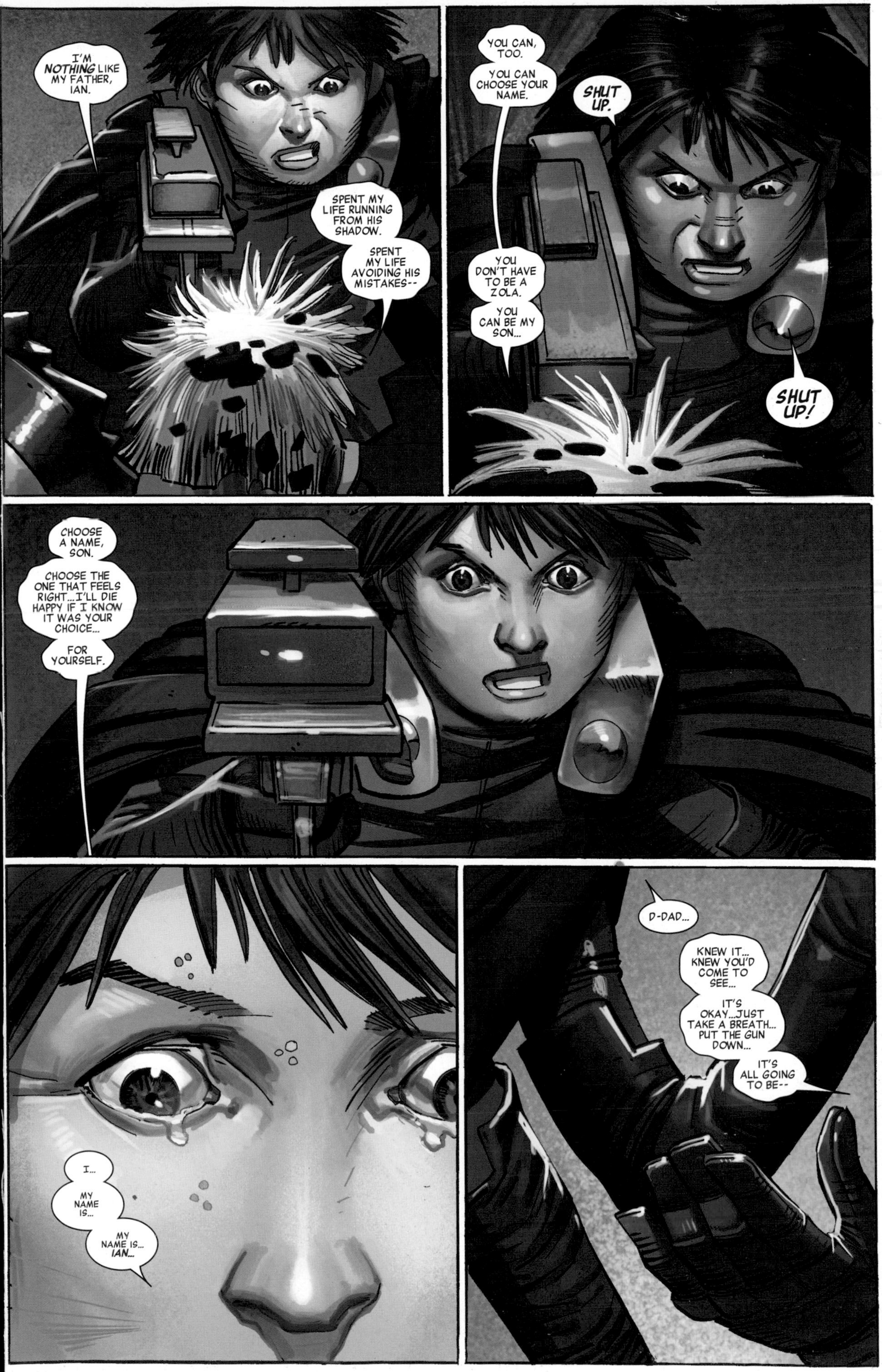
I'M NOTHING LIKE MY FATHER, IAN.
SPENT MY LIFE RUNNING FROM HIS SHADOW.
SPENT MY LIFE AVOIDING HIS MISTAKES--
YOU CAN, TOO.
YOU CAN CHOOSE YOUR NAME.
SHUT UP.
YOU DON'T HAVE TO BE A ZOLA.
YOU CAN BE MY SON...
SHUT UP!
CHOOSE A NAME, SON.
CHOOSE THE ONE THAT FEELS RIGHT...I'LL DIE HAPPY IF I KNOW IT WAS YOUR CHOICE...
FOR YOURSELF.
I...
MY NAME IS...
MY NAME IS... IAN...
D-DAD...
KNEW IT... KNEW YOU'D COME TO SEE...
IT'S OKAY...JUST TAKE A BREATH... PUT THE GUN DOWN...
IT'S ALL GOING TO BE--

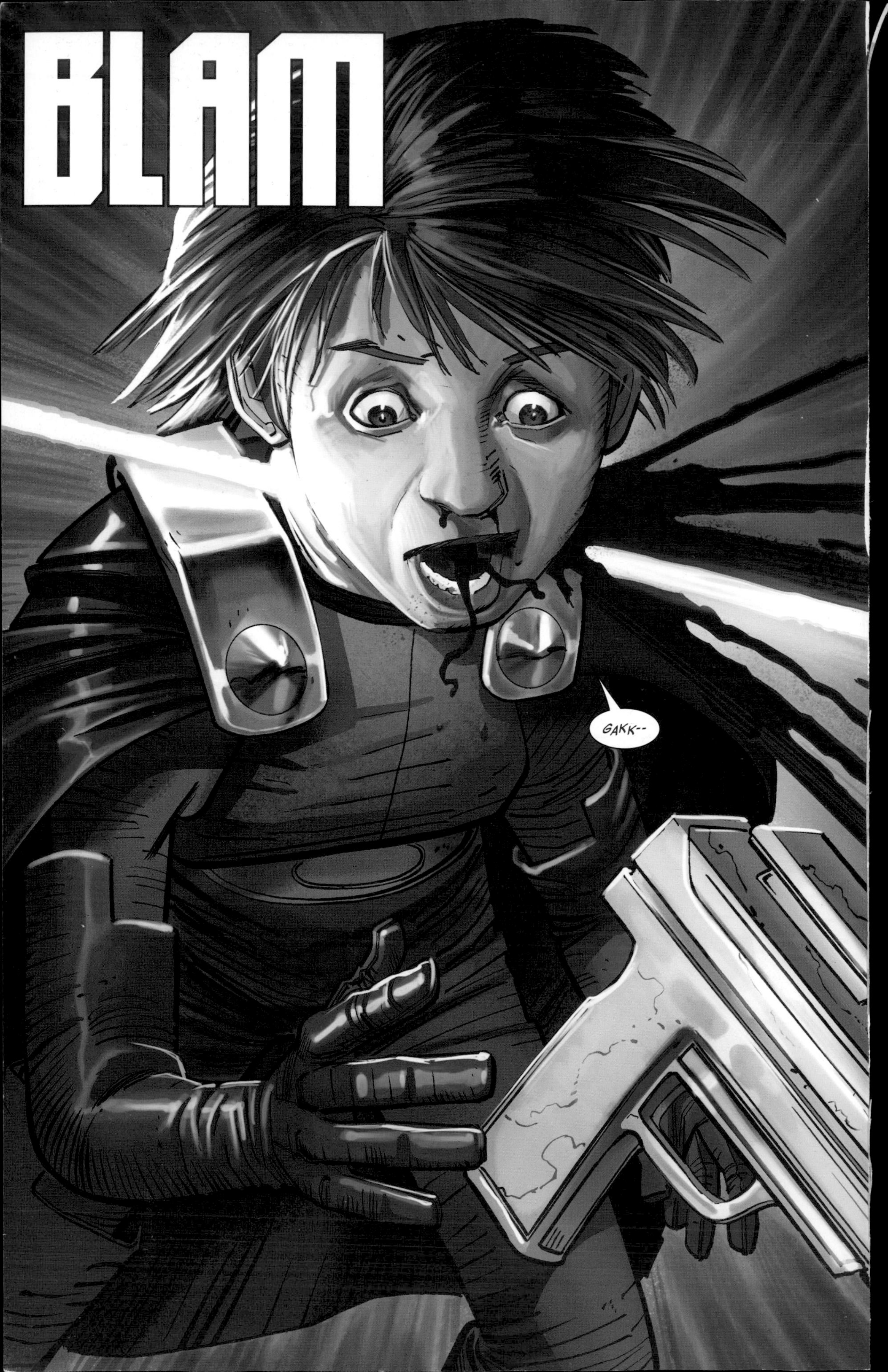
BLAM
GAKK--

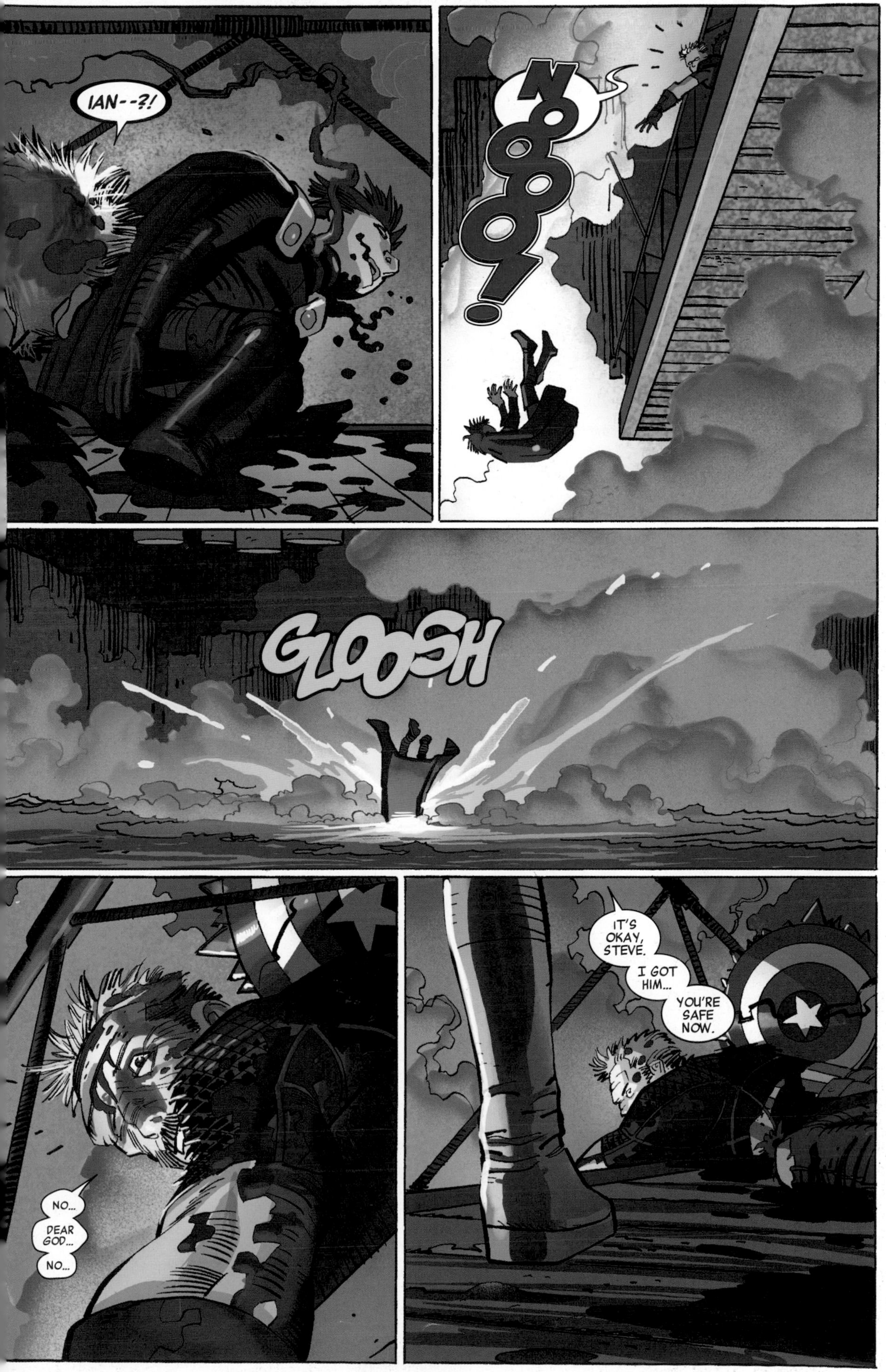
IAN--?!
NOOOO!
GLOOSH
NO...
DEAR GOD...
NO...
IT'S OKAY, STEVE.
I GOT HIM...
YOU'RE SAFE NOW.

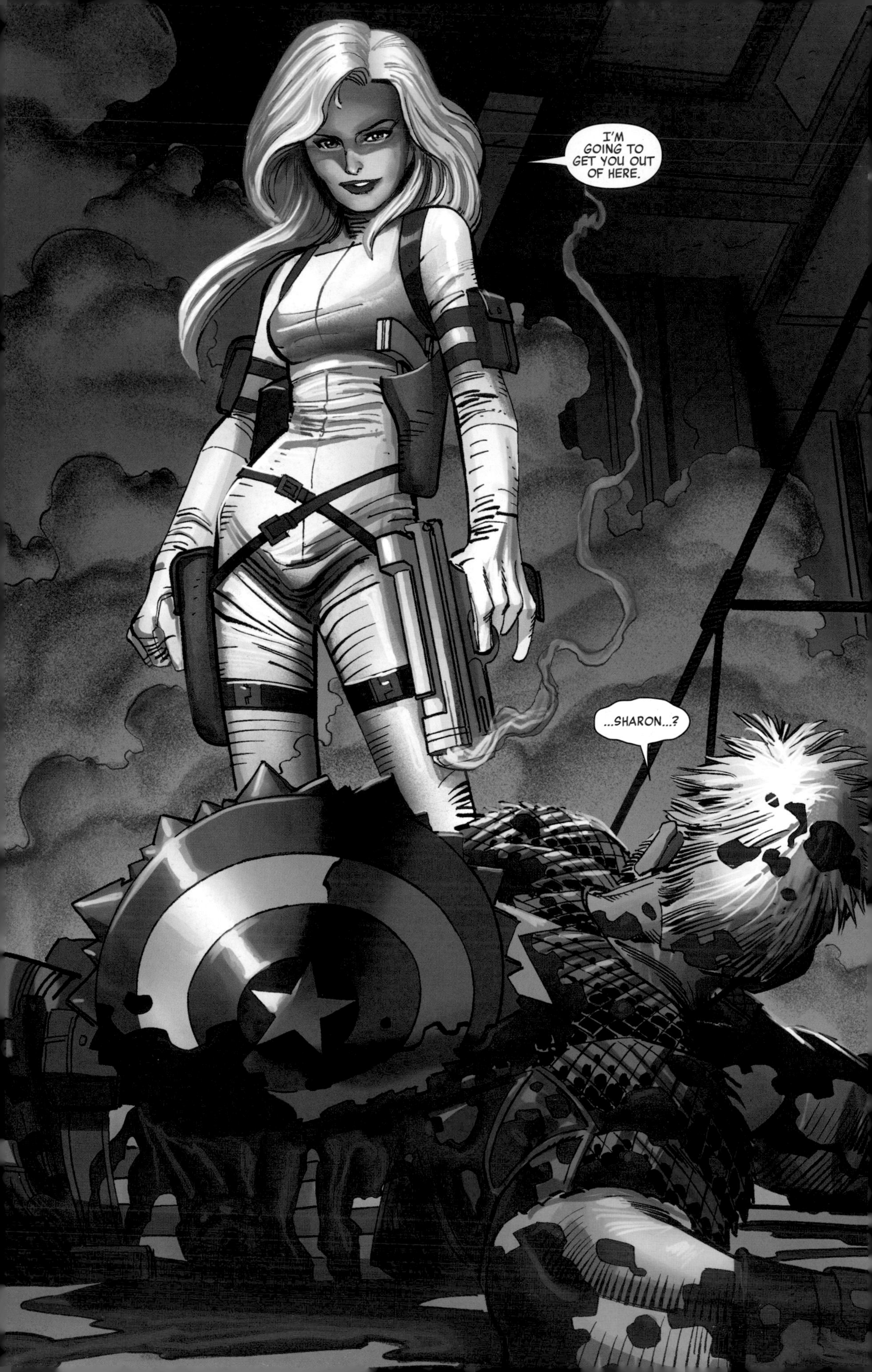
I'M GOING TO GET YOU OUT OF HERE.
...SHARON...?

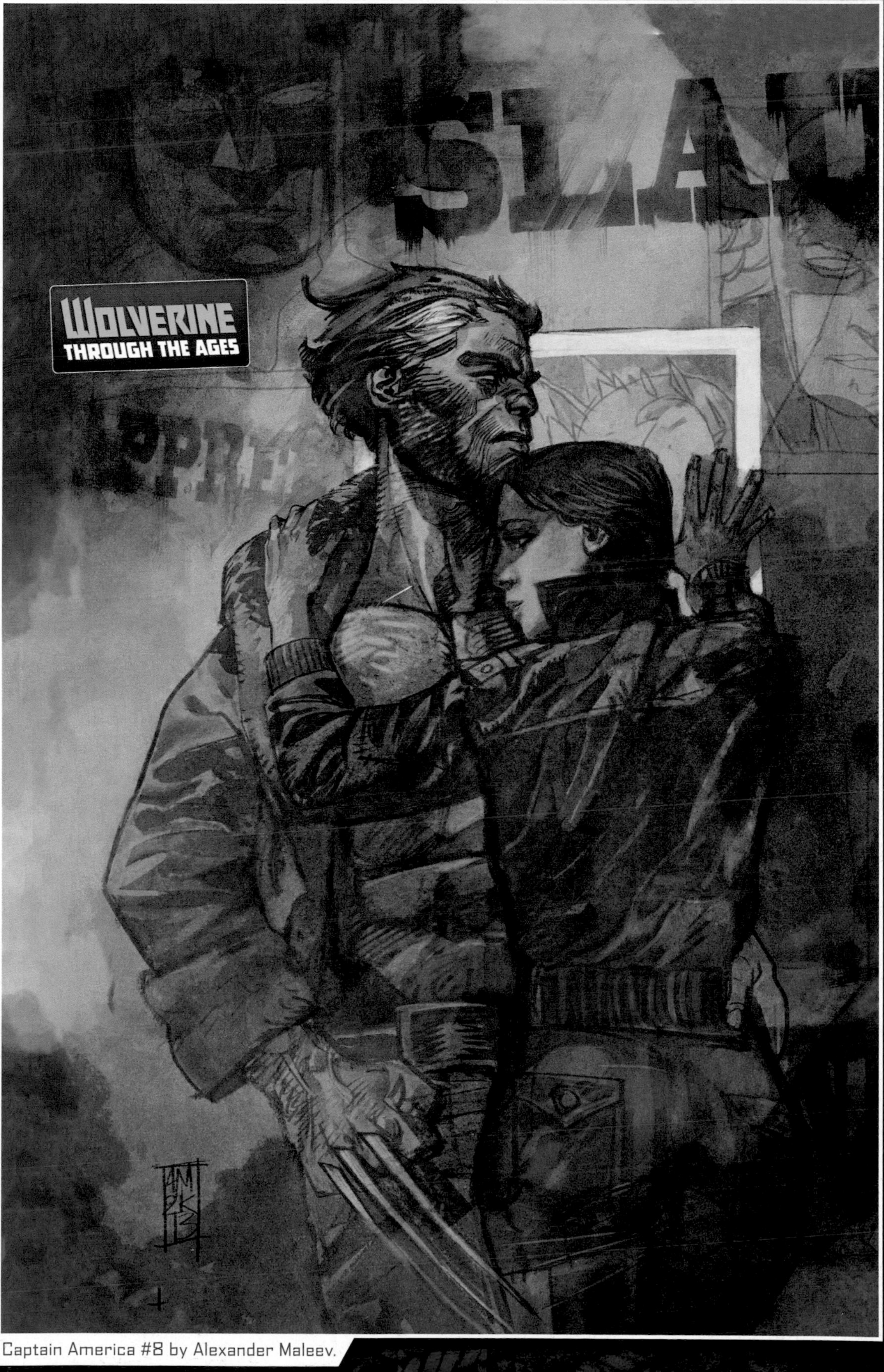
WOLVERINE
THROUGH THE AGES

Captain America #8 by Alexander Maleev.

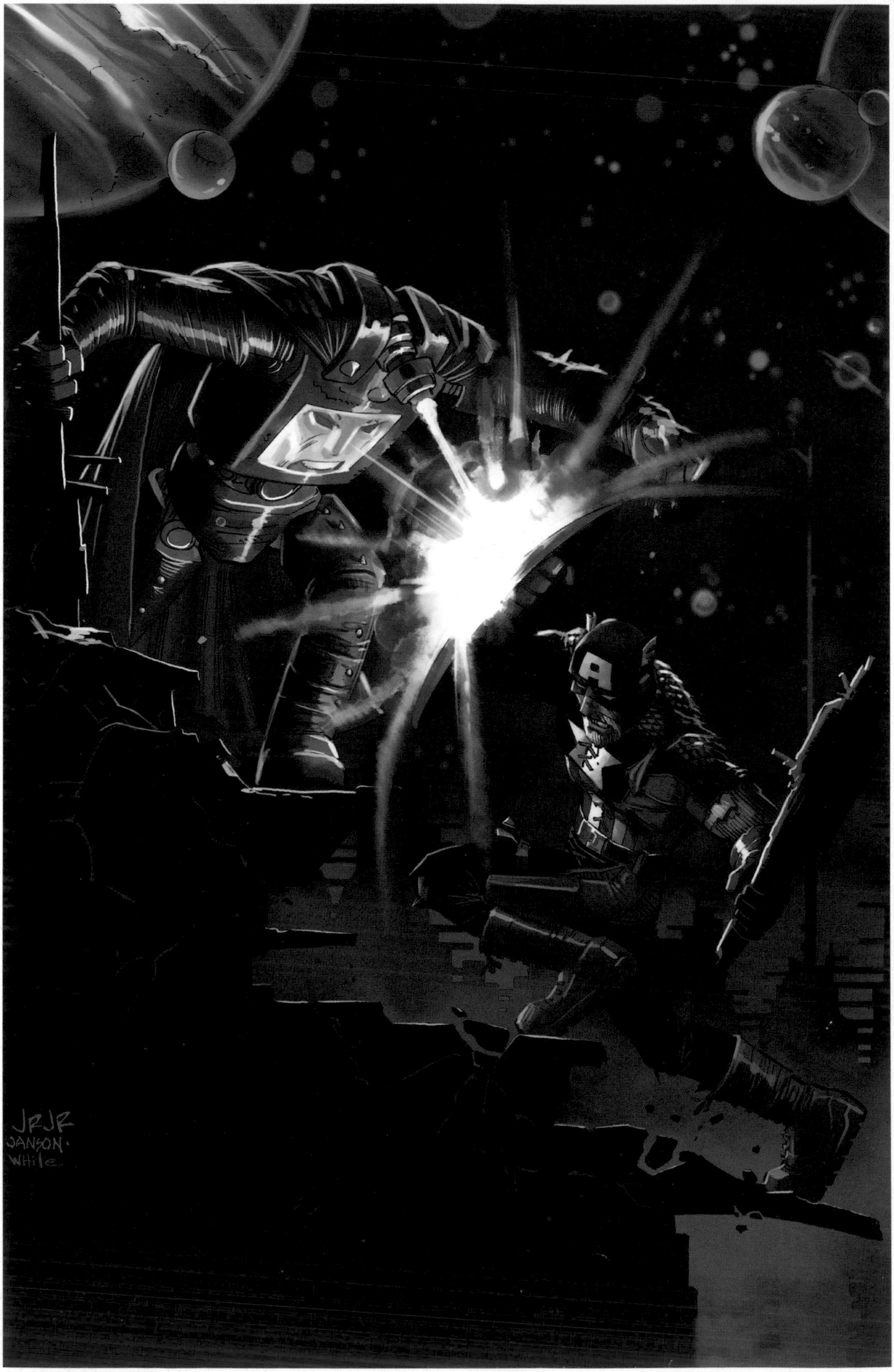
JRJR
JANSON.
White.

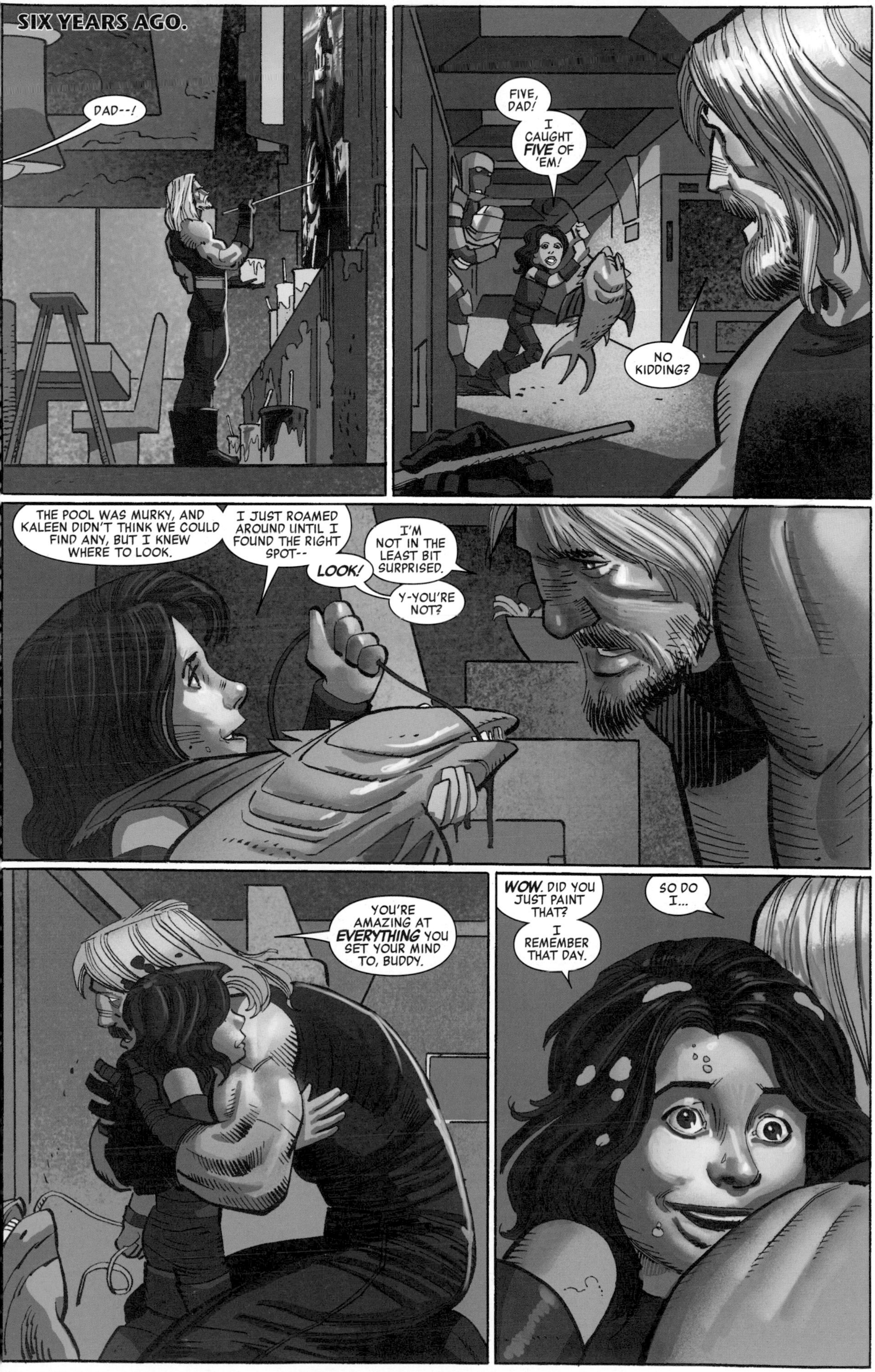
SIX YEARS AGO.
DAD--!
FIVE, DAD!
I CAUGHT FIVE OF 'EM!
NO KIDDING?
THE POOL WAS MURKY, AND KALEEN DIDN'T THINK WE COULD FIND ANY, BUT I KNEW WHERE TO LOOK.
I JUST ROAMED AROUND UNTIL I FOUND THE RIGHT SPOT--
LOOK!
I'M NOT IN THE LEAST BIT SURPRISED.
Y-YOU'RE NOT?
YOU'RE AMAZING AT EVERYTHING YOU SET YOUR MIND TO, BUDDY.
WOW. DID YOU JUST PAINT THAT?
I REMEMBER THAT DAY.
SO DO I...

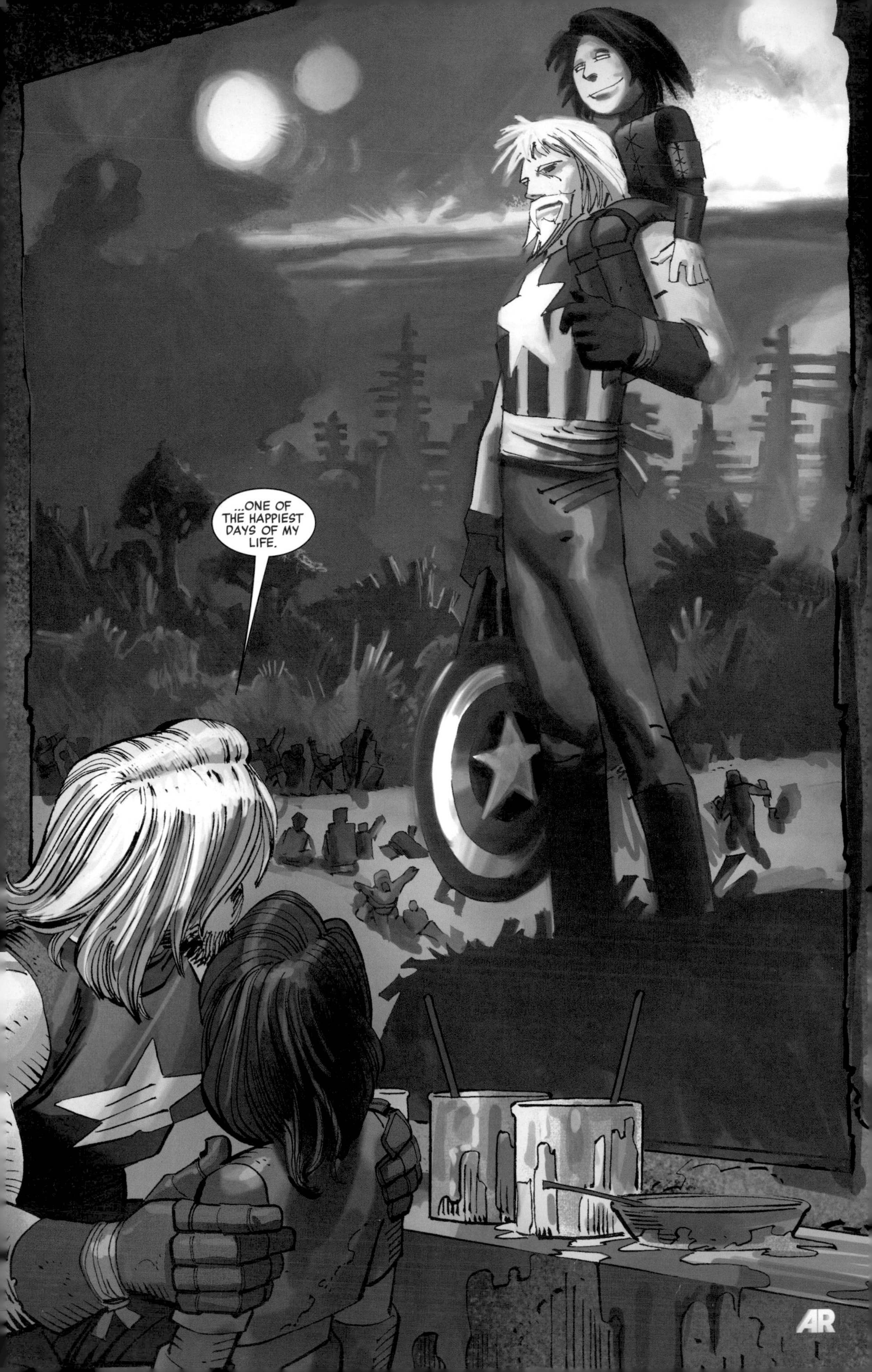
...ONE OF THE HAPPIEST DAYS OF MY LIFE.
AR

NOW.

WE'LL FIGURE IT OUT, STEVE... I PROMISE.

BUT YOU HAVE TO BELIEVE ME...

NOTHING YOU'RE SAYING COULD POSSIBLY BE TRUE.

IT'S ALL ARTIFICIAL MEMORIES ZOLA'S PLANTED INTO YOUR MIND. MEMORIES WE WILL CLEAN OUT.

I-IT'S NOT ARTIFICIAL, SHARON.

I... WE'VE...

...BEEN HERE FOR OVER A DECADE...

=HOKKE= =KOFF=

I-IAN...HE WAS MY SON, SHARON...

MY SON.

YOU HAVE TO LISTEN CLOSELY TO ME NOW. HE WASN'T YOUR SON--AND YOU HAVE NOT BEEN HERE FOR A DECADE.

YOU LEFT ME IN THE TRAIN STATION NOT THIRTY MINUTES AGO. DO YOU UNDERSTAND?

I-IT'S NOT...

NOT POSSIBLE...

I-IAN... I RAISED HIM...

I FOLLOWED RIGHT BEHIND YOU, STEVE. IT'S BEEN MINUTES--NOT YEARS.

WHATEVER YOU THINK HAPPENED, WHATEVER YOU THINK IS GOING ON--IT'S ALL A LIE.

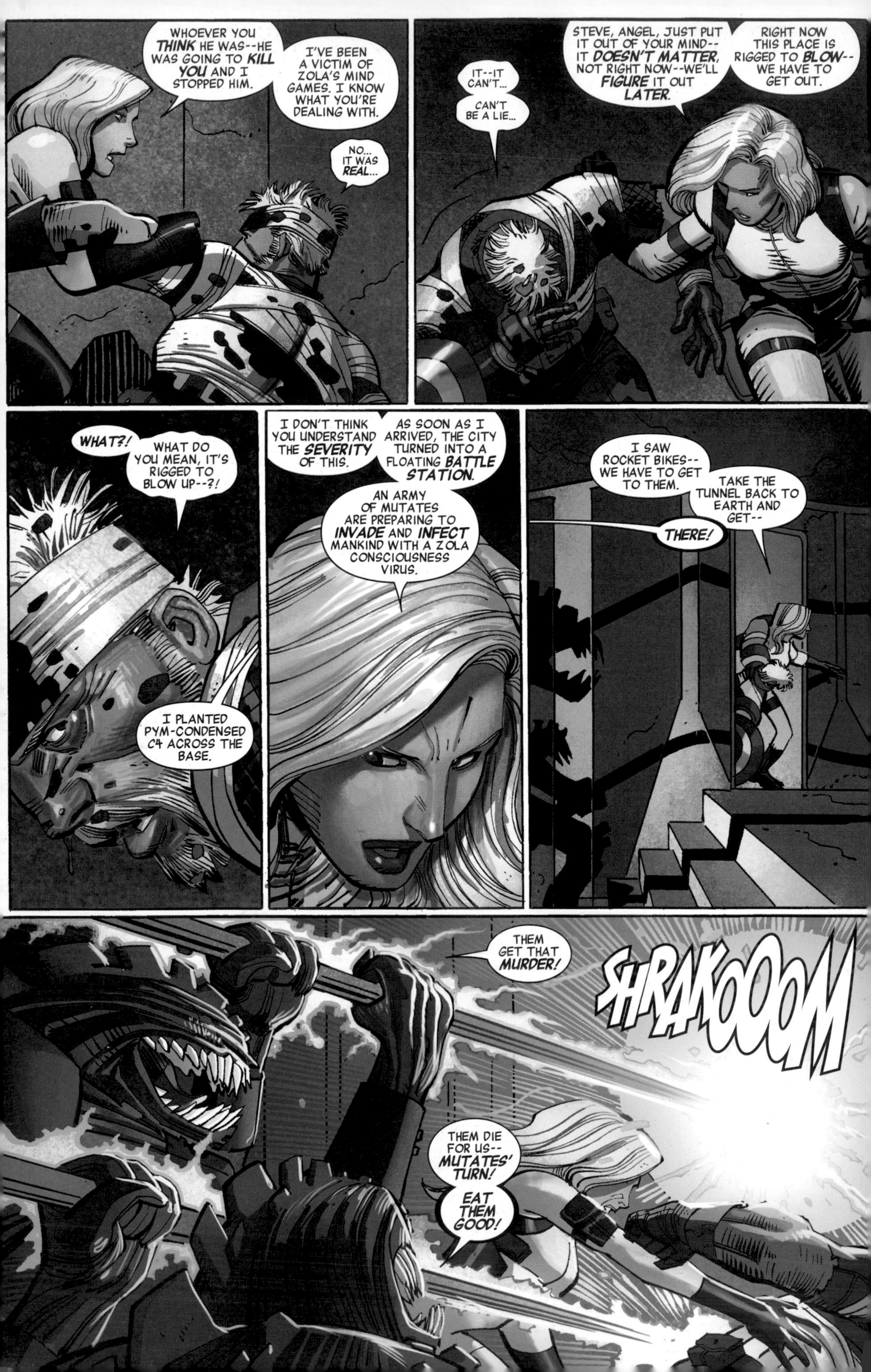
WHOEVER YOU THINK HE WAS--HE WAS GOING TO KILL YOU AND I STOPPED HIM.
I'VE BEEN A VICTIM OF ZOLA'S MIND GAMES. I KNOW WHAT YOU'RE DEALING WITH.
NO... IT WAS REAL...
IT--IT CAN'T...
CAN'T BE A LIE...
STEVE, ANGEL, JUST PUT IT OUT OF YOUR MIND--IT DOESN'T MATTER, NOT RIGHT NOW--WE'LL FIGURE IT OUT LATER.
RIGHT NOW THIS PLACE IS RIGGED TO BLOW--WE HAVE TO GET OUT.
WHAT?!
WHAT DO YOU MEAN, IT'S RIGGED TO BLOW UP--?!
I PLANTED PYM-CONDENSED C4 ACROSS THE BASE.
I DON'T THINK YOU UNDERSTAND THE SEVERITY OF THIS.
AS SOON AS I ARRIVED, THE CITY TURNED INTO A FLOATING BATTLE STATION.
AN ARMY OF MUTATES ARE PREPARING TO INVADE AND INFECT MANKIND WITH A ZOLA CONSCIOUSNESS VIRUS.
I SAW ROCKET BIKES--WE HAVE TO GET TO THEM.
TAKE THE TUNNEL BACK TO EARTH AND GET--
THERE!
THEM GET THAT MURDER!
SHRAKOOOM
THEM DIE FOR US--MUTATES' TURN!
EAT THEM GOOD!

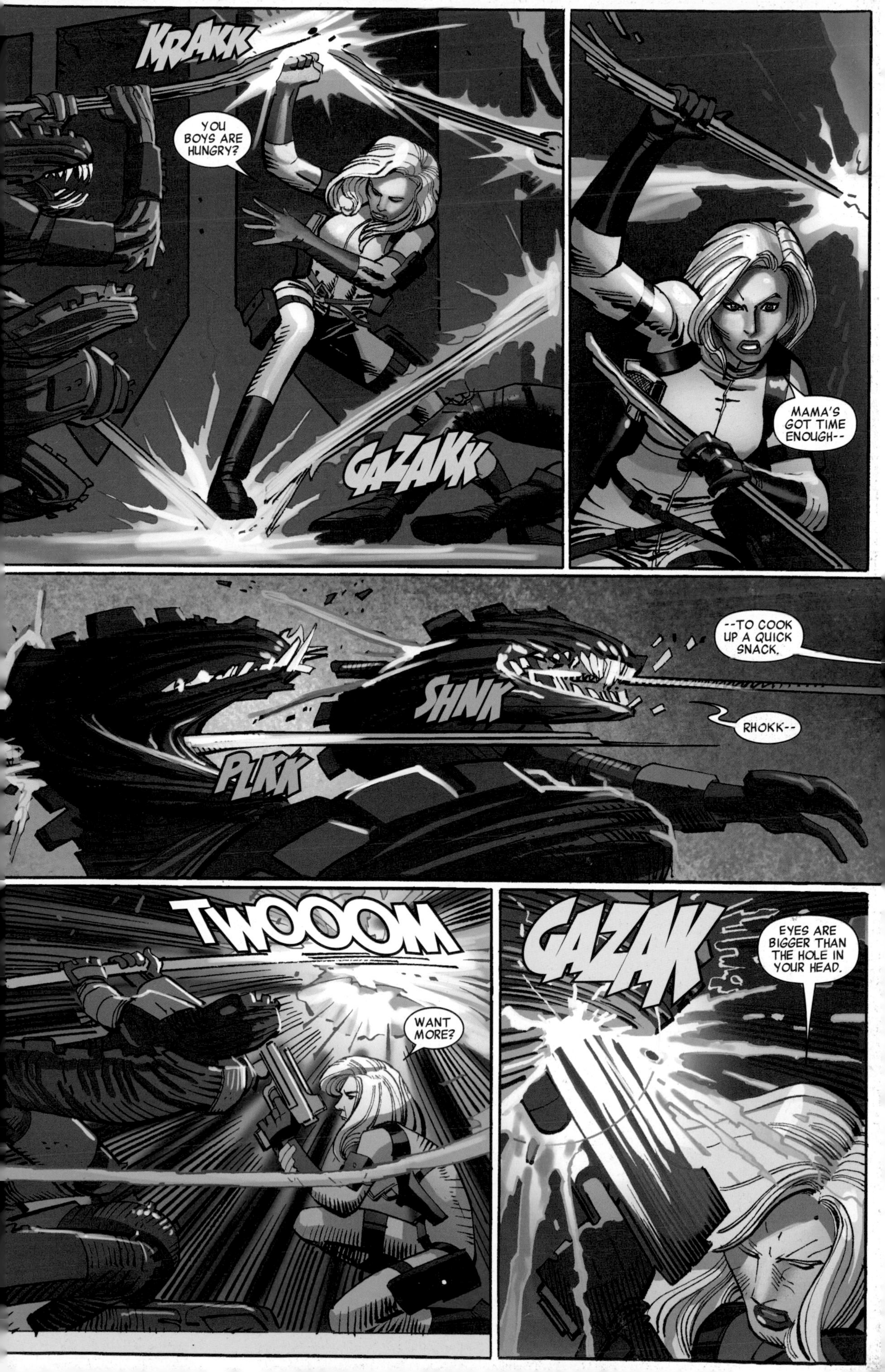
KRAKK
YOU BOYS ARE HUNGRY?
GAZAKK
MAMA'S GOT TIME ENOUGH--
--TO COOK UP A QUICK SNACK.
SHNK
RHOKK--
PLKK
TWOOOM
WANT MORE?
GAZAK
EYES ARE BIGGER THAN THE HOLE IN YOUR HEAD.

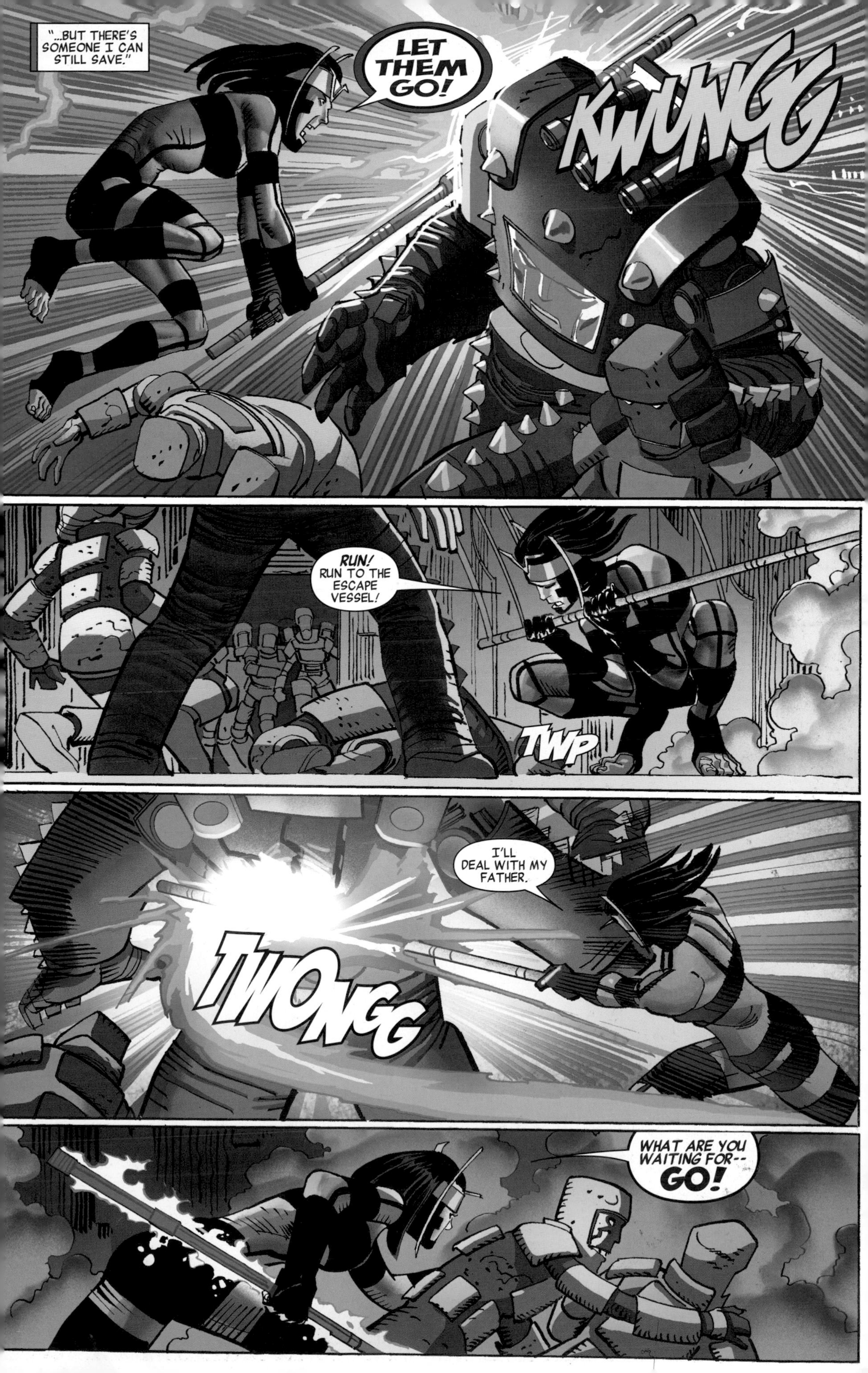
"...BUT THERE'S SOMEONE I CAN STILL SAVE."
LET THEM GO!
KWUNGG
RUN! RUN TO THE ESCAPE VESSEL!
TWP
I'LL DEAL WITH MY FATHER.
TWONGG
WHAT ARE YOU WAITING FOR-- GO!

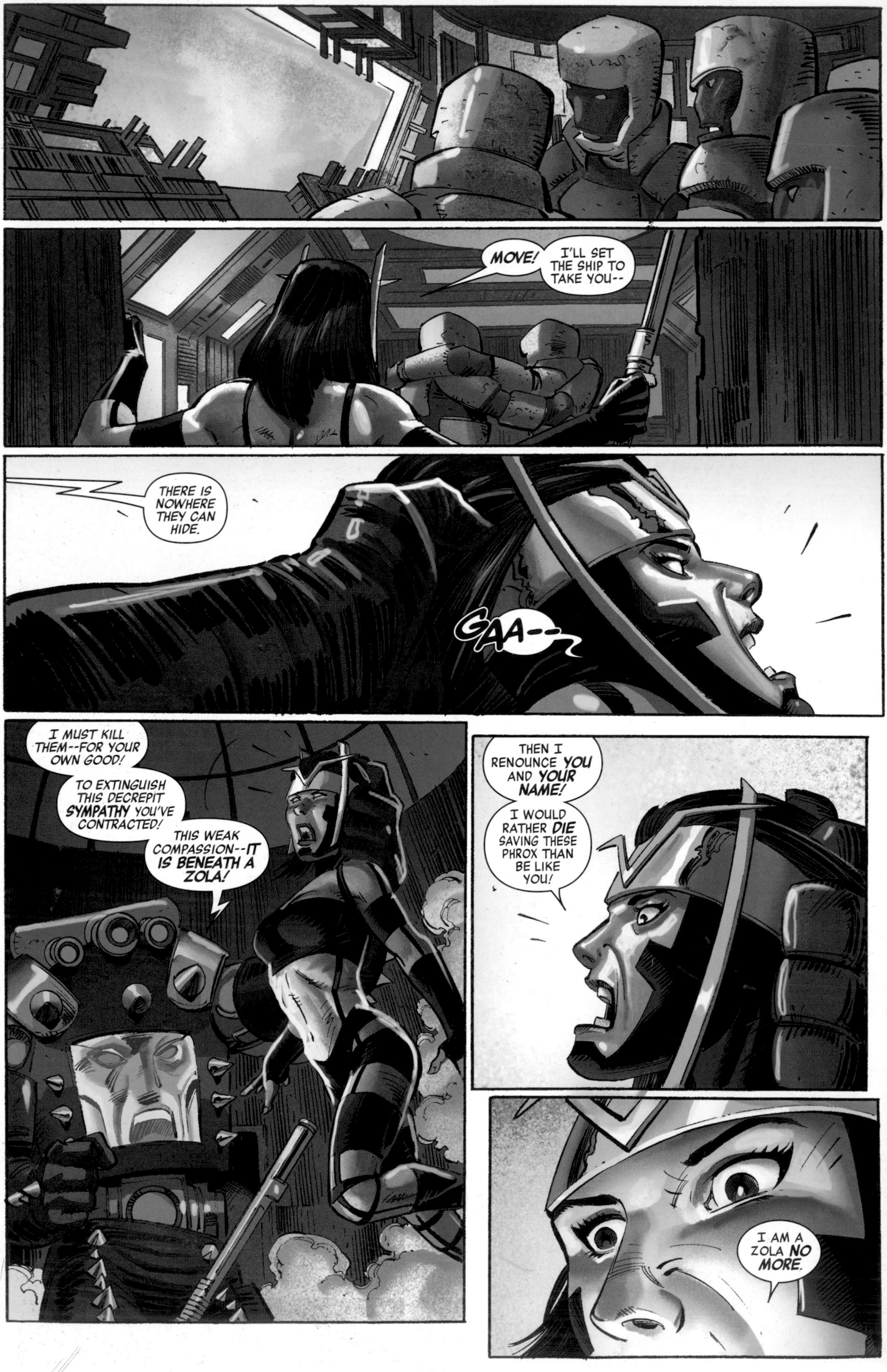
MOVE!
I'LL SET THE SHIP TO TAKE YOU--
THERE IS NOWHERE THEY CAN HIDE.
GAA--
I MUST KILL THEM--FOR YOUR OWN GOOD!
TO EXTINGUISH THIS DECREPIT SYMPATHY YOU'VE CONTRACTED!
THIS WEAK COMPASSION--IT IS BENEATH A ZOLA!
THEN I RENOUNCE YOU AND YOUR NAME!
I WOULD RATHER DIE SAVING THESE PHROX THAN BE LIKE YOU!
I AM A ZOLA NO MORE.

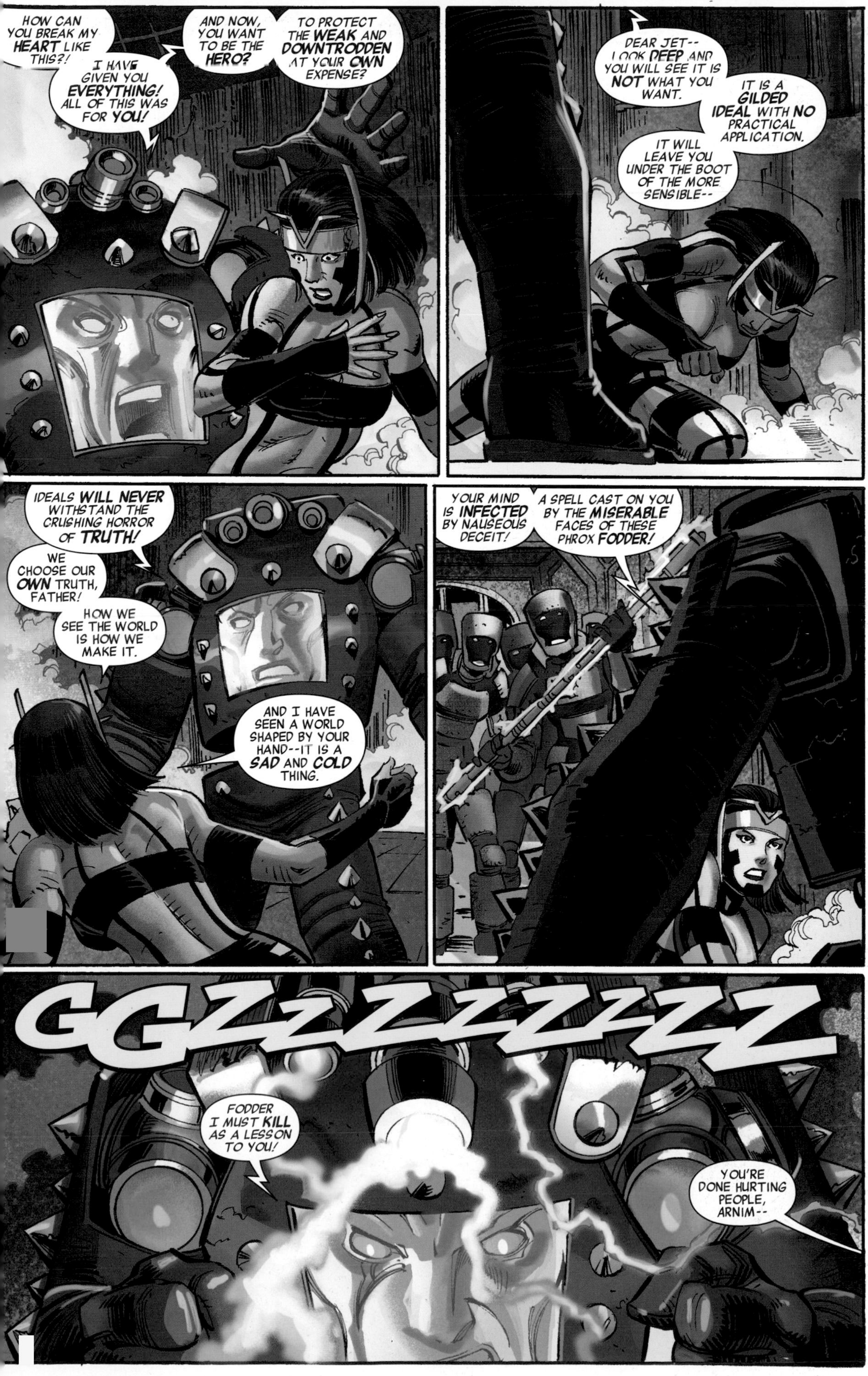
HOW CAN YOU BREAK MY HEART LIKE THIS?!
I HAVE GIVEN YOU EVERYTHING! ALL OF THIS WAS FOR YOU!
AND NOW, YOU WANT TO BE THE HERO?
TO PROTECT THE WEAK AND DOWNTRODDEN AT YOUR OWN EXPENSE?
DEAR JET-- LOOK DEEP AND YOU WILL SEE IT IS NOT WHAT YOU WANT.
IT IS A GILDED IDEAL WITH NO PRACTICAL APPLICATION.
IT WILL LEAVE YOU UNDER THE BOOT OF THE MORE SENSIBLE--
IDEALS WILL NEVER WITHSTAND THE CRUSHING HORROR OF TRUTH!
WE CHOOSE OUR OWN TRUTH, FATHER!
HOW WE SEE THE WORLD IS HOW WE MAKE IT.
AND I HAVE SEEN A WORLD SHAPED BY YOUR HAND--IT IS A SAD AND COLD THING.
YOUR MIND IS INFECTED BY NAUSEOUS DECEIT!
A SPELL CAST ON YOU BY THE MISERABLE FACES OF THESE PHROX FODDER!
GGZZZZZZZZ
FODDER I MUST KILL AS A LESSON TO YOU!
YOU'RE DONE HURTING PEOPLE, ARNIM--

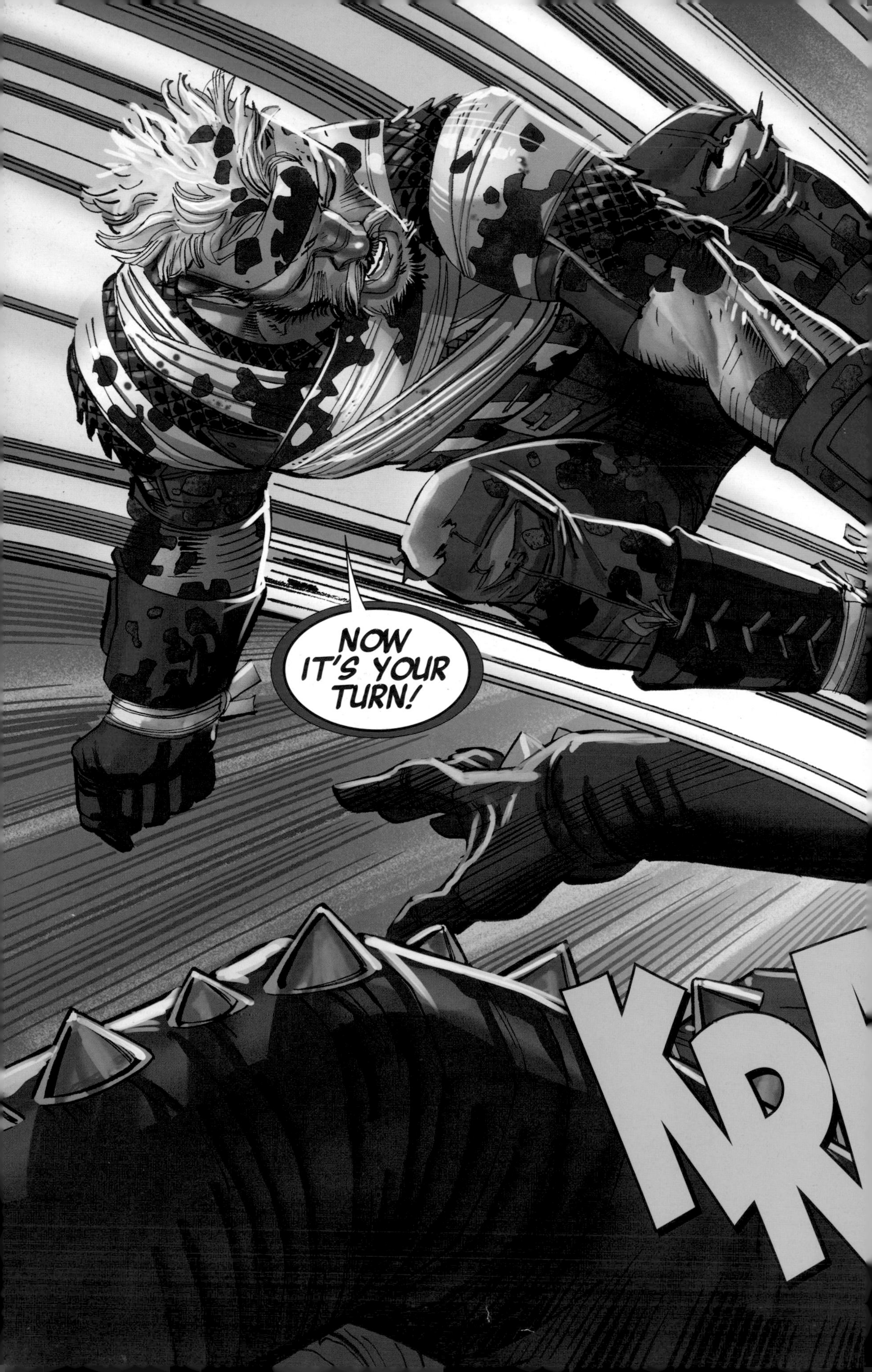
NOW IT'S YOUR TURN!

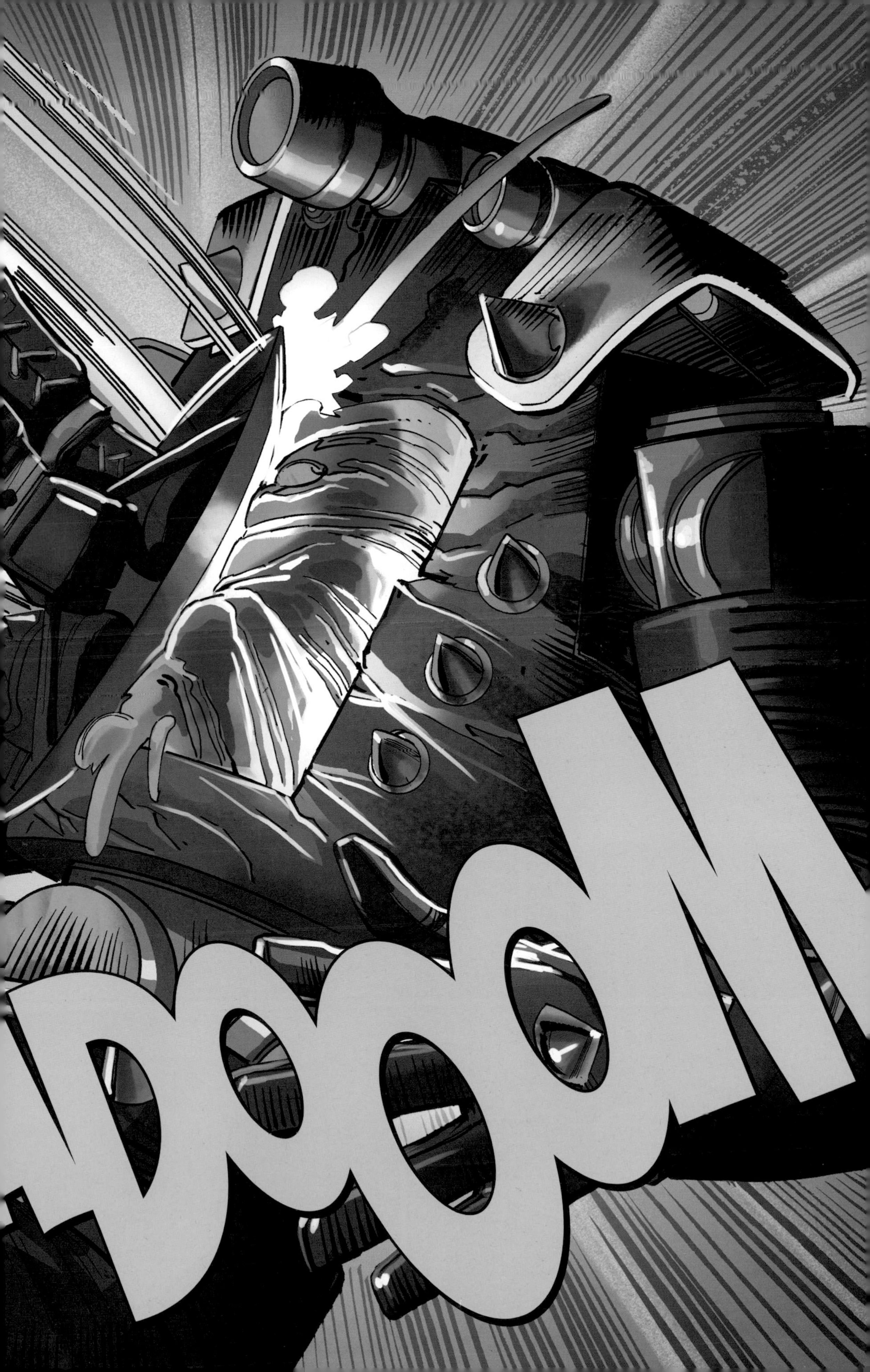
DOOOM

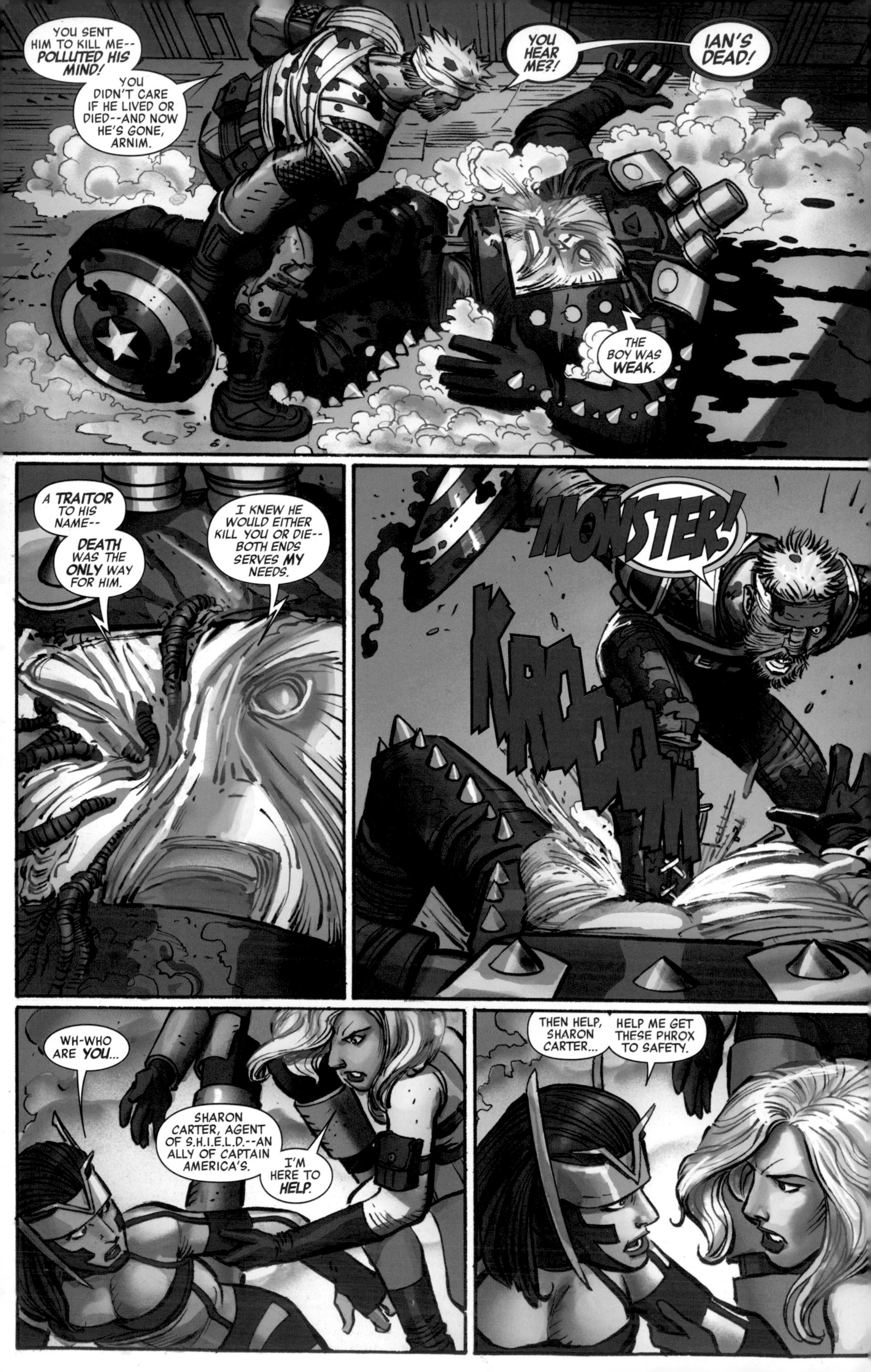
YOU SENT HIM TO KILL ME--POLLUTED HIS MIND!
YOU DIDN'T CARE IF HE LIVED OR DIED--AND NOW HE'S GONE, ARNIM.
YOU HEAR ME?!
IAN'S DEAD!
THE BOY WAS WEAK.
A TRAITOR TO HIS NAME--
DEATH WAS THE ONLY WAY FOR HIM.
I KNEW HE WOULD EITHER KILL YOU OR DIE--BOTH ENDS SERVES MY NEEDS.
MONSTER!
KROOOM
WH-WHO ARE YOU...
SHARON CARTER, AGENT OF S.H.I.E.L.D.--AN ALLY OF CAPTAIN AMERICA'S.
I'M HERE TO HELP.
THEN HELP, SHARON CARTER...
HELP ME GET THESE PHROX TO SAFETY.

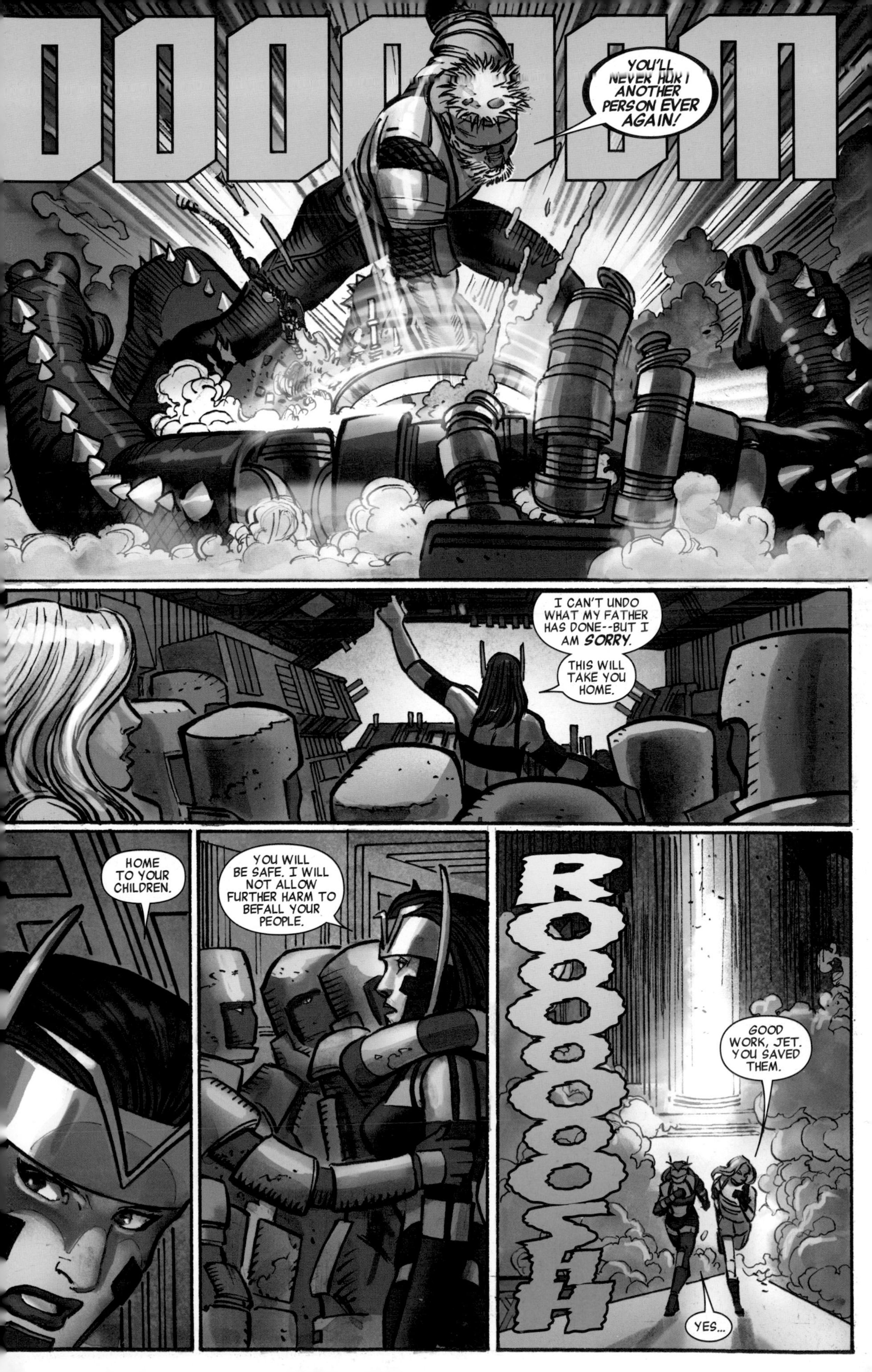
DOOOOM
YOU'LL NEVER HURT ANOTHER PERSON EVER AGAIN!
I CAN'T UNDO WHAT MY FATHER HAS DONE--BUT I AM SORRY.
THIS WILL TAKE YOU HOME.
HOME TO YOUR CHILDREN.
YOU WILL BE SAFE. I WILL NOT ALLOW FURTHER HARM TO BEFALL YOUR PEOPLE.
ROOOOOOSH
GOOD WORK, JET. YOU SAVED THEM.
YES...

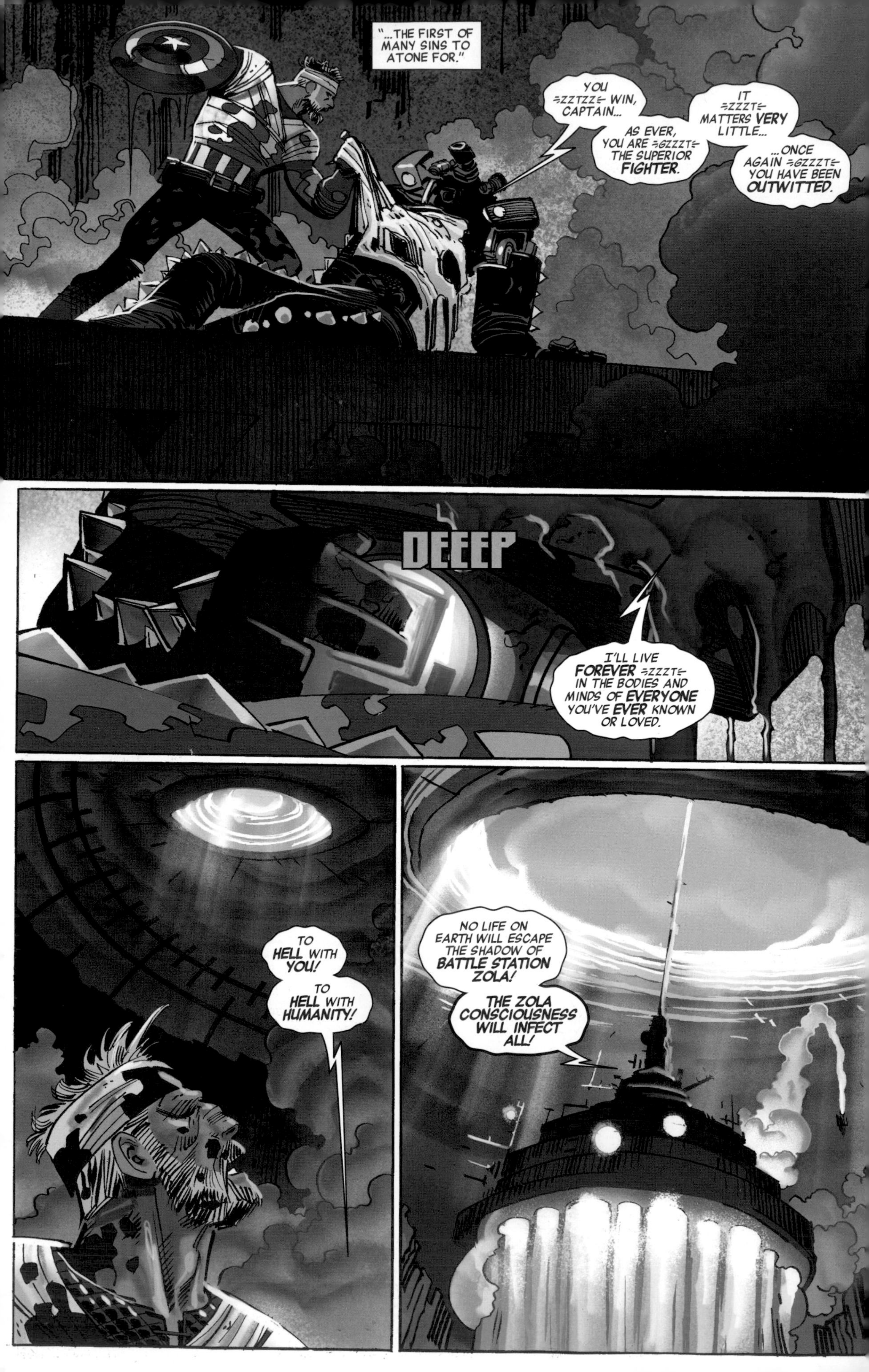
"...THE FIRST OF MANY SINS TO ATONE FOR."
YOU =ZZTZZ= WIN, CAPTAIN...
AS EVER, YOU ARE =GZZZT= THE SUPERIOR FIGHTER.
IT =ZZZT= MATTERS VERY LITTLE...
...ONCE AGAIN =GZZZT= YOU HAVE BEEN OUTWITTED.
DEEEP
I'LL LIVE FOREVER =ZZZT= IN THE BODIES AND MINDS OF EVERYONE YOU'VE EVER KNOWN OR LOVED.
TO HELL WITH YOU!
TO HELL WITH HUMANITY!
NO LIFE ON EARTH WILL ESCAPE THE SHADOW OF BATTLE STATION ZOLA!
THE ZOLA CONSCIOUSNESS WILL INFECT ALL!

OOF--!

AND THIS TIME--

--MANKIND WILL **NOT** HAVE CAPTAIN AMERICA TO LEAD A RESISTANCE!

THE PORTAL TEARS OPEN--

--REVEALING THE BLUE SKIES OF HOME.

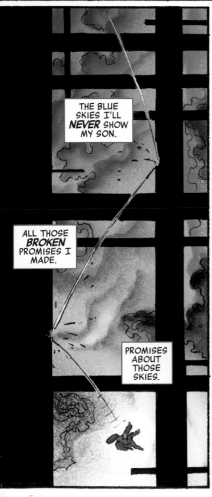

THE BLUE SKIES I'LL **NEVER** SHOW MY SON.

ALL THOSE **BROKEN** PROMISES I MADE.

PROMISES ABOUT THOSE SKIES.

A BLUE THE ATMOSPHERE HERE **NEVER** SHOWS.

A COLOR THAT REPRESENTED A **DREAM** TO HIM.

IN MY PAINTINGS OF HOME, THOSE BLUE SKIES--

IAN WOULD OFTEN BE LOST IN THEM.

TWUPP

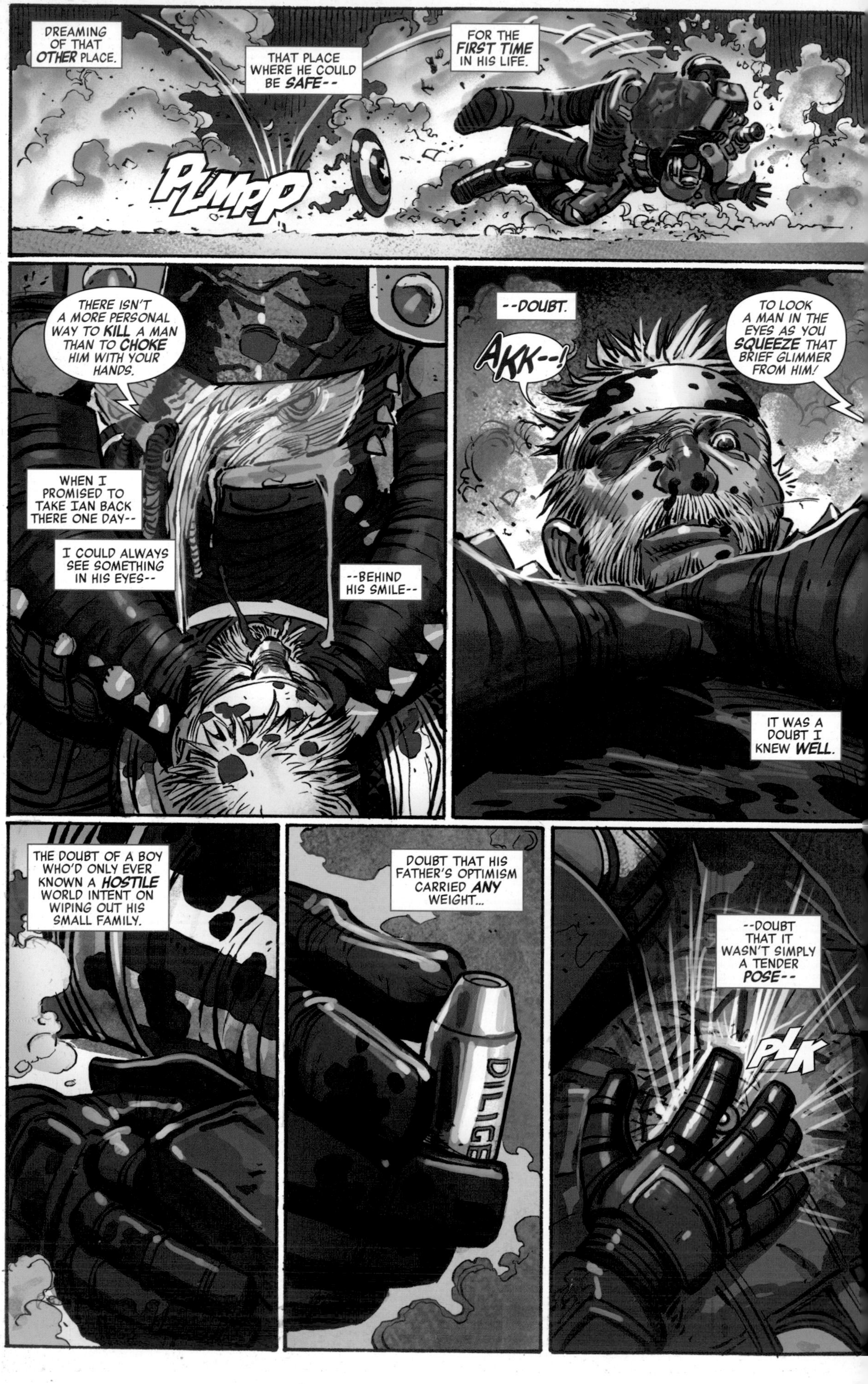

DREAMING OF THAT OTHER PLACE.
THAT PLACE WHERE HE COULD BE SAFE--
FOR THE FIRST TIME IN HIS LIFE.
PLMPP
THERE ISN'T A MORE PERSONAL WAY TO KILL A MAN THAN TO CHOKE HIM WITH YOUR HANDS.
WHEN I PROMISED TO TAKE IAN BACK THERE ONE DAY--
I COULD ALWAYS SEE SOMETHING IN HIS EYES--
--BEHIND HIS SMILE--
--DOUBT.
AKK--!
TO LOOK A MAN IN THE EYES AS YOU SQUEEZE THAT BRIEF GLIMMER FROM HIM!
IT WAS A DOUBT I KNEW WELL.
THE DOUBT OF A BOY WHO'D ONLY EVER KNOWN A HOSTILE WORLD INTENT ON WIPING OUT HIS SMALL FAMILY.
DOUBT THAT HIS FATHER'S OPTIMISM CARRIED ANY WEIGHT...
DILIGE
--DOUBT THAT IT WASN'T SIMPLY A TENDER POSE--
PLK

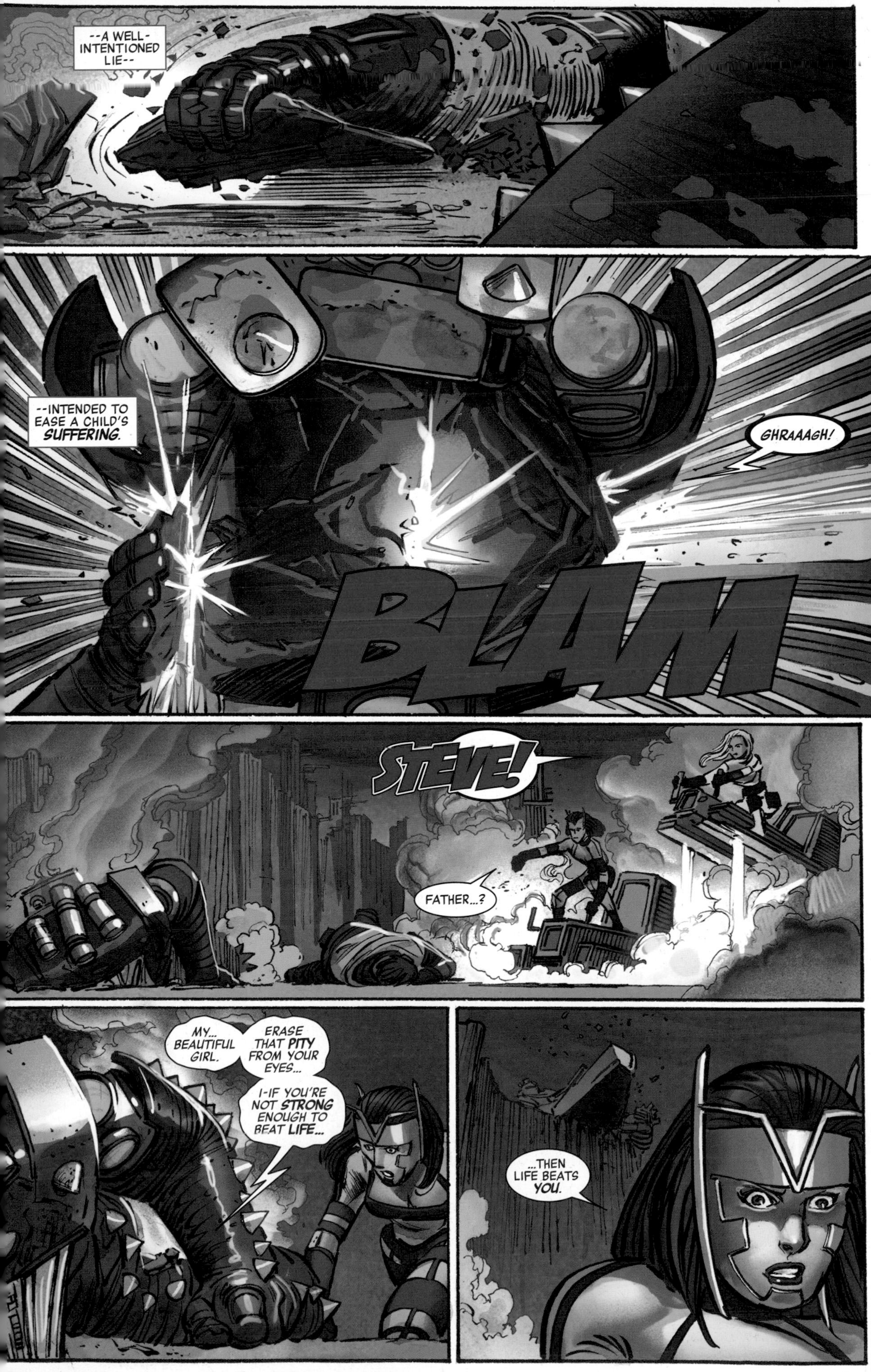
--A WELL-INTENTIONED LIE--
--INTENDED TO EASE A CHILD'S SUFFERING.
GHRAAAGH!
BLAM
STEVE!
FATHER...?
MY... BEAUTIFUL GIRL.
ERASE THAT PITY FROM YOUR EYES...
I-IF YOU'RE NOT STRONG ENOUGH TO BEAT LIFE...
...THEN LIFE BEATS YOU.

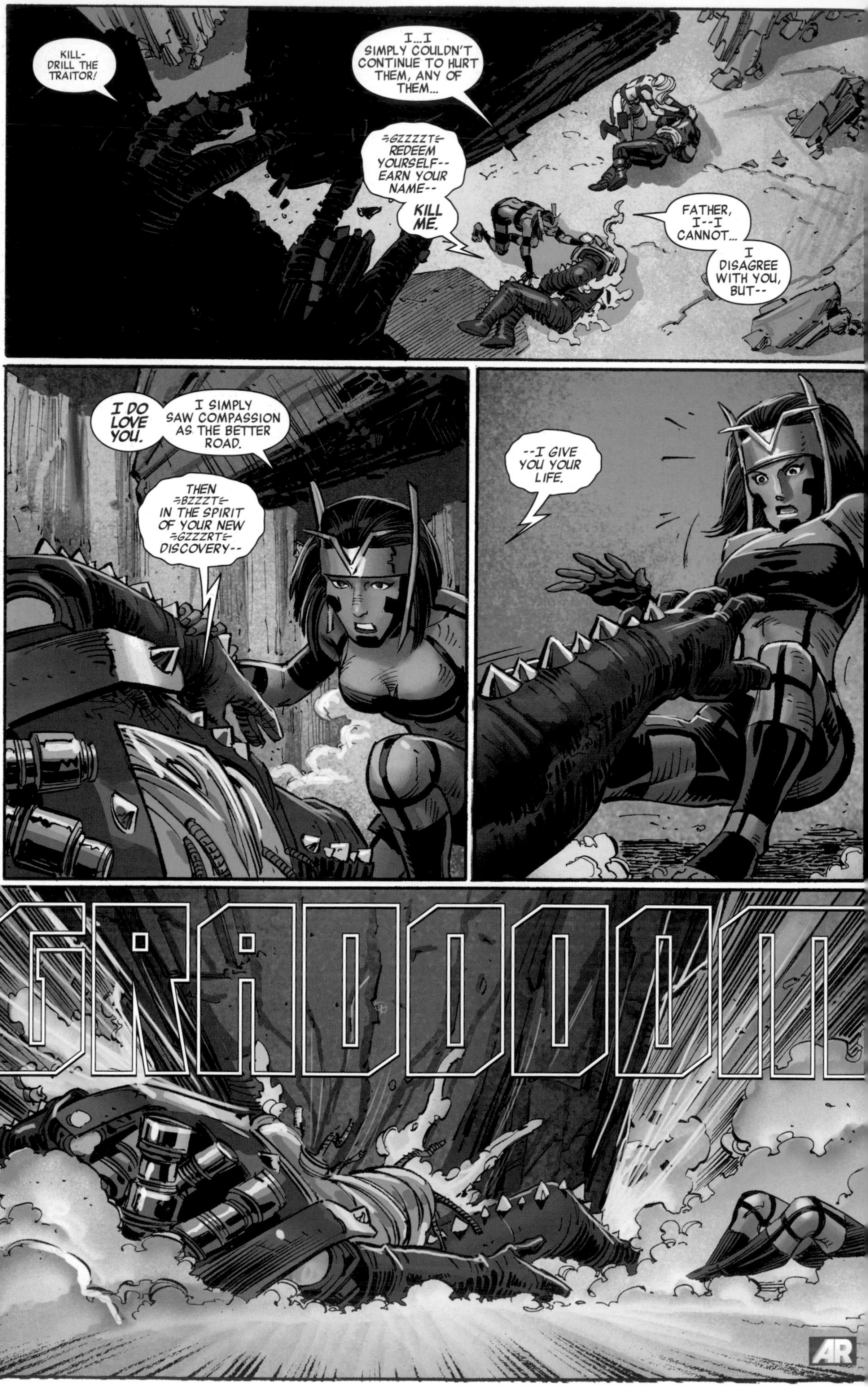

KILL-DRILL THE TRAITOR!
I...I SIMPLY COULDN'T CONTINUE TO HURT THEM, ANY OF THEM...
=GZZZZT= REDEEM YOURSELF--EARN YOUR NAME--
KILL ME.
FATHER, I--I CANNOT...
I DISAGREE WITH YOU, BUT--
I DO LOVE YOU.
I SIMPLY SAW COMPASSION AS THE BETTER ROAD.
THEN =BZZZT= IN THE SPIRIT OF YOUR NEW =GZZZRT= DISCOVERY--
--I GIVE YOU YOUR LIFE.
GRADOOOM
AR

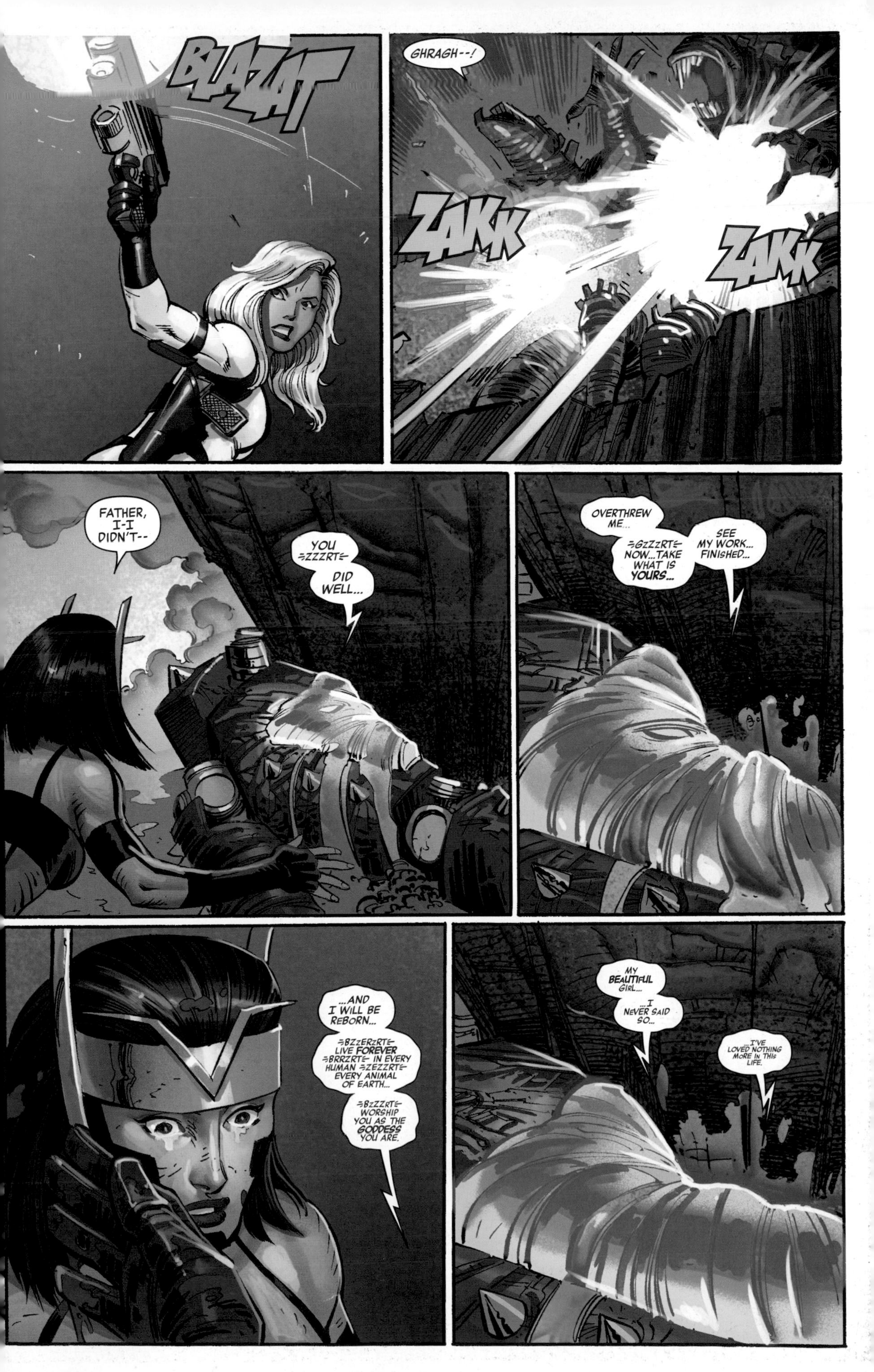
BLAZAT
GHRAGH--!
ZAKK
ZAKK
FATHER, I-I DIDN'T--
YOU =ZZZRT= DID WELL...
OVERTHREW ME...
=GZZZRT= NOW...TAKE WHAT IS YOURS...
SEE MY WORK... FINISHED...
...AND I WILL BE REBORN...
=BZZERZRT= LIVE FOREVER =BRRZRT= IN EVERY HUMAN =ZEZZRT= EVERY ANIMAL OF EARTH...
=BZZZRT= WORSHIP YOU AS THE GODDESS YOU ARE.
MY BEAUTIFUL GIRL...
...I NEVER SAID SO...
...I'VE LOVED NOTHING MORE IN THIS LIFE.

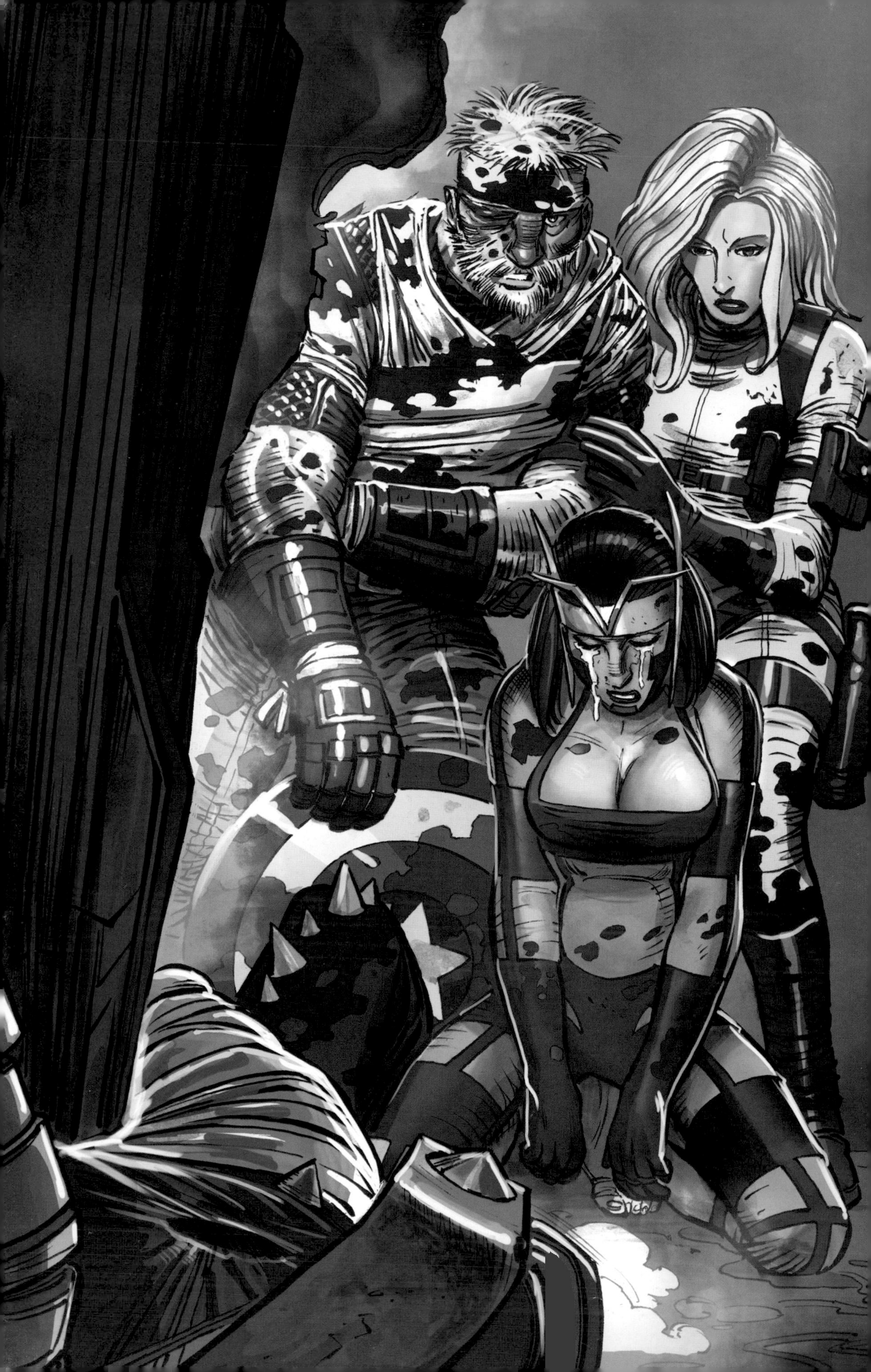

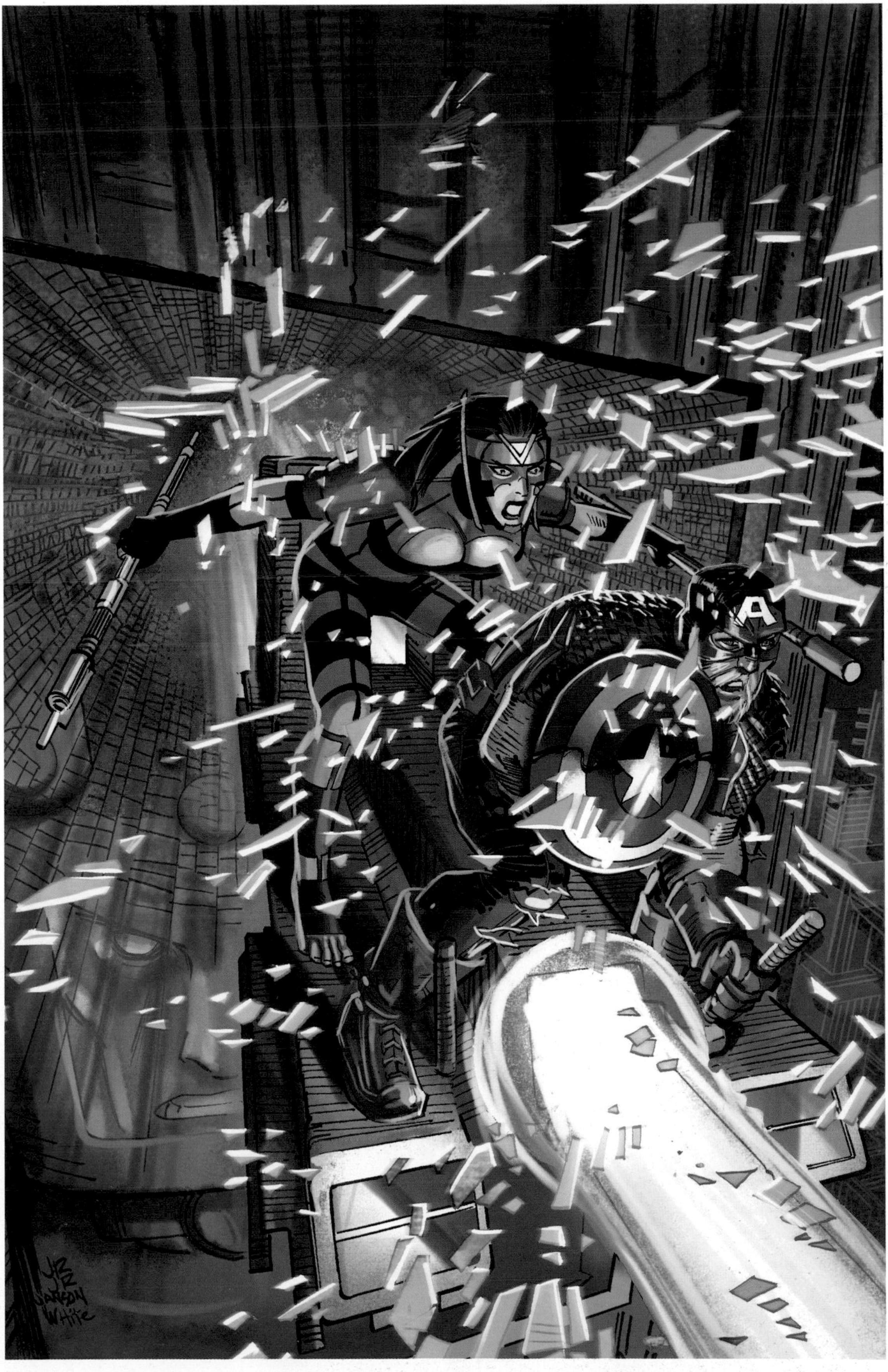
JRJR
JANSON
White

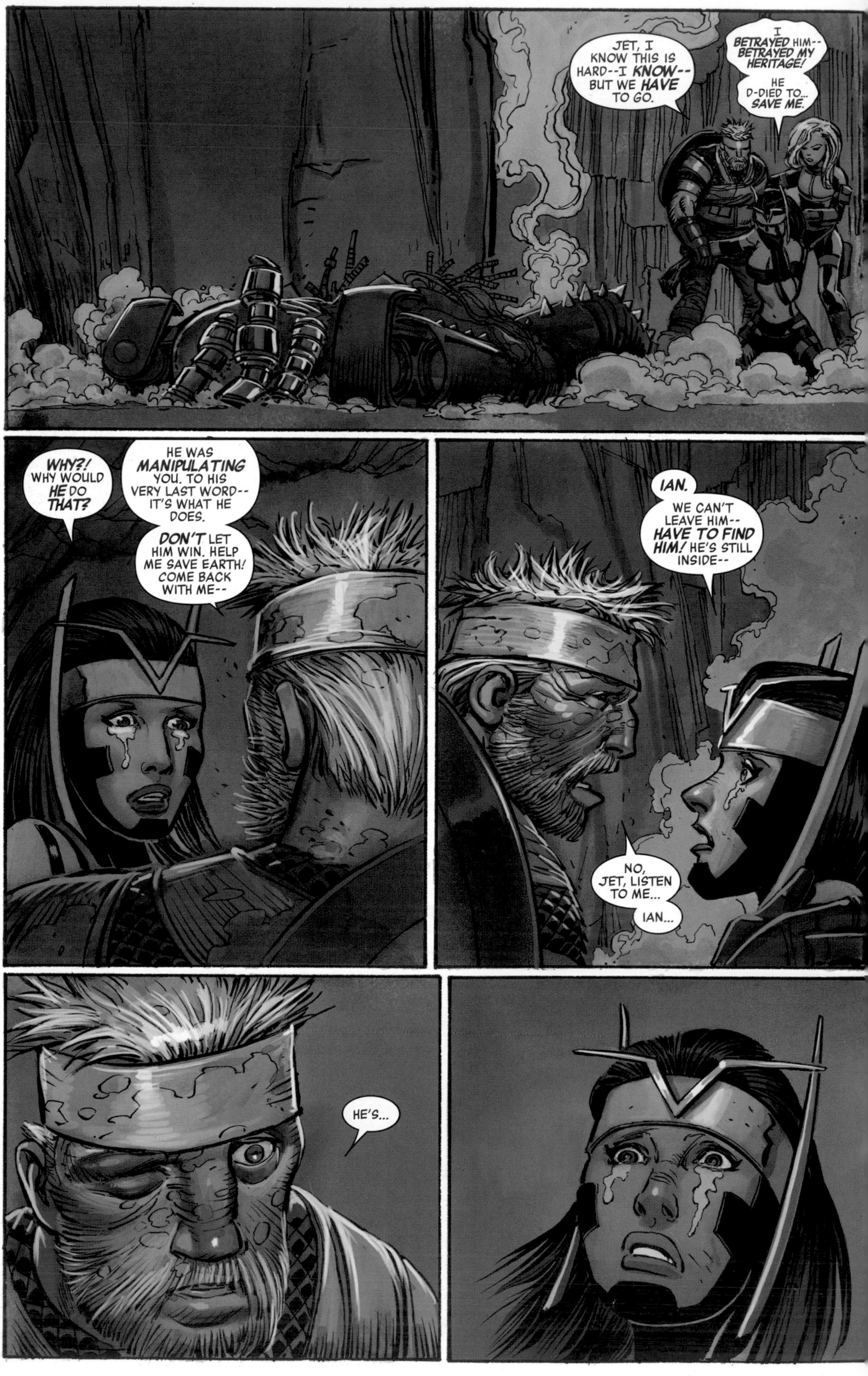
JET, I KNOW THIS IS HARD--I KNOW-- BUT WE HAVE TO GO.
I BETRAYED HIM-- BETRAYED MY HERITAGE!
HE D-DIED TO... SAVE ME.
WHY?! WHY WOULD HE DO THAT?
HE WAS MANIPULATING YOU. TO HIS VERY LAST WORD-- IT'S WHAT HE DOES.
DON'T LET HIM WIN. HELP ME SAVE EARTH! COME BACK WITH ME--
IAN.
WE CAN'T LEAVE HIM-- HAVE TO FIND HIM! HE'S STILL INSIDE--
NO, JET, LISTEN TO ME...
IAN...
HE'S...

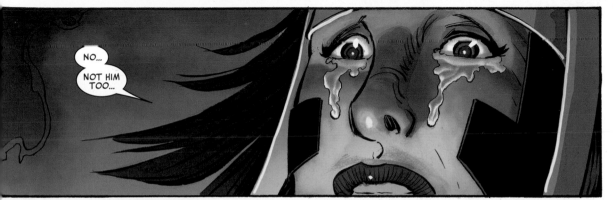

NO...

NOT HIM TOO...

I'M SORRY-- *BUT WE HAVE TO GO!*

IF WE HAVEN'T MADE IT TO THE CAVE PORTAL LEADING HOME WHEN I DETONATE THAT BATTLE STATION-- *WE WILL ALL BE BLOWN RIGHT TO HELL.*

AND I *WILL NOT* ALLOW THAT THING TO GET THROUGH TO EARTH.

EVEN IF IT MEANS WE *ALL DIE.*

SO WE HAVE TO GET TO THE PORTAL BEFORE I PULL THIS TRIGGER.

YOU'VE RIGGED MY HOME WITH EXPLOSIVES?!

YOUR HOME IS A *MOBILE BATTLE STATION* ON ITS WAY TO DELIVER A PAYLOAD HORDE OF *MUTATES* TO EARTH-- YOU'RE *DAMN* RIGHT I DID, SISTER.

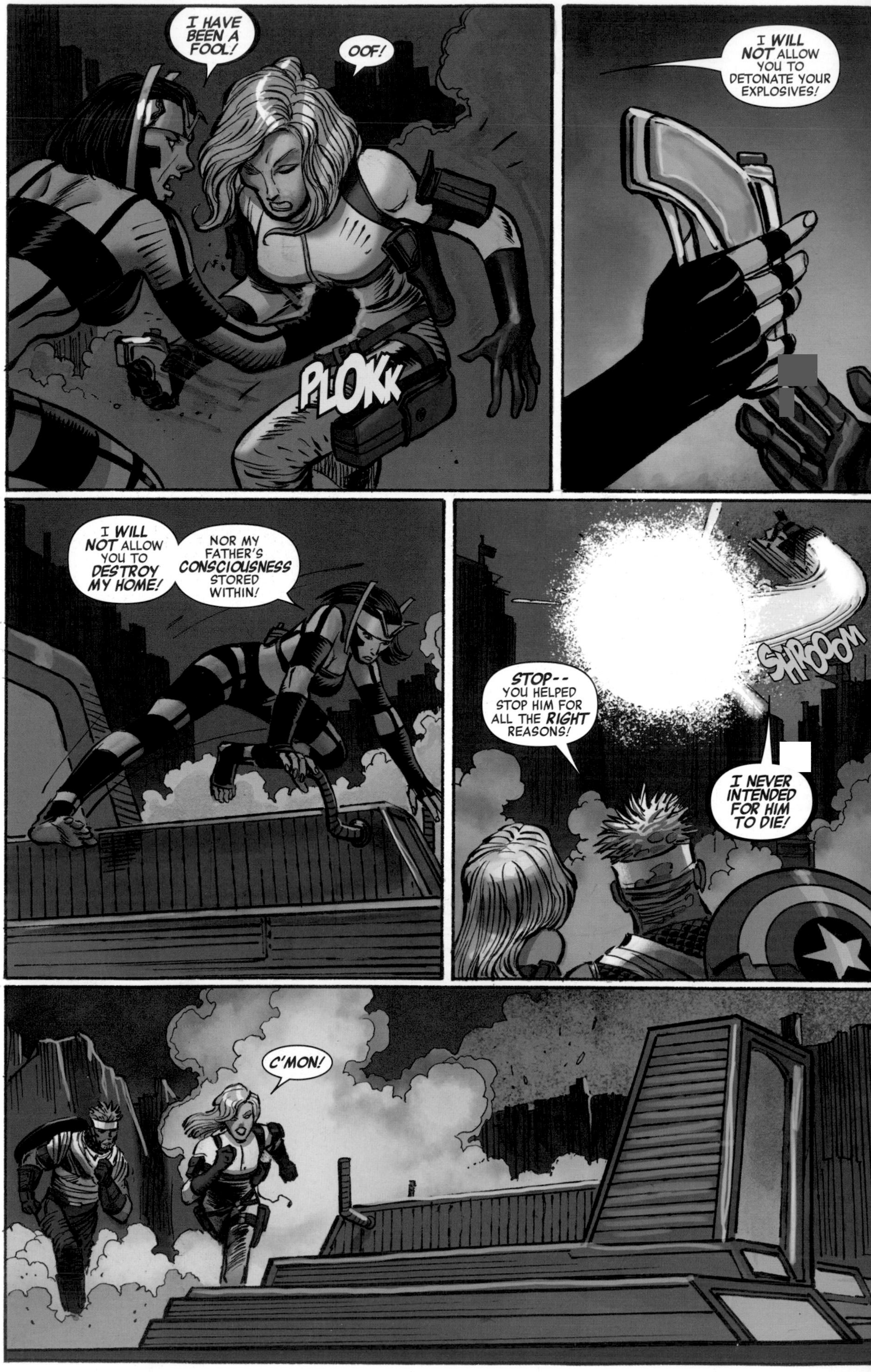
I HAVE BEEN A FOOL!
OOF!
PLOKK
I WILL NOT ALLOW YOU TO DETONATE YOUR EXPLOSIVES!
I WILL NOT ALLOW YOU TO DESTROY MY HOME!
NOR MY FATHER'S CONSCIOUSNESS STORED WITHIN!
SHROOOM
STOP-- YOU HELPED STOP HIM FOR ALL THE RIGHT REASONS!
I NEVER INTENDED FOR HIM TO DIE!
C'MON!

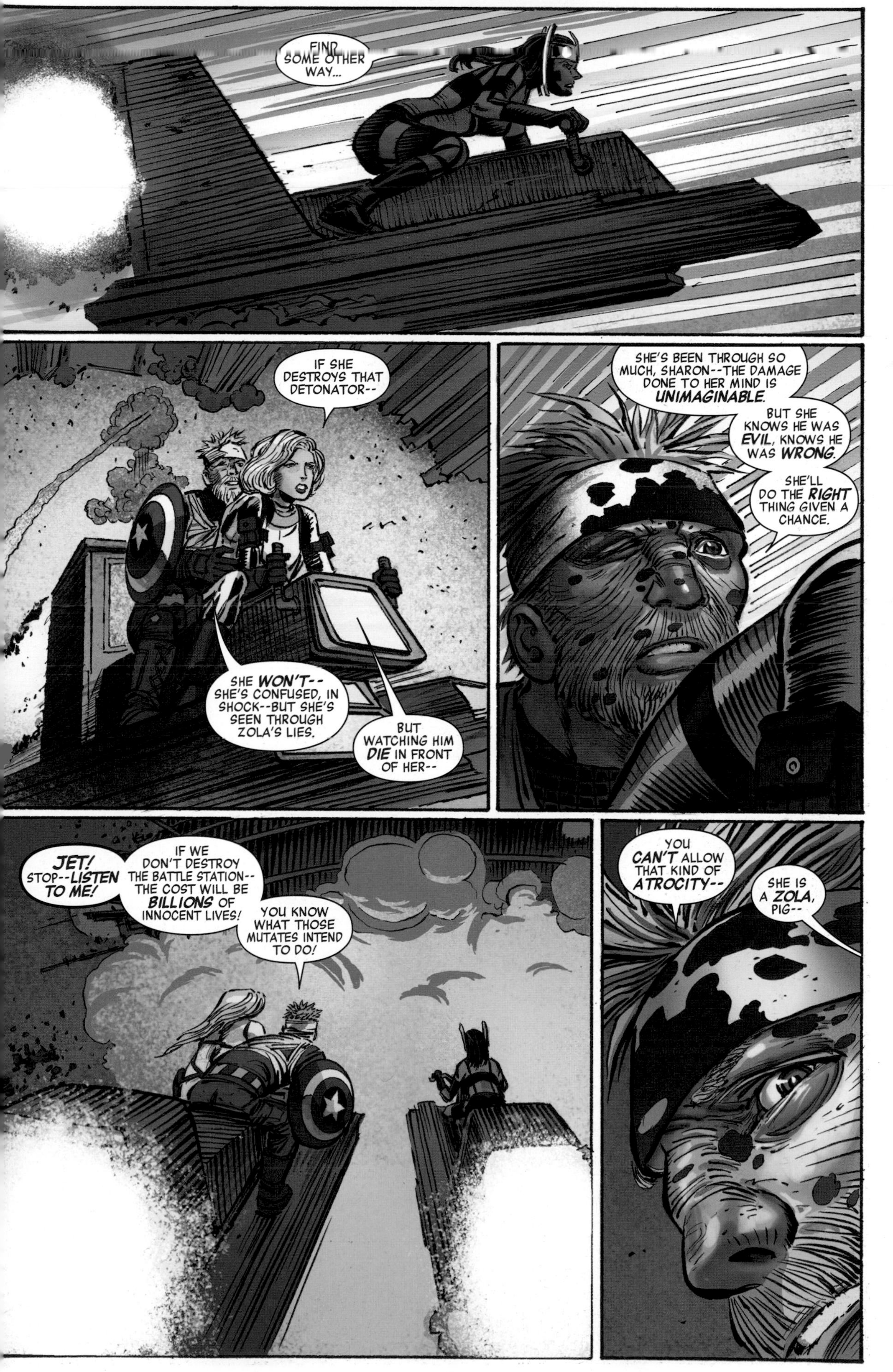
FIND SOME OTHER WAY...
IF SHE DESTROYS THAT DETONATOR--
SHE WON'T--SHE'S CONFUSED, IN SHOCK--BUT SHE'S SEEN THROUGH ZOLA'S LIES.
BUT WATCHING HIM DIE IN FRONT OF HER--
SHE'S BEEN THROUGH SO MUCH, SHARON--THE DAMAGE DONE TO HER MIND IS UNIMAGINABLE.
BUT SHE KNOWS HE WAS EVIL, KNOWS HE WAS WRONG.
SHE'LL DO THE RIGHT THING GIVEN A CHANCE.
JET! STOP--LISTEN TO ME!
IF WE DON'T DESTROY THE BATTLE STATION--THE COST WILL BE BILLIONS OF INNOCENT LIVES!
YOU KNOW WHAT THOSE MUTATES INTEND TO DO!
YOU CAN'T ALLOW THAT KIND OF ATROCITY--
SHE IS A ZOLA, PIG--

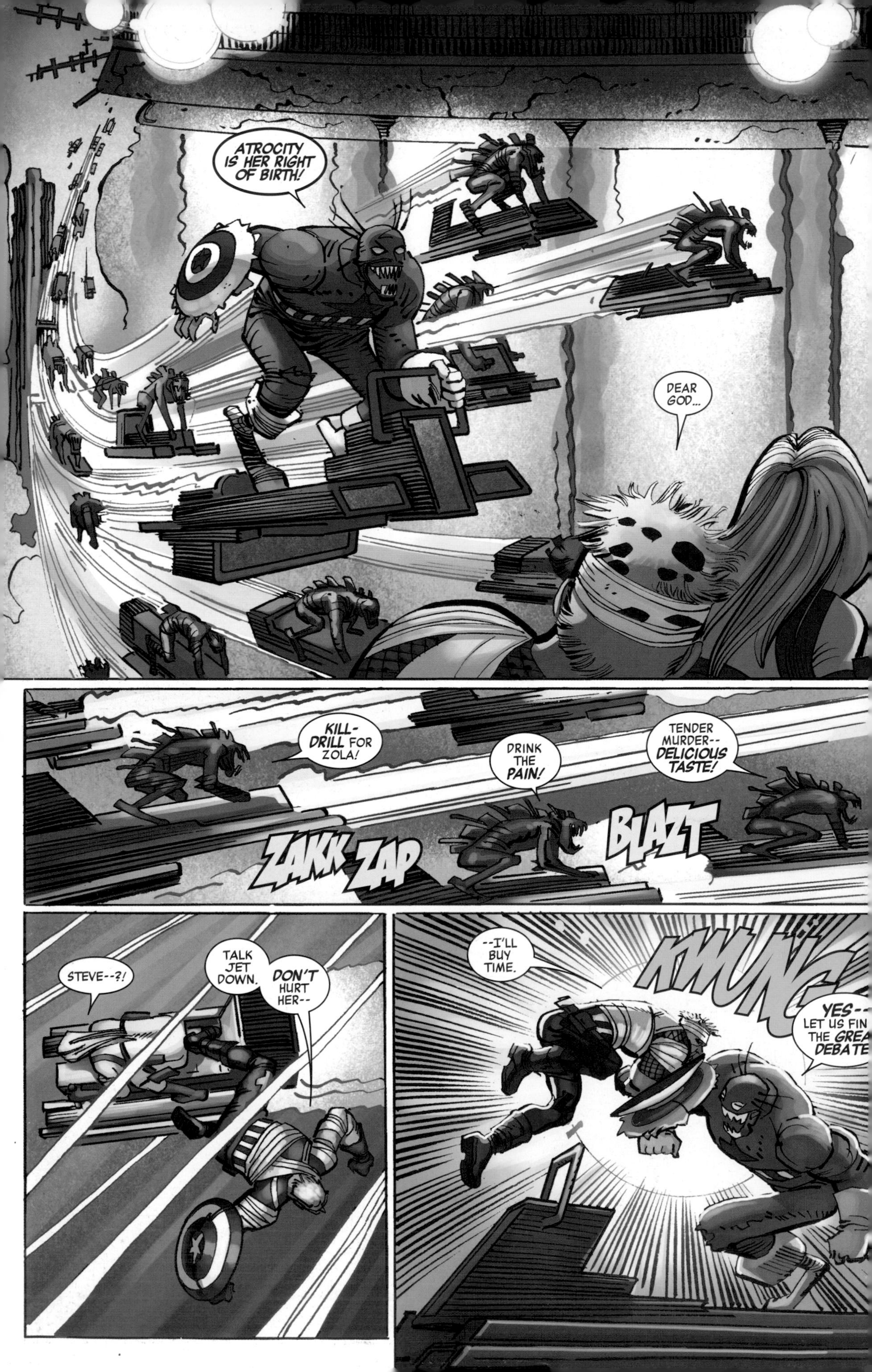
ATROCITY IS HER RIGHT OF BIRTH!
DEAR GOD...
KILL-DRILL FOR ZOLA!
DRINK THE PAIN!
TENDER MURDER--DELICIOUS TASTE!
ZAKK
ZAP
BLAZT
STEVE--?!
TALK JET DOWN.
DON'T HURT HER--
--I'LL BUY TIME.
KMUNG
YES--LET US FIN
THE GREA
DEBATE

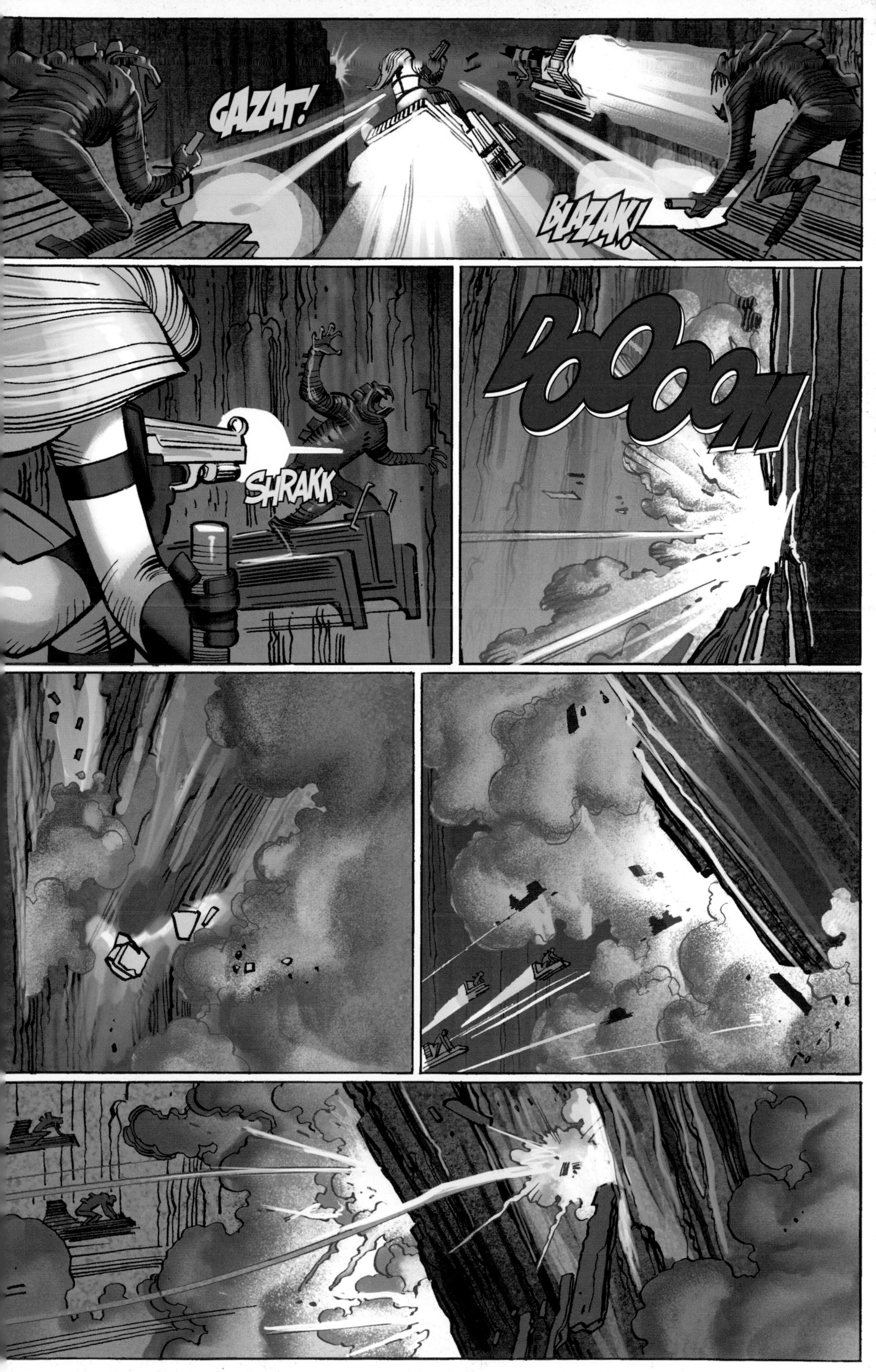
GAZAT!
BLAZAK!
SHRAKK
BOOOOM

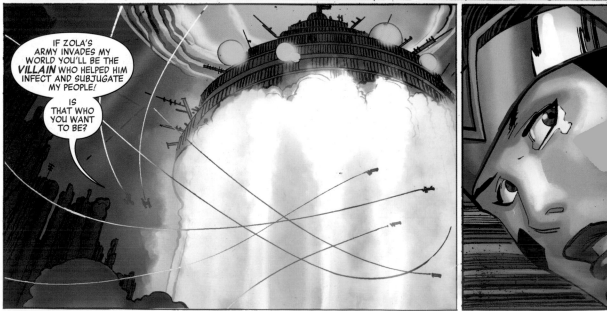

DOOOM

GRAB HOLD!

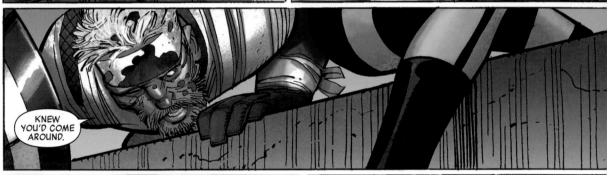

KNEW YOU'D COME AROUND.

NOW LET'S GET TO THE PORTAL HOME AND BLOW THESE MONSTERS TO--

YOU HAVE FAILED ME *UTTERLY*, DAUGHTER.

YOU HAVE *FAILED* YOUR *FINAL* TEST.

FAILED TO EARN YOUR *NAME*.

FAILED TO MOVE PAST *WEAKNESS*--

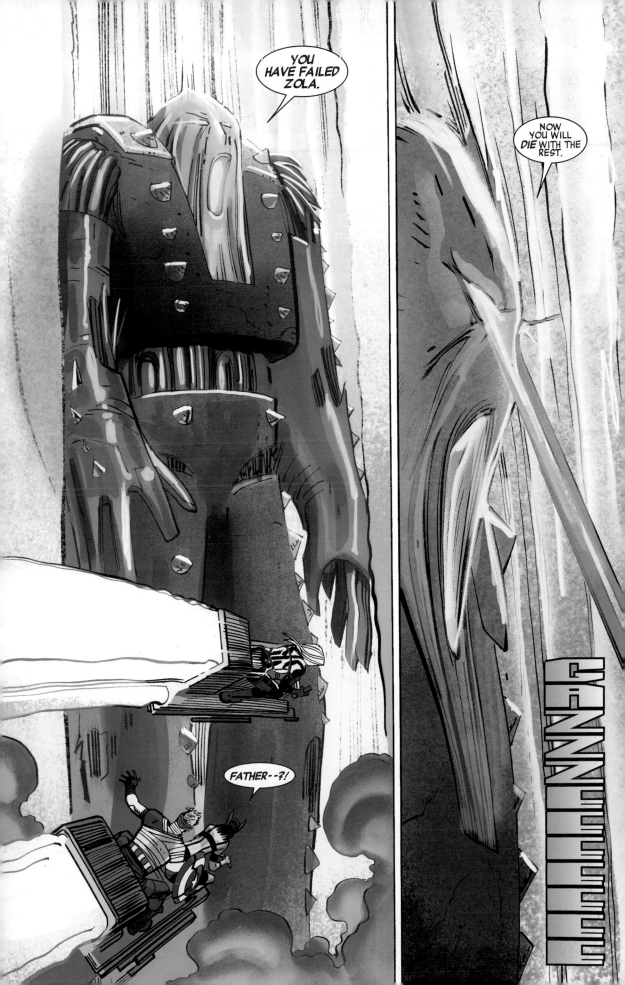

GHA--!

SHARON!

HOLD ON!

SO MUCH TIME *WASTED* ON YOU, MY DAUGHTER!

SO MANY *FAILED* OPPORTUNITIES TO *EARN* YOUR NAME!

I *LOVED* YOU WITH ALL OF MY HEART--

--AND YOU CHOSE TO SIDE WITH MY *GREATEST ENEMY!*

YOU CHOSE *FRAILTY* OVER *POWER!*

PUNCH IT, JET! HE'S ALMOST ON US!

DOOOM

ZAKK

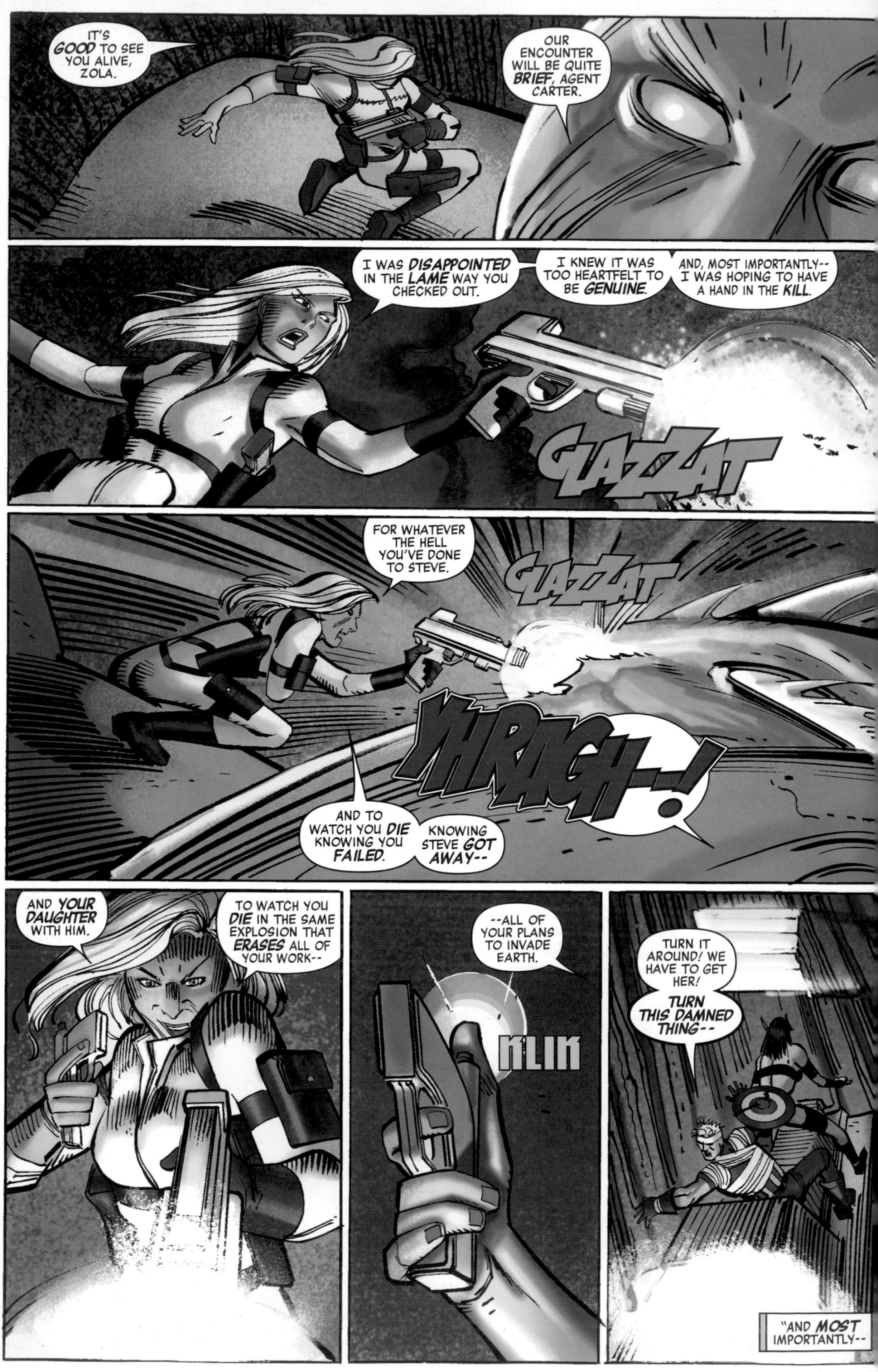
IT'S GOOD TO SEE YOU ALIVE, ZOLA.
OUR ENCOUNTER WILL BE QUITE BRIEF, AGENT CARTER.
I WAS DISAPPOINTED IN THE LAME WAY YOU CHECKED OUT.
I KNEW IT WAS TOO HEARTFELT TO BE GENUINE.
AND, MOST IMPORTANTLY-- I WAS HOPING TO HAVE A HAND IN THE KILL.
GLAZZAT
FOR WHATEVER THE HELL YOU'VE DONE TO STEVE.
GLAZZAT
YHRAGH--!
AND TO WATCH YOU DIE KNOWING YOU FAILED.
KNOWING STEVE GOT AWAY--
AND YOUR DAUGHTER WITH HIM.
TO WATCH YOU DIE IN THE SAME EXPLOSION THAT ERASES ALL OF YOUR WORK--
--ALL OF YOUR PLANS TO INVADE EARTH.
KLIK
TURN IT AROUND! WE HAVE TO GET HER!
TURN THIS DAMNED THING--
"AND MOST IMPORTANTLY--

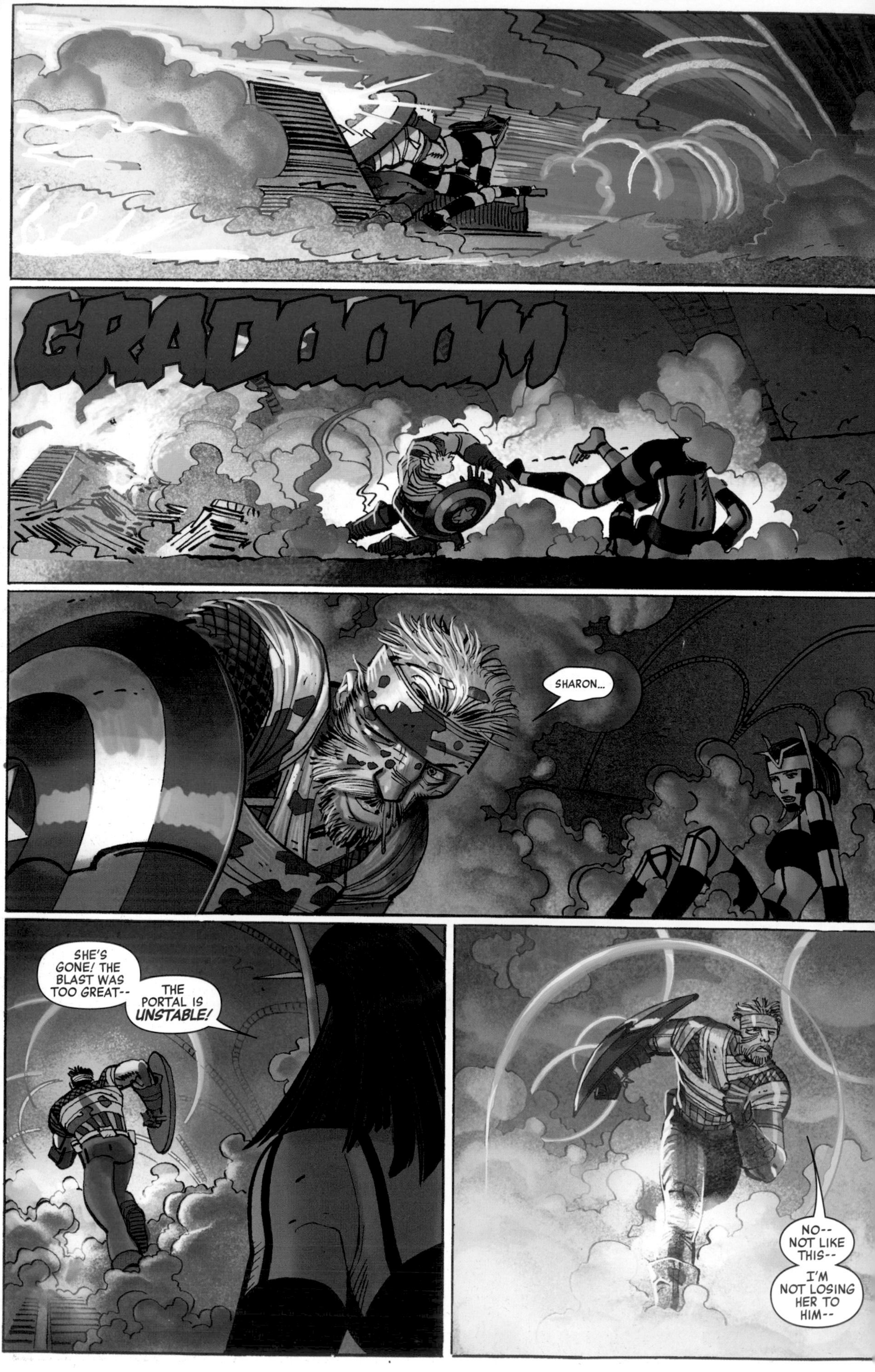

GRADOOOM
SHARON...
SHE'S GONE! THE BLAST WAS TOO GREAT--
THE PORTAL IS *UNSTABLE!*
NO-- NOT LIKE THIS--
I'M NOT LOSING HER TO HIM--

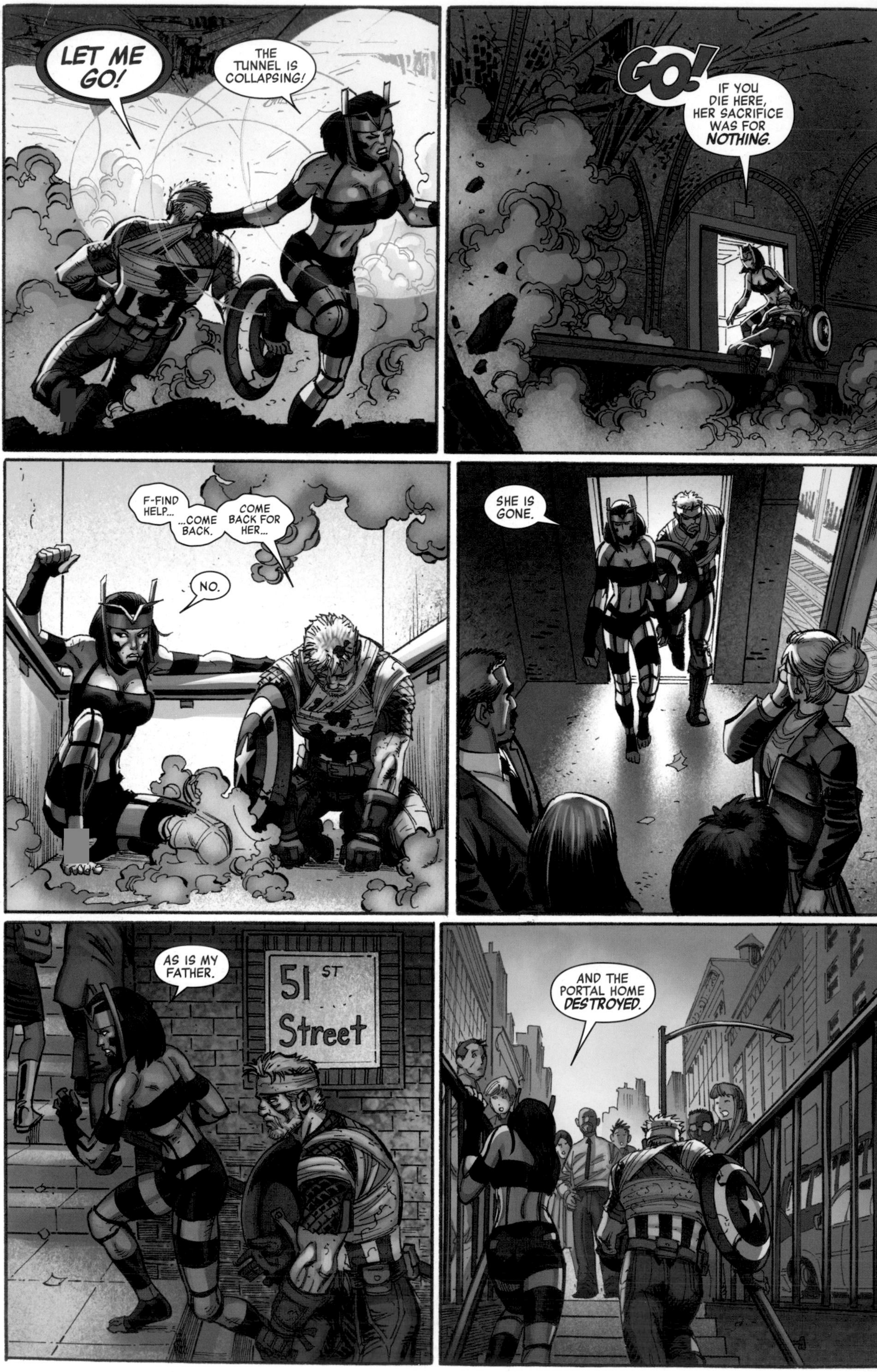
LET ME GO!
THE TUNNEL IS COLLAPSING!
GO!
IF YOU DIE HERE, HER SACRIFICE WAS FOR NOTHING.
F-FIND HELP...
...COME BACK.
COME BACK FOR HER...
NO.
SHE IS GONE.
AS IS MY FATHER.
51 ST Street
AND THE PORTAL HOME DESTROYED.

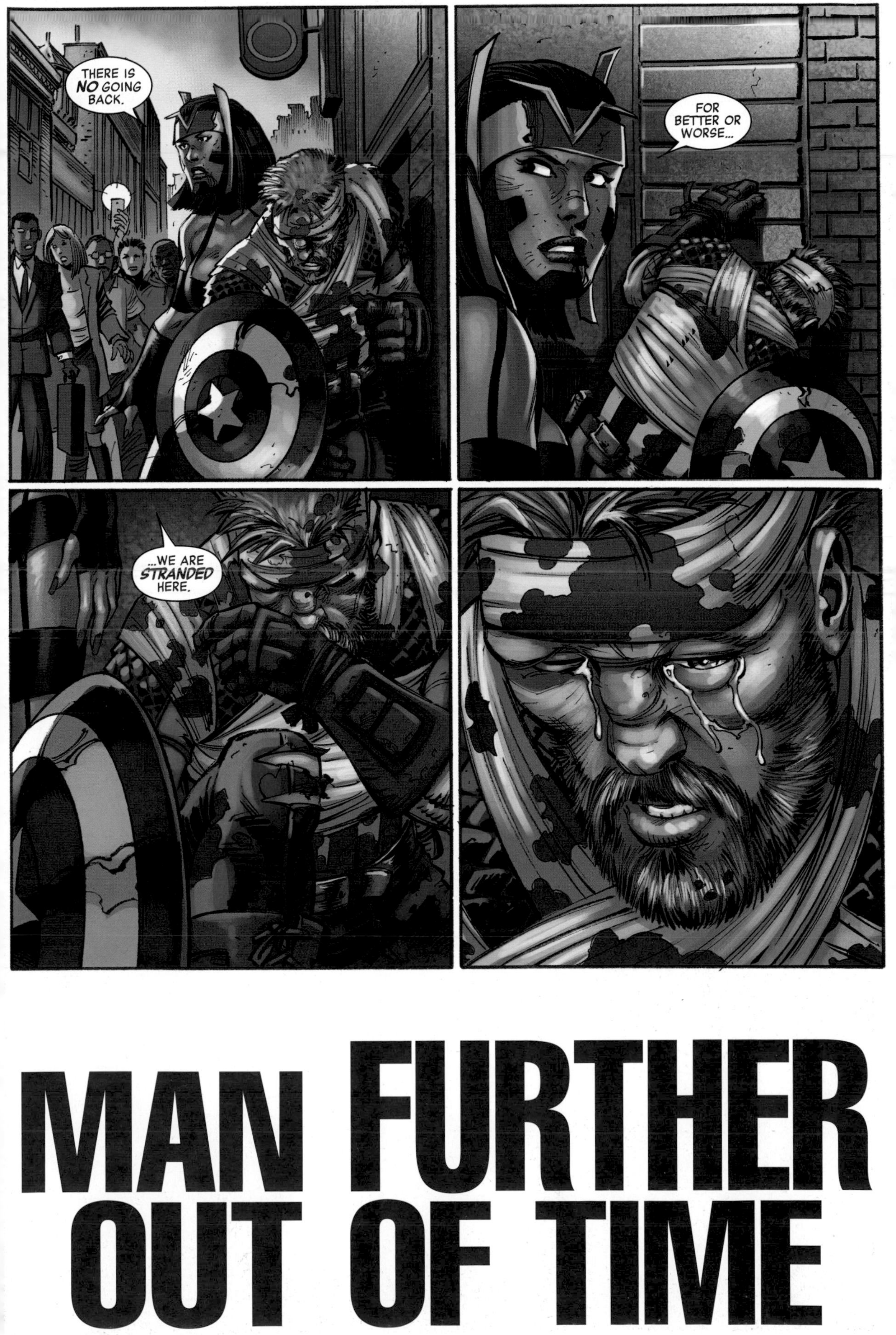
THERE IS NO GOING BACK.
FOR BETTER OR WORSE...
...WE ARE STRANDED HERE.

MAN FURTHER OUT OF TIME

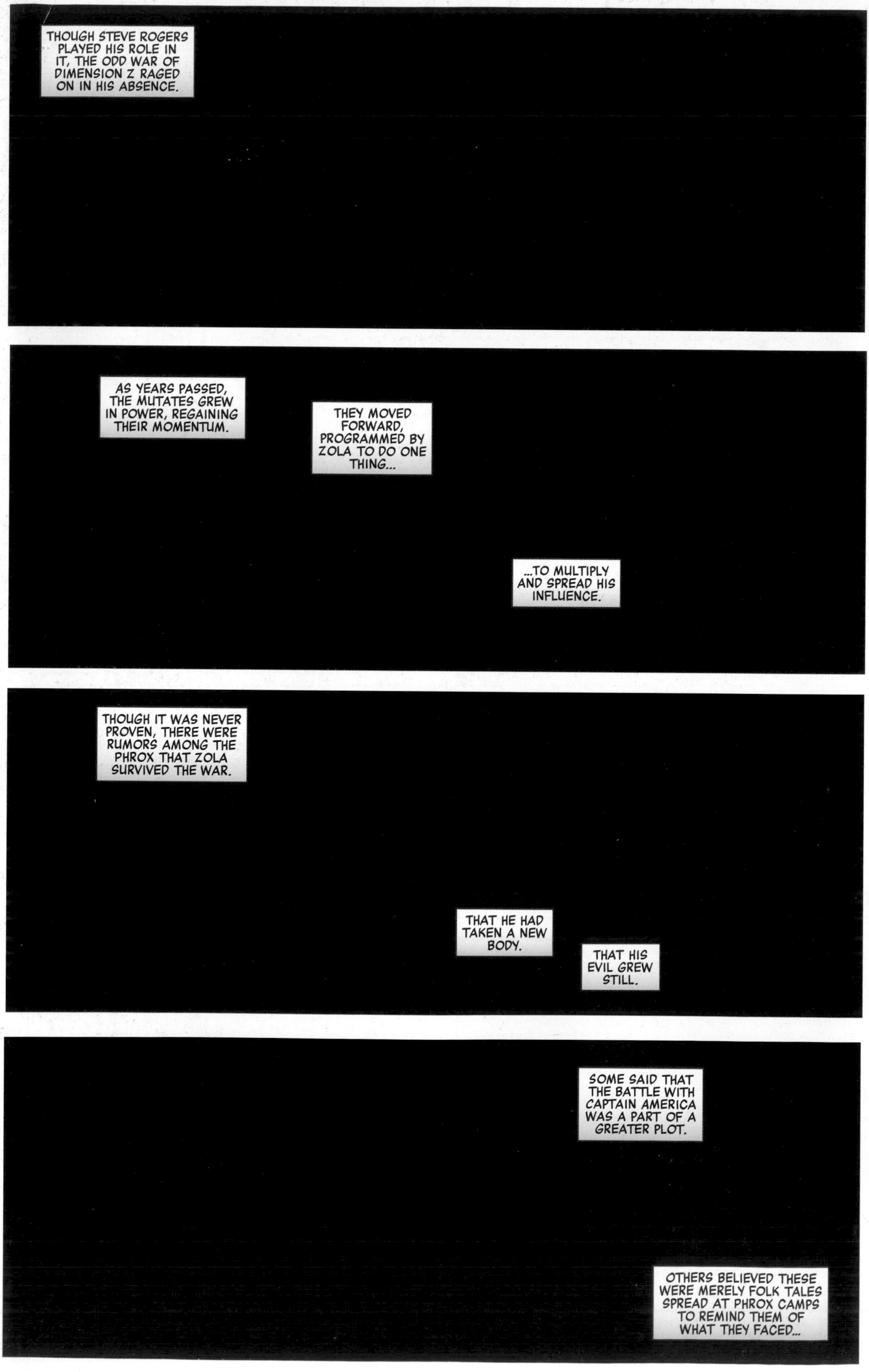
THOUGH STEVE ROGERS PLAYED HIS ROLE IN IT, THE ODD WAR OF DIMENSION Z RAGED ON IN HIS ABSENCE.
AS YEARS PASSED, THE MUTATES GREW IN POWER, REGAINING THEIR MOMENTUM.
THEY MOVED FORWARD, PROGRAMMED BY ZOLA TO DO ONE THING...
...TO MULTIPLY AND SPREAD HIS INFLUENCE.
THOUGH IT WAS NEVER PROVEN, THERE WERE RUMORS AMONG THE PHROX THAT ZOLA SURVIVED THE WAR.
THAT HE HAD TAKEN A NEW BODY.
THAT HIS EVIL GREW STILL.
SOME SAID THAT THE BATTLE WITH CAPTAIN AMERICA WAS A PART OF A GREATER PLOT.
OTHERS BELIEVED THESE WERE MERELY FOLK TALES SPREAD AT PHROX CAMPS TO REMIND THEM OF WHAT THEY FACED...

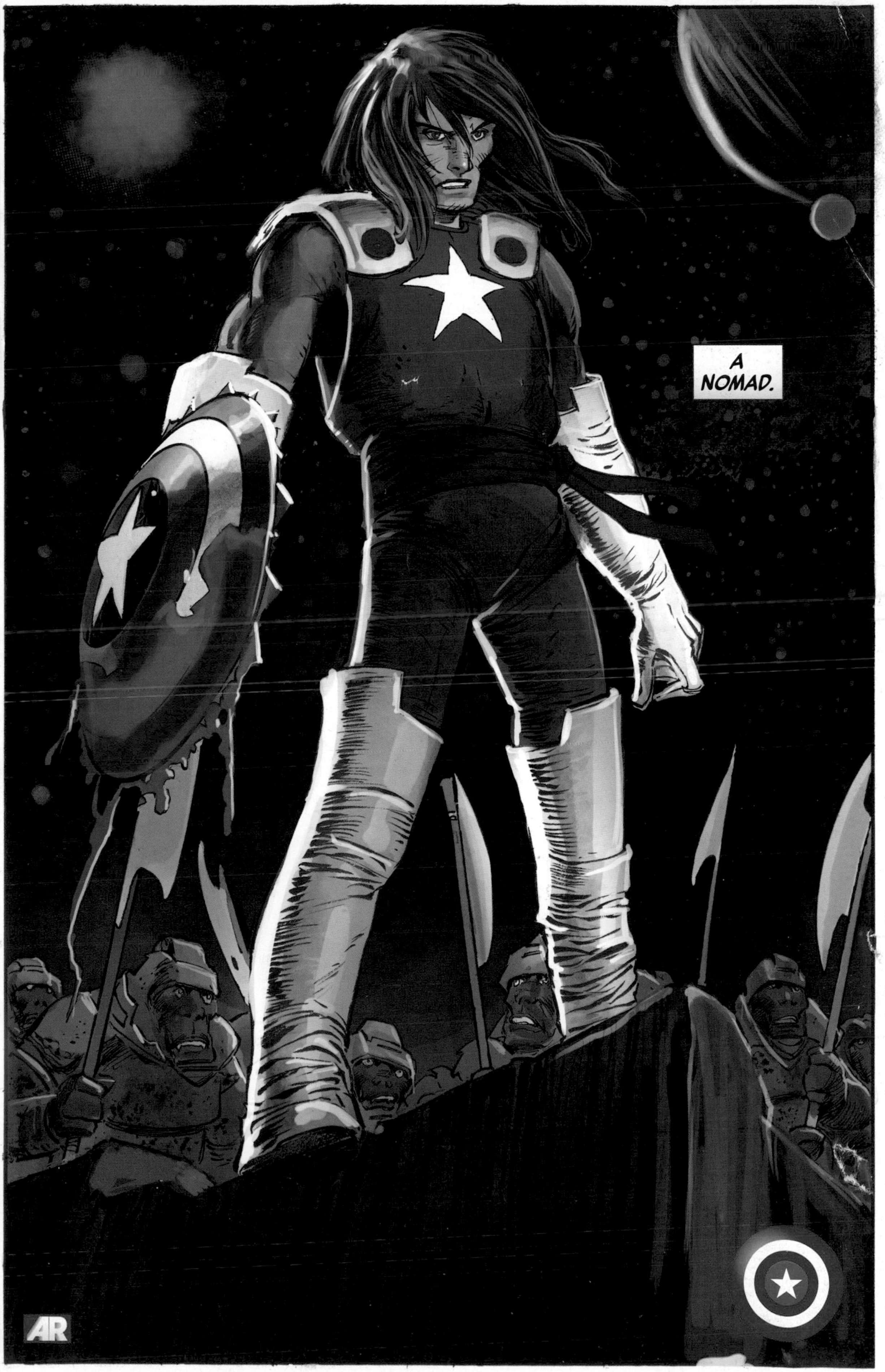
A NOMAD.

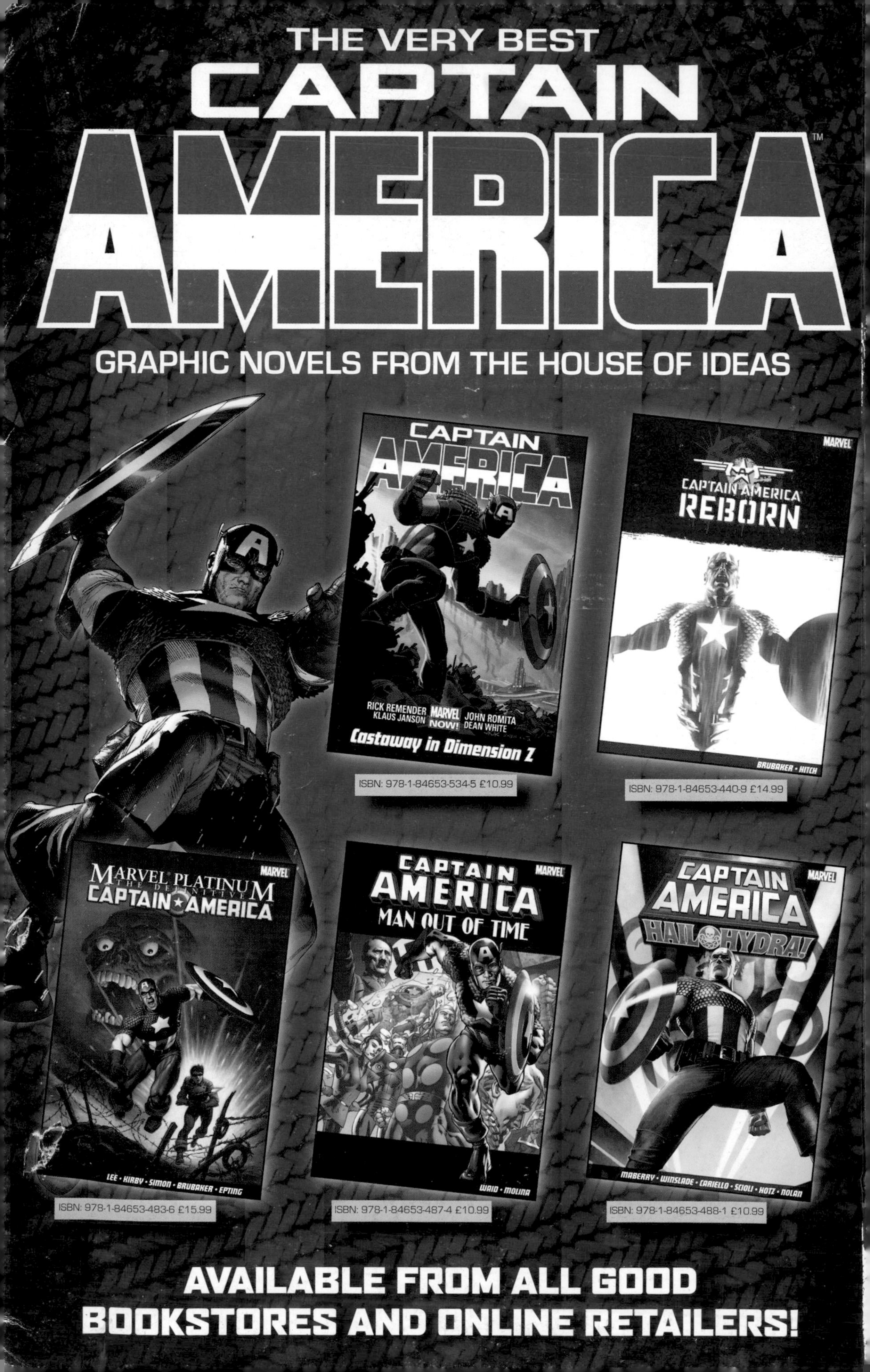
THE VERY BEST
CAPTAIN
AMERICA™
GRAPHIC NOVELS FROM THE HOUSE OF IDEAS
CAPTAIN AMERICA
RICK REMENDER KLAUS JANSON MARVEL NOW! JOHN ROMITA DEAN WHITE
Castaway in Dimension Z
ISBN: 978-1-84653-534-5 £10.99
MARVEL
CAPTAIN AMERICA REBORN
BRUBAKER • HITCH
ISBN: 978-1-84653-440-9 £14.99
MARVEL
MARVEL PLATINUM THE DEFINITIVE CAPTAIN AMERICA
LEE • KIRBY • SIMON • BRUBAKER • EPTING
ISBN: 978-1-84653-483-6 £15.99
MARVEL
CAPTAIN AMERICA
MAN OUT OF TIME
WAID • MOLINA
ISBN: 978-1-84653-487-4 £10.99
MARVEL
CAPTAIN AMERICA
HAIL HYDRA!
MABERRY • WINSLADE • CARIELLO • SCIOLI • HOTZ • NOLAN
ISBN: 978-1-84653-488-1 £10.99
AVAILABLE FROM ALL GOOD
BOOKSTORES AND ONLINE RETAILERS!